THE CONCISE OXFORD

DICTIONARY OF

AUSTRALIAN HISTORY

THE CONCISE OXFORD

DICTIONARY OF

AUSTRALIAN HISTORY

JAN BASSETT

Melbourne
Oxford University Press

Oxford University Press

Oxford New York Toronto
Delhi Bombay Calcutta Madras Karachi
Petaling Jaya Singapore Hong Kong Tokyo
Nairobi Dar es Salaam Cape Town
Melbourne Auckland and associates in
Beirut Berlin Ibadan Nicosia

Oxford is a trademark of Oxford University Press.
© Jan Bassett, 1986

First published 1986

National Library of Australia
Cataloguing-in-Publication data:

Bassett, Jan, 1953–
The concise Oxford dictionary of Australian history.

ISBN 0 19 554422 6.

1. Australia — History — Dictionaries.   I. Title.

994′.003′21

Designed by Peter Shaw
Typeset by Post Typesetters, Brisbane
Printed by Impact Printing, Melbourne
Published by Oxford University Press,
253-275 Normanby Road, South Melbourne

Preface

This concise dictionary contains about 550 entries. Intended as a general reference book, it is designed particularly to assist students of Australian history.

The selection of entries was a major consideration when compiling the dictionary. The principal people, institutions, places, ideas, movements, events, artefacts and documents generally considered to be historically significant in Australia's history to 1975 are represented as far as is possible within the constraints of the book's length and objectives. Some entries concerning international events, with emphasis upon Australian involvement, are included.

The entries are arranged in alphabetical order of their headwords up to the first punctuation mark. Cross-references are denoted by an asterisk preceding the headword of another entry in which relevant information may be found. They are not usually given for the names of states and capital cities, nor for commonly used terms such as First World War.

Responsibility for this dictionary rests with the author, but I would like to acknowledge in particular the generous assistance of Professor A. G. L. Shaw and Dr L. L. Robson.

Jan Bassett

Acknowledgements

I wish to acknowledge the assistance afforded by officers of many institutions, including the Australian Atomic Energy Commission, the Australian Elizabethan Theatre Trust, the Australian War Memorial, the Australian Workers' Union, the Big Brother Movement, the Commonwealth Grants Commission, the Country Women's Association, the Department of Aboriginal Affairs, the Department of Immigration and Ethnic Affairs, the Hydro-Electric Commission of Tasmania, the National Council of Women of Victoria, New Norcia, the Returned Services League, the Victorian Department of the Premier and Cabinet, and the various state libraries. I also wish to thank Olga Abrahams, John Bangsund, Jill Davies, Garry Disher, David Elder, Jim Ellison, Sue Ellison, Dr Charlie Fox, Dr Robin Gerster, Frank Lyons, Una Lyons, Dr Ross McMullin, Neil McPhee, Dr Carolyn Rasmussen, Professor Henry Reynolds, Dr Lloyd Robson, Professor A. G. L. Shaw and Dr David Stockley for their much appreciated assistance.

A

AAEC: *Australian Atomic Energy Commission

ABC: *Australian Broadcasting Commission

Aboriginal Flag: Flag of the Australian Aboriginal people. It is divided horizontally in half, the top black and the bottom red, with a solid yellow circle in the centre. The black represents the Aboriginal people, the red the earth, and the yellow the sun. Harold Thomas, an Aranda elder from Central Australia, designed the flag, which apparently was first flown at *land rights demonstrations in Adelaide during the late 1960s. Aborigines at the tent embassy in Canberra in 1972 decided that they should fly an Aboriginal flag; a number of designs were considered, and Thomas's was chosen. It is not a registered flag.

Aborigines: Term used to describe the original inhabitants of a country, as opposed to colonists. Australian Aborigines are believed to have come from South-East Asia to Australia, then part of a much larger land mass, which included *New Guinea, more than 40,000 years ago. Migration probably took place over thousands of years. Most prehistorians now believe that there were two human types in prehistoric Australia who merged to form the modern Aboriginal race. The Australian Aborigines were semi-nomadic hunters and gatherers. Their systems of belief emphasized the Dreamtime and the spiritual significance of the land. Some 300 different languages were spoken. White settlement, which began in 1788, proved disastrous for the Aborigines. The Aboriginal population in 1788 has been estimated at about 30,000, but recent research suggests that it may have been much higher. Within a hundred years the population had declined to about 50,000, and virtually all of the Tasmanian Aborigines were dead. The main reasons suggested for this decline include loss of land, adoption of European habits, such as drinking alcohol, effects of European

1

diseases, such as *smallpox, influenza, respiratory diseases and venereal diseases, declining birth-rates, and violence between Europeans and Aborigines. Such violence (for example, at the Battle of *Pinjarra, at *Myall Creek, and that caused by the *Native Police) led to deaths on both sides. It is estimated that about 2500 whites and about 20,000 Aborigines were killed as a result of direct conflict. During the nineteenth and twentieth centuries, official white policies toward Aborigines have included, at various times, 'protection', segregation, assimilation and integration. Aborigines have faced legal, political, economic and social discrimination. A referendum proposing that Aborigines should be included in the census count, and that the Commonwealth Government should be given the power to legislate for Aborigines, was passed overwhelmingly in 1967. Most 'protective' and discriminatory legislation has been repealed. The *land rights movement, which began in the 1960s, continued to be significant in the 1980s.

ACT: *Australian Capital Territory

ACTU: *Australian Council of Trade Unions

Adelaide, the capital city of *South Australia, lies between the Mount Lofty Ranges in the east and Gulf St Vincent in the west. *Flinders explored the coast in 1801 and 1802, Collet Barker the land in 1831. The Colonization Commission instructed *Light, South Australia's first Surveyor-General, to select the site for the new province's capital. He did so in 1836. His choice of site was the cause of some controversy. He also planned the capital (which was named after Queen Adelaide), surrounding the central area with a wide band of parklands. Adelaide's municipal corporation, the first in Australia, was established in 1840. The population of Adelaide was 546 in 1836, 118,000 in 1886, and 882,520 in 1981.

'Advance Australia Fair', the Australian national anthem since 1984, was composed by Peter Dodds McCormick, a Scot, about 1878. It was first played at a concert in Sydney, arranged by the Highland

Society of New South Wales, on St Andrew's Day, 30 November 1878. The words of the first stanza are as follows:

Australians all let us rejoice,
For we are young and free;
We've golden soil and wealth for toil;
Our home is girt by sea;
Our land abounds in nature's gifts
Of beauty rich and rare;
In hist'ry's page let every stage
Advance Australia Fair.
In joyful strains then let us sing
Advance Australia Fair.

Age: *Syme, David

AIF: *Australian Imperial Force

Air Force: *Royal Australian Air Force

Albany: Town situated on King George Sound in Western Australia. George Vancouver visited and named the sound (originally King George the Third's Sound) in 1791. The British, motivated partly by fears that the French might settle in the area, established the first white settlement in the western part of Australia there in 1826. Major Edmund Lockyer, who led the first settlers, a small group of troops and convicts from New South Wales, named the settlement Frederickstown (after Frederick, Duke of York and Albany). It became known officially as Albany in 1832. The troops and convicts were withdrawn in 1831, the year in which the recently founded colony of Western Australia took responsibility for the settlement. Albany was Western Australia's most important port for many years.

Alice Springs: Town in the Northern Territory, close to the centre of Australia. The original Alice Springs, springs on the Todd River some kilometres from the present-day town, were first discovered by white people in 1871, during preparation for construction of the *Overland Telegraph Line, and were named after Charles Todd's wife. The telegraph station was also named Alice Springs. The town, which was surveyed in 1888, was originally named Stuart (after John McDouall *Stuart), but became popularly known as Alice Springs, and its name was officially changed in 1933. Alice Springs was the administrative centre of Central Australia when the latter was a separate territory between 1926 and 1931. The town was connected by rail with Port Augusta in the south in 1929, and by a bitumen road to Darwin in the north (a distance of more than 1500 kilometres) during the Second World War. The Joint Defence Space Research Facility at Pine Gap, near Alice Springs, was established following the signing of an agreement between the Australian and United States Governments in 1966. In the early 1980s Alice Springs served mainly the tourist, cattle and mining industries. Its population in 1981 was 18,395.

All for Australia League: *United Australia Party

'All the way with LBJ': *Vietnam War

ALP: *Australian Labor Party

ANA: *Australian Natives' Association

Angas, George Fife: *South Australian Company

Anglo–Japanese Alliance: Treaty between Britain and Japan, first signed in 1902 and renewed in 1905 and 1911. The treaty, the initial purpose of which was to prevent Russian expansion in the East, was a factor leading to Japan's involvement in the First World War. It was ended at the Washington Conference, during which several treaties were signed, including one between the United States of America, Britain, Japan and France in 1921.

Ansett Airlines of Australia: One of Australia's two main domestic airlines, the other being the government-owned *Trans Australia Airlines. Reginald (later Sir Reginald) Myles Ansett founded

4

Ansett Roadways in Victoria in 1931. He began
Ansett Airways, with a Hamilton–Melbourne air service relying upon one aircraft, in 1936. The size of
the fleet and the extent of the services increased in
the next few years. Ansett merged his Pioneer Tours,
a tourist coach service, and Ansett Airways to form
Ansett Transport Industries in 1946. The latter
bought Australian National Airways (ANA), a major
competitor, in 1957 to form Ansett-ANA, which later
became Ansett Airlines of Australia. A group of other
companies took over Ansett Transport Industries in
1981.

Antarctic Treaty: Treaty signed in 1959 by Argen-
tina, Australia, Belgium, Chile, France, Japan, New
Zealand, Norway, South Africa, the United Kingdom
and the United States of America. It came into effect
in 1961 and other countries later acceded to it. The
treaty reserves Antarctica for peaceful purposes,
pledges international scientific co-operation and pro-
hibits nuclear explosions. It does not affect prior
territorial claims, of which Australia has made the
largest, the *Australian Antarctic Territory, nor can
activities during its term be used to support claims.

Anzac: Name derived from the initials of the Australian and New Zealand Army Corps, which fought
in the First World War. It is reputed to have been
coined by clerks at General Birdwood's headquarters
in Cairo and was in use by early 1915. The place
where the Anzacs landed on the Gallipoli peninsula
on 25 April 1915 soon become known as Anzac Cove.
Originally the name was applied to those members
of the corps who took part in the *Gallipoli campaign,
but eventually it was applied to all Australian and
New Zealand troops who fought in the First World
War.

Anzac Day (25 April) commemorates the Anzac landing on the Gallipoli peninsula on 25 April 1915, during the *Gallipoli campaign. It has been observed
every year since 1916, becoming a holiday in one
state after another from about the mid-1920s. Its

function has been broadened to commemorate the dead of other wars. Anzac Day rituals include dawn services, marches, wreath-laying and speeches.

Anzac Legend: A significant theme in twentieth-century Australian history. It rests upon the assumption that Australia 'came of age' as a nation when the *Anzacs landed on Gallipoli on 25 April 1915. The Anzacs have been described thus:

They made a distinctive tradition—brave and tough in battle, excelling at any task to which they set their hands, careless of authority, hostile to most convention, proud of their distinctiveness and their country. For them the real Australian was the Anzac, the bushman on the stage of the world.[1]

Ellis Ashmead Bartlett (a British war correspondent), *Bean, the *Australian War Memorial and the *Returned Services League are among those people and institutions credited with helping to develop and maintain the Anzac Legend.

Anzac Pact: Security treaty between Australia and New Zealand, signed in 1944. It was also known as the Australia–New Zealand Agreement, and in New Zealand as the Canberra Pact. The South Pacific Commission was established under it in 1947. The Anzac Pact was virtually superseded by the *ANZUS Pact in 1951.

ANZAM: Popular name given to an arrangement by which Australia, New Zealand and Britain stationed defence forces in Malaya and Singapore. The arrangement began during the *Malayan Emergency, and continued after Malaya became independent in 1957, and after Malaysia was created in 1963. ANZAM was superseded by the Five Power Defence Arrangement in 1971.

ANZUS Pact: Security treaty between Australia, *New Zealand and the United States of America,

---

[1] Bill Gammage, 'Anzac', in John Carroll (ed.), *Intruders in the Bush, The Australian Quest for Identity* (Oxford University Press, Melbourne, 1982), p. 63.

signed at San Francisco in 1951 and ratified by Australia in 1952. It states that each party

recognizes that an armed attack in the Pacific Area on any of the Parties would be dangerous to its own peace and safety and declares that it would act to meet the common danger in accordance with its constitutional processes.

Related agreements have allowed the United States to establish bases in Australia, for example at North West Cape, at Pine Gap, and in the Woomera area. Controversy, and doubts about the future of the ANZUS Pact, arose in 1984 when New Zealand decided to ban nuclear vessels (including American) from its ports.

Archibald, Jules François (1856-1919), journalist, was born at Kildare, near Geelong, Victoria. He was baptized John Feltham, but later adopted the names Jules François. His father was a police sergeant. Archibald attended schools in Warrnambool before becoming an apprentice in the printery of the *Warrnambool Examiner* in 1870. From 1872 he worked in the printery of the *Warrnambool Standard*, and wrote some pieces for the *Hamilton Spectator* and the *Port Fairy Gazette*. In 1874 Archibald moved to Melbourne, where he worked as a stone-hand on the *Herald* and as a reporter on the *Echo* and then on the *Daily Telegraph*. He held several clerical positions, with the Victorian Education Department (1876-8), with a Queensland engineering firm, and with the *Evening News* in Sydney. He became a reporter on the latter newspaper. Archibald and John Haynes, a fellow journalist on the *Evening News*, founded the **Bulletin* in 1880. After being jailed for failure to pay costs in a libel action, Archibald and Haynes became employees of William Henry Traill, who took over as proprietor and editor of the *Bulletin* in 1882. Archibald visited England, France and the USA in 1883. When Traill sold out, Archibald and William McLeod took over as proprietors of the *Bulletin* in 1886 and Archibald was its editor until 1902. He spent some time in the Callan Park Asylum between 1906 and 1910. Archibald eventually sold his share in the *Bulletin* in 1914. He worked on *Smith's Weekly* for some months in 1919 before his final illness. He died in Sydney. He left an annual prize for portrait painting.

Army: Britain provided troops for garrison duties in Australia between 1788 and 1870. The first were marines with the *First Fleet; then came the *New South Wales Corps, and finally members of various regiments. These troops were mainly used to control groups such as convicts during the *transportation period, *diggers during the *gold-rushes, and *bushrangers. They were used, for example, to suppress the *Castle Hill Uprising, the *Eureka Rebellion and the *Lambing Flat Riots. All of the Australian colonies began to raise local forces during the mid-nineteenth century (there had been some earlier short-lived attempts to do so in New South Wales and South Australia), and they maintained them, in some cases intermittently, for the rest of the nineteenth century. Some Australian colonists went individually to the *Maori Wars, to which British armed forces were sent. A *Sudan Contingent was formed. Australians were also involved in the *Boer War. Following Federation in 1901, the newly created Commonwealth Government assumed responsibility for defence, and so the various colonial forces were amalgamated. The Royal Military College, at Duntroon, was founded in 1911. During the First World War the *Australian Imperial Force was formed, and a second Australian Imperial Force was formed during the Second World War. Women, other than those in the medical services, were not accepted in the army until 1941. Since the end of the Second World War, Australian troops have been sent to various conflicts, including the *Korean War, the *Malayan Emergency and the *Vietnam War. Various forms of *conscription (sometimes called national service) have been used at times to supplement numbers in the army. Australia's other armed forces are the *Royal Australian Navy and *Royal Australian Air Force.

Arthur, Sir George (1784–1854), soldier and colonial administrator, was born at Plymouth, England.

He joined the army in 1804, and subsequently served in several countries. He administered British Honduras from 1814 to 1822, and was Lieutenant-Governor of *Van Diemen's Land from 1824 to 1836. During his period in office there, Van Diemen's Land was separated administratively from New South Wales (1825), large land grants were given out, notably to the *Van Diemen's Land Company, the *Black Line was formed, and *Port Arthur was established. Arthur, a strong believer in transportation as a punishment, greatly improved the administration of the convict system, and the colony flourished under his rule. He went on to become Lieutenant-Governor of Upper Canada (1837-41) and Governor of Bombay (1842-6). He died in London. His publications include *Observations upon Secondary Punishment* (1833) and *Defence of Transportation* (1835).

ASEAN: *Association of South-East Asian Nations

Ashes, The: *Cricket

ASIO: *Australian Security Intelligence Organization

Assignment: *Transportation

Association of South-East Asian Nations (ASEAN): Alliance formed in Bangkok in 1967. Its members are Indonesia, Malaysia, the Philippines, Singapore and Thailand. Its aims are to foster stability and economic co-operation in South-East Asia.

Australia Day (26 January) commemorates the landing of *Phillip and the *First Fleet at Sydney Cove in 1788. It was first declared a holiday in 1838. In the past, different states have called it different names, such as Anniversary Day and Foundation Day. The Monday following Australia Day is a national holiday.

Australia Felix was the early name used for the present-day Western District of Victoria. In 1836 Thomas *Mitchell so named the area (*felix* being a Latin word meaning happy) because of its beauty and fertility.

Australia First Movement: A short-lived organization formed in Sydney in 1941, during the Second World War. P. R. Stephensen was the president of the organization, which expounded extreme nationalist and neo-fascist views. Four people with links with the organization were arrested on charges of conspiring to assist Japan in Western Australia in 1942. Two were convicted, imprisoned and later interned; the others were acquitted, but interned. Sixteen men, mostly members, were interned in New South Wales in 1942. (Two other people, one a member, the other an ex-member, were also interned in New South Wales and Victoria, but other factors were said to be involved in their cases.) Most of the sixteen were released in 1942, two in 1944, and Stephensen in 1945. Mr Justice Clyne, who conducted a commission of inquiry (1944–5) into the affair, found that the four Western Australians had been guilty, that the detention of eight of the sixteen had been unjustified and that they deserved financial compensation (which was paid), that there was fair opportunity for the sixteen to appeal, that restrictions imposed after release were fair, and that no further action should be taken.

Australian Agricultural Company: An agricultural and pastoral organization formed by a London syndicate in 1824. Its stated aim was 'the Cultivation and Improvement of the Waste Lands in the Colony of New South Wales'.[1] Its first agent, Robert Dawson, began operations at Port Stephens, north of *Newcastle, in 1826. Its activities, which have included raising and breeding of stock, leasing and selling of land, and coal-mining, continued in the 1980s.

Australian Airlines: *Trans Australia Airlines

---

[1]This extract from the Company's charter is cited in Stephen H. Roberts, *History of Australian Land Settlement, 1788–1920* (Macmillan, Melbourne, first edition 1924, reissued 1968), p. 57.

Australian Antarctic Territory: A large area of Antarctica claimed and administered by Australia as an external territory. It covers the islands and territories between 45°E and 136°E, and 142°E and 160°E. The area was claimed, following Antarctic exploration by *Mawson and other Australians, by a British Order-in-Council in 1933. The *Australian Antarctic Territory Acceptance Act* 1933 was ratified in 1936. Australia conducts scientific and other research in Antarctica, and bases were established at Mawson in 1954, Davis in 1957, and Casey in 1969. Australia's claim to the Australian Antarctic Territory, and other such claims, were suspended under the provisions of the *Antarctic Treaty.

Australian Atomic Energy Commission (AAEC): Statutory authority established under the *Atomic Energy Act* 1953. Its main functions, in general terms, are

development of uranium resources, operation of reactors, research in connection with uranium and atomic energy, sale of radioisotopes, training in nuclear science, and publication of research work.[1]

Its activities have included the control of uranium mining at *Rum Jungle, the establishment of uranium mining at Mary Kathleen and elsewhere, and the creation of the Lucas Heights research centre near Sydney.

Australian Ballet: *Australian Elizabethan Theatre Trust; *Borovansky, Edouard

Australian Ballot: *Secret Ballot

Australian Broadcasting Commission (ABC): Statutory authority established in 1932, replacing the Australian Broadcasting Company. Listeners' licence fees originally paid for it. It began broadcasting with eight capital-city and four regional radio

---

[1]Australian Atomic Energy Commission, *Thirty-First Annual Report, Being the Commission's Report for the Year Ended 30 June 1983*, p. 9.

Australian Broadcasting Corporation

stations in 1932. It founded studio orchestras throughout Australia and began to hold subscription concerts in the 1930s, and later established symphony orchestras in the state capitals. An overseas radio broadcasting service, known as Radio Australia, began in 1939. In 1948 an annual appropriation from the Commonwealth Parliament was introduced to pay most of the Commission's costs. Its television broadcasting began with channels in Sydney and Melbourne in 1956, followed by others elsewhere in later years. Colour television broadcasting began in 1975. Its FM (frequency modulation) radio broadcasting began in 1976. The Commission was renamed the Australian Broadcasting Corporation and restructured in 1983.

Australian Broadcasting Corporation: *Australian Broadcasting Commission

Australian Capital Territory (ACT): A federal territory in which *Canberra, Australia's national capital, is situated. A site in the Yass–Canberra district of New South Wales was chosen in 1908, and transferred to the Commonwealth in 1911. A small area of land at Jervis Bay, on the New South Wales coast, was included in the expectation that it would become a federal port; this area was increased in 1915.

Australian Colonies' Government Act (1850) is the usual name given to a British Act of Parliament that granted a limited form of self-government to *Victoria, *New South Wales, *South Australia and *Van Diemen's Land. Its actual name was *Act for the better Government of Her Majesty's Australian Colonies*. It separated the *Port Phillip District (renaming it Victoria) from New South Wales, and granted Legislative Councils (two-thirds of whose members were to be elected, one-third nominated) to Victoria, South Australia and Van Diemen's Land. New South Wales had already been granted such a Legislative Council in 1842. Franchise requirements were less strict than those imposed in New South Wales in 1842. The Legislative Councils could

12

make some laws, could change their franchise and membership qualifications, and (subject to Royal Assent) could split into upper and lower houses. Provision was made for similar measures in Western Australia in the future.

Australian Council of Trade Unions (ACTU): The main organization governing Australian trade unions. About 130 trade unions were affiliated with it in the late 1970s. The Australasian (from 1943, Australian) Council of Trade Unions was formed in 1927. It has played, and continues to play, a significant role in Australian industrial and political affairs.

Australian Country Party: *National Party

Australian Elizabethan Theatre Trust: Arts organization established in 1954 (commemorating the first visit of Queen Elizabeth II to Australia) to develop the performing arts in Australia. A non-profit-making public company, it was founded by public subscription and a Commonwealth Government grant. The Trust, acting in an entrepreneurial role, has presented many productions, including drama, opera, ballet, musicals and concerts, with performers from Australia and other countries. It established the Elizabethan Trust Opera Company (1956), from which the Australian Opera (1970) developed; the Marionette Theatre of Australia; the Elizabethan Sydney Orchestra (1967) and the Elizabethan Melbourne Orchestra (1969), to accompany the Australian Opera and the Australian Ballet; and the Theatre of the Deaf (1979). It also helped to establish the Australian Ballet (1962) and many theatre companies in various parts of Australia. The Trust's other main role has been to provide administrative services. The Australian Council for the Arts (founded 1968, succeeded in 1973 by the Australia Council) took over some of the Trust's functions. The Trust had about 7000 members in the early 1980s.

Australian Flying Corps: *Royal Australian Air Force

Australian Imperial Force (AIF): The name given to two military forces whose members were all volunteers. The first AIF was the main Australian expeditionary force during the First World War. *Bridges, who organized it in 1914, also named it. The second AIF was the comparable body during the Second World War.

Australian Labor Party: Australia's oldest political party. It is a democratic socialist party. The trade union movement organized colonial political parties from 1891 onwards. The failure of the *Maritime Strike and the *Shearers' Strikes acted as a catalyst in the formation of such parties. The Trades and Labor Council formed Labor Electoral Leagues in New South Wales, the Trades Hall Council formed the Progressive Political League in Victoria and similar bodies, with various names, were formed in other colonies. The Labor Party has governed federally a number of times (1904, 1908-9, 1910-13, 1914-16, 1929-32, 1941-9, 1972-5, 1983-   ), and for longer periods in some of the states. During the First World War it split, basically over the issue of *conscription, when *Hughes and his supporters left and helped to form the *Nationalist Party. During the *Great Depression it split again, basically over the issue of fiscal measures to combat the Depression; *Lyons and his supporters left and helped to form the *United Australia Party. In the mid-1950s it split for a third time, basically over the issue of communism; expelled members formed the Australian Labor Party (Anti-Communist), which later became the *Democratic Labor Party. Federal parliamentary leaders (to the mid-1980s) have been *Watson (1901-7), *Fisher (1907-15), *Hughes (1915-16), Frank Gwynne Tudor (1917-22), Matthew Charlton (1922-8), *Scullin (1928-35), *Curtin (1935-45), *Forde (1945), *Chifley (1945-51), *Evatt (1951-60), *Calwell (1960-7), *Whitlam (1967-78), William George Hayden (1978-83) and *Hawke (1983-   ).

Australian National Flag: A flag that has been in use for most of the twentieth century. The flag is described in the following way:

Australian-New Zealand Agreement

The Australian National Flag is the British Blue Ensign, consisting of a blue flag with the Union Jack occupying the upper quarter next the staff, differenced by a large white star (representing the six States of Australia and the Territories of the Commonwealth) in the centre of the lower quarter next the staff and pointing to the centre of the St George's Cross in the Union Jack and five white stars, representing the Southern Cross, in the fly, or half of the flag farther from the staff.[1]

In 1901 the Commonwealth Government joined a magazine entitled *The Review of Reviews* in holding a competition to choose a design for a national flag. The Havelock Tobacco Company also contributed to the prize money, which totalled £200. The competition attracted almost 33,000 designs from Australia and elsewhere. Five different competitors submitted the same winning design, which formed the basis for the present flag. The design was given royal approval in 1903, was changed slightly in 1909, and was officially adopted in 1953.

Australian Natives' Association (ANA): A friendly society ('for mutual insurance against distress in sickness or old age'). The Victorian Natives' Society (later Association) was founded in Melbourne in 1871. It restricted its membership to Victorian-born men over sixteen. In 1872 it changed its name to Australian Natives' Association and admitted Australian-born men over sixteen. Women were not admitted as members until 1964. The Association has been active in public debate, advocating causes that it has seen as being patriotic, notably federation, female *suffrage, defence, restriction of *immigration, and conservation. Numerous prominent Australians have been members.

Australian-New Zealand Agreement: *Anzac Pact

---

[1]From the *Flags Act* (1953), cited in Frank Cayley in 'Flags', in *The Australian Encyclopaedia*, volume 3 (The Grolier Society of Australia, Sydney, third edition, 1977, revised 1979), p. 48.

Australian Opera

Australian Opera: *Australian Elizabethan Theatre Trust

Australian Patriotic Association: An 'essentially emancipist organisation',[1] formed in New South Wales in 1835. Its leading members included Sir John Jamison (president), *Wentworth (vice-president) and Dr William Bland, and its London agent was Charles Buller. Its main purpose was to campaign for representative government. This was achieved, to some extent, with the passing of *An Act for the Government of New South Wales and Van Diemen's Land* (1842), which provided for a New South Wales Legislative Council consisting of thirty-six members, of whom twenty-four were to be elected and twelve nominated.

Australian Rules Football: *Football

Australian Security Intelligence Organization (ASIO): One of Australia's main security organizations. It was established by the Chifley Labor Government in 1949.

Australian War Memorial (AWM): A statutory authority. *Bean was largely responsible for its establishment. Its building in Canberra was opened in 1941. The Australian War Memorial's main functions are to commemorate the Australians who served in the wars in which Australia has participated, to collect records and promote research, and to display relics and art. It has become one of Canberra's major tourist attractions.

Australian Workers' Union (AWU): A large trade union. William Guthrie *Spence was mainly responsible for its founding in 1894, when a number of bush unions in New South Wales, Victoria, South Australia and Queensland merged. They included the Amalgamated Shearers' Union and the General

---

[1]W. G. McMinn, *A Constitutional History of Australia* (Oxford University Press, Melbourne, 1979), p. 28.

Labourers' Union. The estimated original membership was 30,000 men. The AWU, Australia's largest trade union for many years, did not affiliate with the *Australian Council of Trade Unions until 1967. In 1983 its membership, drawn from a diversity of industries, was about 123,000.

'Australia Will Be There': A popular Australian song during the First World War. Its publishers described it as 'Australia's Battle Song', the 'Australian War Song' and 'Australia's Marseillaise'. Its title became used as a patriotic slogan.

Australind: A proposed model settlement, to be based upon *Wakefield's ideas, on the Leschenault Estuary (near present-day Bunbury) in Western Australia. The Western Australian Company, which was constituted in 1840, planned to sell the land from England. The settlement collapsed within three or four years of the arrival of its first settlers in 1841. Suggested reasons for its failure include lack of labour, the settlers' lack of farming experience, financial mismanagement on the part of the Company, and the unsuitability of the area for small farms. A small town, also named Australind, now exists on the site.

AWM: *Australian War Memorial

AWU: *Australian Workers' Union

B

Baby Bonus: Popular name given to a maternity allowance introduced by the Commonwealth Parliament in 1912. Most Australian mothers (some groups, such as *Aborigines and Asians, were excluded) were paid a lump sum, originally £5, on the birth of each child. There was no means test. During the *Great Depression the amount was reduced and a means test was introduced. The Baby Bonus was abolished in 1978.

Ballarat Reform League

Ballarat Reform League: *Eureka Rebellion

Bank of New South Wales: The first bank established in Australia. When the bank opened for business in 1817, in premises in Macquarie Place, Sydney, the colony of New South Wales lacked a stable local currency. The bank was to have a nominal capital of £20,000; £1425 was subscribed when it opened. *Macquarie, who strongly supported the establishment of such a bank, granted it a charter of incorporation. The British Government declared the charter invalid, but an amended charter was issued in 1823. The Bank of New South Wales was reconstituted and incorporated under an Act of the Legislative Council in 1850, and eventually branches were established throughout Australia and elsewhere. The bank remained open throughout the bank crashes of 1893, one of the few to do so, and during the *Great Depression it led the way in devaluing the Australian pound in 1931. Over the years, it took over various smaller banks. It merged with the Commercial Bank of Australia in 1981, and in the following year adopted the name Westpac Banking Corporation. In the mid-1980s Westpac was one of Australia's major private banks.

Bank Nationalization: A controversial political issue in Australia between 1945 and 1949. The *Banking Act* 1945 gave the Commonwealth Government increased control over the banking system, but in 1947 the *High Court found some parts of the legislation to be invalid. The *Chifley Labor Government then passed the *Banking Act* 1947, which provided for the nationalization of the banking system. This move led to controversy and opposition, and in 1948 the High Court found some of this legislation, too, to be invalid. The Privy Council upheld the High Court's ruling in 1949. The bank nationalization issue has been seen as a major factor in the defeat of the Chifley Government in 1949.

Banks, Sir Joseph (1743–1820), naturalist, was born in England and was educated at Harrow, Eton and Oxford. He inherited considerable wealth. He studied natural science for much of his life, taking part in many expeditions and amassing large collections of animals, plants, rocks and other objects, and acted as a patron to many collectors and explorers. Banks, who has been described as the 'Father of Australia', took part in James *Cook's expedition in the *Endeavour* (1768-71), recommended *Botany Bay as the site for a proposed convict settlement to a British House of Commons committee in 1779, and later gave advice about the new settlement. He corresponded with *Phillip, *Hunter, *King, *Bligh, *Macquarie and early colonists, and he paid the expenses of collectors and explorers such as Alan Cunningham. He also pursued similar interests in other parts of the world. He was President of the Royal Society from 1778 until his death at Isleworth, England. His publications include *The Propriety of Allowing a Qualified Exportation of Wool* (1782), published anonymously, *A Short Account of the Causes of the Disease in Corn Called by Farmers the Blight, the Mildew, and the Rust* (1805), and a number of articles. J. C. Beaglehole edited *The Endeavour Journals of Joseph Banks 1768-1771* (1962).

Barcaldine: A town in central western Queensland. During the *Shearers' Strike of 1891, shearers established a number of camps, the best-known of which was at Barcaldine, where about 1000 shearers, said to be armed and advocating incendiarism, were camped. They flew the *Eureka flag. A number of union leaders were sentenced to terms of imprisonment following their arrests at Barcaldine.

Barry, Sir Redmond (1813-80), lawyer, was born in Ireland, was educated there and in England, and was appointed to the Irish Bar in 1838, before migrating to Australia in 1839. He practised as a barrister in Melbourne, and became Commissioner of the Court of Requests in 1843, Victoria's first Solicitor-General in 1851, and a judge of the Victorian Supreme Court in 1852. Well-known trials over which he presided include those of Raffaello Carboni and others involved in the *Eureka Rebellion, and that of *Kelly. Barry's many contributions to Melbourne's

development include helping to found the Melbourne
*Mechanics' Institute, the University of Melbourne
(of which he was the first Chancellor, from 1853 until
his death), the Public Library and the Art Gallery.
He died in Melbourne.

Barton, Sir Edmund (1849-1920), politician, was
born in Sydney. His father was a financial agent
and sharebroker; his mother ran a girls' school during the 1860s. Barton was educated at Fort Street
Model School, Sydney Grammar School, and the University of Sydney. He was admitted to the Bar in
1871 and was appointed Queen's Counsel in 1889.
He entered state politics in 1879 and was a Member
of the Legislative Assembly (1879-87, 1891-4, 1899-
1900) and the Legislative Council (1887-91, 1897-8).
He held various portfolios. Barton became the
acknowledged leader of the *federation movement
in New South Wales. During the late 1880s and 1890s
he played a prominent role in conferences, set up
branches of the Australasian Federation League and
campaigned for the referendums. In 1900 he led the
Australian delegation to London to explain the Commonwealth of Australia Constitution Bill. Barton
was Australia's first Prime Minister and Minister
for External Affairs (1901-3), leading a Protectionist
Ministry. The first Commonwealth Parliament was
noted for legislation relating to tariffs, *immigration
and defence. Barton was the senior puisne justice
on the new *High Court of Australia from 1903 until
his death. He supported controversial judgements
maintaining states' rights before 1914.

Barwick, Sir Garfield Edward John (1903-   ),
politician and lawyer, was born at Stanmore, New
South Wales. His father was a compositor. Barwick
was educated at Fort Street High School and the
University of Sydney. He was admitted to the Bar
in 1927, and was appointed King's Counsel in 1941.
He was the leading counsel for the banks in the *bank
nationalization controversy. Barwick also entered
federal politics, and was a Liberal Member of the
House of Representatives from 1958 to 1964. He was
Attorney-General (1958-64) and Minister for External Affairs (1961-4). Barwick was the Chief Justice

of the *High Court from 1964 to 1981; his judgements tended to favour a strict interpretation of legislation controlling industry and imposing taxation. He gave the Governor-General an opinion during the political crisis of 1975, an act seen by some people as controversial.

Basic Wage: A principle introduced by the *Harvester Judgement, made by the President of the *Commonwealth Conciliation and Arbitration Court, *Higgins, in 1907. Higgins defined it as being sufficient to cover 'the normal needs of the average [male] employee regarded as a human being living in a civilised community'. It was supposed to be for a family of about five, until the introduction of child endowment during the Second World War. Margins (as they became called) for skills were added to the basic wage, and cost-of-living adjustments were made automatically after 1913. A Royal Commission recommendation in 1920 that the basic wage should be higher was not implemented. During the *Great Depression, the real basic wage was reduced by 10 per cent in 1931, much of the reduction being restored in 1934. In 1937 the basic wage was divided into a needs wage and a prosperity loading. A basic wage for women, comprising 75 per cent of the male wage, was introduced in 1950. Automatic cost-of-living adjustments were dropped in 1953; it was no longer considered to be a needs wage, being above such a minimum. By then the real basic wage was about 50 per cent higher than in 1911, and the working week had decreased by about 20 per cent.[1] The Commonwealth Conciliation and Arbitration Commission replaced the basic wage with the total wage in 1967, a minimum wage for men also being prescribed. The various states also adopted the principle of the basic wage, and later that of the total wage, although some variations occurred.

Bass, George (1771-1803?), naval surgeon and explorer, was born in Lincolnshire, England, and

[1]These figures are taken from A. G. L. Shaw, *The Story of Australia* (Faber and Faber Ltd, London, fourth edition, 1972), p. 284.

arrived in New South Wales in the *Reliance* in 1795. In that year Bass, *Flinders and William Martin explored parts of *Botany Bay in the *Tom Thumb*. In 1796 the three sailed south to present-day Lake Illawarra, in a second *Tom Thumb*. Bass unsuccessfully attempted to cross the Blue Mountains, and made various other explorations on land. After sailing in the *Reliance* to South Africa, Bass searched successfully for coal at Coalcliff. Late in 1797 he travelled about 1930 kilometres south in a whaleboat, discovered the Shoalhaven River, Twofold Bay, Wilson's Promontory and Western Port, and deduced the existence of a strait between the mainland and *Van Diemen's Land. Bass and Flinders sailed south in the *Norfolk* in 1798, confirmed the existence of the strait (now called Bass Strait) and circumnavigated Van Diemen's Land, before returning to Port Jackson in 1799. Bass also undertook scientific investigation, and was elected a member of the Linnean Society in London in 1799. In that year he left New South Wales, on medical grounds, and returned to England, where he was given leave. He and Charles Bishop became partners in several commercial ventures. They bought the *Venus* and sailed for New South Wales with a cargo of goods to sell, but the venture failed. They then bought pork and salt in the South Pacific islands for *King; this venture was successful. Bass sailed in the *Venus*, with contraband to sell in South America, in 1803. Nothing more was heard of him or the *Venus*.

Batavia: A Dutch East India Company ship. In 1625 she left Holland for Batavia (present-day Jakarta), under Francisco Pelsaert's command, carrying more than 300 soldiers, crew and passengers. In 1629 she struck a reef off the Houtman Abrolhos (some seventy-five kilometres from present-day Geraldton, Western Australia). Some of those on board drowned; others reached nearby islands. Pelsaert, with a number of others, sailed an open boat to Batavia, about 3220 kilometres away. Meanwhile the ship's supercargo, Jerome Cornelius, led a group of mutineers who planned to take silver from the cargo, murder some of the survivors and seize the rescue ship. They killed more than 125 men, women and children. Webbye Hayes, a soldier, led a group calling itself the 'Defenders', which captured Cornelius and killed some of the mutineers. When Pelsaert returned, in the *Saerdam*, the mutineers were tried and tortured. Seven, including Cornelius, were hanged, and two others were marooned on the mainland. Pelsaert and the survivors sailed for Batavia. Some of the mutineers were punished during the voyage, and, some were retried in Batavia, where there were further hangings in 1630. The wreck of the *Batavia* was discovered in 1961 and some relics have been recovered from her.

Bates (née O'Dwyer), **Daisy May** (1863-1951), anthropologist and welfare worker, was born in Tipperary, Ireland. She lived in Australia from 1884 to 1894. She worked as a governess in New South Wales, married Jack Bates in 1885, and bore a son. She then lived in England from 1894 to 1899, during which time she worked as a journalist in London. After her return to Australia in 1899, she spent most of her life living with *Aborigines in Western Australia and South Australia, doing research and welfare work. Daisy Bates died in Adelaide. She wrote some 270 articles about Aborigines, and *The Passing of the Aborigines* (1938), which is autobiographical. Her papers are in the National Library of Australia, Canberra.

Batman, John: *Port Phillip Association

Battle of Brisbane: *Brisbane, Battle of

Battle of Pinjarra: *Pinjarra, Battle of

'Battle of the Plans': *Great Depression

Baudin, Thomas Nicolas (1754-1803), French navigator and naturalist, joined the French navy in 1774. He took part in several scientific expeditions before leading a cartographic and scientific expedition, generally considered to have been fairly unsuccessful, to *New Holland. His ships, the *Géographe* and

Naturaliste, arrived on the west coast, via Mauritius, in 1801. Baudin surveyed from Cape Leeuwin to Cape Levêque; Hamelin, commanding the *Naturaliste*, surveyed from Cape Leeuwin to Shark Bay. After visiting Timor, they sailed to *Van Diemen's Land, arriving there early in 1802, and surveyed the D'Entrecasteaux Channel. Baudin surveyed the south coast of New Holland, westwards from Wilson's Promontory, and met *Flinders at Encounter Bay. He believed that he was the first European to discover this coast, which he named Terre Napoléon, but in fact was the first to discover only the section from Cape Banks to Encounter Bay. After sailing south around Van Diemen's Land he arrived in Sydney in mid-1802. Hamelin surveyed Port Dalrymple and Western Port. Baudin sent the *Naturaliste* back to France from Sydney, and continued the expedition, having bought the *Casuarina*, which he placed under Freycinet's command, from *King. The expedition proceeded to King Island (where the British made it clear that Van Diemen's Land was a British possession), then surveyed *Kangaroo Island, the west coast of New Holland, and part of the north-west coast. In 1803 the two vessels reached Mauritius, where Baudin died shortly afterwards. The *Casuarina* was left there, but the *Géographe* arrived back in France in 1804. Baudin's expedition exacerbated British fears that the French might settle in New Holland or Van Diemen's Land.

Baynton (née Lawrence)**, Barbara Jane (Janet Ainsleigh)** (1857–1929), writer, was born to Irish parents at Scone, New South Wales, and was educated at home. She worked as a governess before the first of her three marriages. Barbara Baynton (who is known by her second husband's surname) alternated between residence in Australia and England. She died in Melbourne. She is best known for *Bush Studies* (1902), a collection of six stories of Australian outback life.

Bean, Charles Edwin Woodrow (1879–1968), journalist and historian, was born at Bathurst, New

South Wales, where his father was the headmaster of All Saints' College. Bean was educated in Australia and England, and graduated from Oxford before being called to the Bar of the Inner Temple, London, in 1903. He taught at Brentwood School, and as a travelling tutor, before returning to Australia, where he was admitted to the Bar in New South Wales in 1904. He again taught, this time at Sydney Grammar School, before going on circuit as a judge's associate in New South Wales from 1905 to 1907. Bean then turned to journalism; he became a reporter on the *Sydney Morning Herald* in 1908, and represented that newspaper in London from 1910 to 1912. Bean was the Official War Correspondent with the *Australian Imperial Force during the First World War; he went to Egypt with the first contingent, landed on 25 April 1915 at Gallipoli, where he was later wounded, and continued on to France, where he worked from 1916 to 1918. He then became the Official War Historian, a position that occupied him for many years. Bean played an important role in the creation of the *Australian War Memorial, and became chairman of its board in 1952. He founded the Parks and Playgrounds Movement of New South Wales. During the Second World War, Bean worked for the Department of Information for some time. He also chaired the Commonwealth Archives Committee in 1942. He chaired the promotion appeals board for the *Australian Broadcasting Commission from 1947 until 1958. He died in Sydney. Bean has been credited with being one of the main creators of the *Anzac Legend, and is best known for his work on the publication of *The Official History of Australia in the War of 1914-1918* (12 volumes, 1921–42), of which he wrote six volumes and edited the remainder. He wrote a number of other books about the First World War and other subjects.

Bennelong (1764?-1813), an *Aborigine, was captured on Governor *Phillip's orders and brought to Sydney Cove for observation in 1789. He escaped in 1790, but later returned to the settlement. A hut was built for him at Sydney Cove in 1791. Its site is now known as Bennelong Point. Phillip took Bennelong to England in 1792, where he was presented to King George III. Bennelong returned to Sydney in 1795. He died at Kissing Point.

BHP: *Broken Hill Proprietary Company Limited

Big Brother Movement: A migration assistance organization, founded in 1925 by Sir Richard Linton and others in Australia. Its purpose was to assist boys and young men wishing to work in rural occupations (later expanded to cover other occupations) in Australia. Members are known as Big Brothers, migrants as Little Brothers. The organization, which has mainly been privately funded, provides accommodation, food, welfare services and assistance to find employment, but not fares. The Big Brother Movement had sponsored some 12,500 boys and young men, almost all from Britain, by the beginning of 1983.

Bigge, John Thomas (1780–1843), judge and royal commissioner, was born in Northumberland, England, and educated at Newcastle Grammar School, Westminster School and Oxford. He pursued a legal career, and was Chief Justice of Trinidad from 1813 until his appointment in 1819 to inquire into the colony of *New South Wales. He visited New South Wales and *Van Diemen's Land for about eighteen months between 1819 and 1821, and produced three official reports in 1822 and 1823. These are usually referred to as the *Bigge reports. Bigge then helped to conduct a similar inquiry into Cape Colony, Ceylon and Mauritius (1823–9). His health was very poor when he returned to England in 1829. He died in London.

Bigge Reports (1822–3): Popular name given to *Bigge's findings following his inquiry, held between 1819 and 1821, into the colony of *New South Wales. Criticisms have been made of the way in which the inquiry was conducted. The three reports, *The State of the Colony of New South Wales* (1822), *The Judicial Establishment of New South Wales and of Van*

Diemen's Land (1823) and *The State of Agriculture and Trade in the Colony of New South Wales* (1823),

collectively prompted the insertion in the New South Wales Act (4 Geo. IV, c. 96) of clauses to set up limited constitutional government through a Legislative Council, to establish Van Diemen's Land as a separate colony, to enable extensive legal reforms and to make new provisions for the reception of convicts from England.[1]

Other recommendations, many of which were implemented, included the encouragement, by a variety of means, of the pastoral industry. Bigge was critical of *Macquarie, especially with regard to his treatment of convicts and *emancipists, which Bigge saw as being excessively lenient, and also of his expensive program of public works.

Bjelke-Petersen, Sir Johannes (1911–), politician, was born in New Zealand. He farmed in Queensland before becoming a Member of the Queensland Legislative Assembly in 1947, representing the Country Party (later renamed the *National Party). He became Premier in 1968.

Blackbirding: A practice that involved trafficking in coloured labour. Employers in Australia, Fiji and Samoa recruited Pacific Islanders (then more commonly known as Kanakas, from the Hawaiian word for 'man', South Sea Islanders or Polynesians) during the nineteenth century. An early attempt, in 1847, to use Pacific Islanders on New South Wales sheep stations was short-lived. Some 57,000 Pacific Islanders were brought to Queensland and northern New South Wales between 1863 and 1904, mainly from the New Hebrides (present-day Vanuatu) and the Solomon Islands. Most worked on sugar plantations, although a few worked on stations and cotton plantations. Their wages were low. In theory, they voluntarily entered contracts to work in Australia for fixed

---

[1] J. M. Bennett, 'John Thomas Bigge', in Douglas Pike (ed.), *Australian Dictionary of Biography*, volume 1 (Melbourne University Press, Melbourne, 1966), p. 100.

terms. In practice, they were subjected to abuses that included kidnapping, slavery and murder. From the 1860s onwards the Queensland Government passed various Acts relating to the recruitment and employment of Pacific Islanders. The Colonial Office in London also made some attempts to control the situation. It insisted on the inclusion of government agents on recruiting ships in 1871. The British Government passed the *Pacific Islanders Protection Act* in 1872 and strengthened it in 1875. A Queensland Government Royal Commission, held in 1884, led to a ban on the introduction of Pacific Islanders after the end of 1890, but the ban was lifted in 1892. The Commonwealth Government legislated to ban the introduction of Pacific Islanders from 1904 onwards, and to deport those who were already in Australia after 1906. Some who fulfilled certain qualifications were allowed to remain.

Black Friday: Popular name given to Friday, 13 January 1939, a day on which disastrous bushfires in Victoria reached a climax. There had been bushfires in December 1938 and the early days of January, and on several days, including Black Friday, high temperatures and strong winds prevailed. Seventy-one people died in the bushfires. A number of towns, including Noojee, were destroyed, stock losses were high and much property was lost, including many timber mills. Bushfires occurred elsewhere in Australia during the same period.

Black Line: A cordon of about 2000 white soldiers and civilians, formed in 1830 when Governor *Arthur decided to capture all of the *Aborigines living in the eastern part of *Van Diemen's Land, or to drive them on to Tasman's Peninsula, in the south-east of the island, where they were to be confined. The Black Line operated for about seven weeks. Only two Aborigines were captured.

Black Police: *Native Police

Black Thursday: Popular name given to Thursday, 6 February 1851, a day on which disastrous bushfires occurred in the colony of Victoria. There had been other bushfires in the preceding weeks, but those on Black Thursday were the worst. It was a day of extreme heat—the temperature in Melbourne at 11 a.m. was 47°C in the shade—and there were strong northerly winds. Many areas of the colony were burnt. At least ten people, including a woman and her five children, were killed. Stock losses were very high, and much property was destroyed.

Black Wednesday: The name given to Wednesday, 8 January 1878, when the Berry Ministry dismissed several hundred Victorian public servants, including judges and magistrates. The Legislative Assembly and the Legislative Council had reached a deadlock over reform of the latter and *payment of members. The Legislative Council had refused to pass the Appropriation Bill (which included provision for payment of members). Berry claimed that he could not pay those dismissed, because his government had not been voted funds, but he was not unwilling to attack his opponents. Some of those dismissed were later reinstated.

Blamey, Sir Thomas Albert (1884-1951), soldier, was born near Wagga Wagga, New South Wales. He was a schoolteacher before joining the *army. He studied, and then served, in India from 1911 onwards. During the First World War he took part, as a member of the *Australian Imperial Force, in the *Gallipoli campaign and in fighting in Europe. He held various positions, including that of chief-of-staff of the Australian Corps in France in 1918. He retired from the army in 1925, and was Chief Commissioner of Police in Victoria from 1925 to 1936. He later chaired the Manpower Committee. During the Second World War he commanded in turn the 1st Australian Corps, the Australian Imperial Force in the Middle East, and the Anzac Corps. He became Deputy Commander-in-Chief, Middle East, after the fall of Greece. In 1942 he became Commander-in-Chief of the Australian Military Forces and Commander of the Allied Land Forces in the South-West Pacific. He commanded operations in *New Guinea.

Blamey retired from the army in late 1945. In 1950 he became the first Australian to be promoted to the rank of field-marshal.

Blaxland, Gregory: *Blue Mountains, Crossing of the

Bligh, William (1754–1817), naval officer and *governor, was born at Plymouth in England. He pursued a naval career, sailing with James *Cook's last voyage, surviving the *Bounty* mutiny, and commanding ships in the battles of Camperdown (1797) and Copenhagen (1801). He was made a Fellow of the Royal Society in 1801, and succeeded *King as Governor of New South Wales in 1806. His conflict with the *New South Wales Corps culminated in the *Rum Rebellion of 1808. After his return to England in 1810, Bligh was virtually exonerated. He died in England.

Bloody Friday: Popular name given to Friday, 19 June 1931, when policemen and anti-evictionists fought a violent battle at a house in the Sydney suburb of Newtown. During the *Great Depression, many tenants who were unable to pay their rents were evicted. The Communist-led Unemployed Workers' Movement prevented some such evictions. The police, instructed by the *Lang Labor Government, attempted to stop the activities of the Unemployed Workers' Movement, and on the morning of 19 June about forty policemen attempted to enforce an eviction order at 143 Union Street, Newtown. About eighteen people were defending the house. The policemen were armed with guns; the anti-evictionists were armed with makeshift weapons, such as bricks and iron bars. A crowd said to consist of many thousands watched the battle that ensued. Eventually the policemen overpowered the anti-evictionists. Fourteen anti-evictionists and thirteen policemen were injured; some of those injured received fractured skulls. A further demonstration took place at Railway Square in the evening. More than twenty people were arrested on Bloody Friday.

Blue Mountains, Crossing of the: A major feat of exploration in 1813. The Blue Mountains, which form part of the Great Dividing Range, prevented westward expansion of white settlement in New South Wales. Numerous attempts to cross them failed. In 1813, Gregory Blaxland, William Lawson and *Wentworth discovered a possible route, but did not actually cross the main range. George William Evans, using the same route, did so later in the year. William Cox, acting on *Macquarie's instructions, supervised the building of the first road across the Blue Mountains in 1814 and 1815. The crossing of the Blue Mountains led to extensive pastoral expansion.

Bodyline Series (1932–3): A controversial Test *cricket series played between England and Australia during the Great Depression. Douglas Jardine captained the English team, Bill Woodfull the Australian. Harold Larwood and Bill Voce used bodyline (or fast leg theory, as the English called it) bowling against the Australians. It consisted of fast, short-pitched deliveries, aimed (according to the Australians) at the batsman's body rather than the wicket, with the fieldsmen placed in a leg-side position. The batsman could defend his body and risk being caught, or risk being hit by the ball. The Australians saw it as an attempt to curb *Bradman's high scoring, all other methods having failed. Press and public protest became vigorous during the third Test, in Adelaide, when Woodfull and W. A. Oldfield were injured. After being injured, Woodfull made his now-famous comment in the dressing-room to Pelham Warner, the English manager, that one team was playing cricket and the other was not. During the Test, the Australian Cricket Board of Control cabled the Marylebone Cricket Club, in London, claiming that bodyline bowling was unsportsmanlike and that 'Unless stopped at once it is likely to upset the friendly relations existing between Australia and England.'[1] The Marylebone Cricket Club rejected

---

[1]Cited in numerous places, including J. H. Fingleton, *Cricket Crisis* (Cassell and Company Ltd, London, 1946), p. 20.

Australia's claims and stated that they would agree
to cancellation of the rest of the series if Australia
wished. The series continued. England won the
Ashes, having lost only the second Test, in Melbourne. The Marylebone Cricket Club altered its rules
in 1935, banning such bowling.

Boer War (1899-1902): The second of two wars
between the British and the Boers in South Africa.
The Australian colonies, as parts of the British
Empire, became involved. Enthusiasm was keen,
even before the war began; Queensland offered
troops, Victoria and New South Wales followed suit,
and the military commandants of the six colonies
conferred in Melbourne and agreed upon a scheme
to send men if necessary. In total, about 16,500 men,
of whom about 6800 were Bushmen (mostly un-
trained volunteers, paid either by public subscription
or, later, by the British Government), left Australia
for South Africa. After Federation in 1901, the Commonwealth took responsibility for the defence forces;
accordingly, those fighting in South Africa became
known as the Australian Commonwealth Horse. The
defence of the Elands River at Brakfontein was the
most significant fighting in which the Australians
were involved. The war ended with the signing by
the British and the Boers of the Treaty of Vereeniging
at Pretoria on 31 May 1902. Five hundred and eighty-
eight Australians had been killed or had died from
disease. The execution of 'Breaker' Morant and Peter
Joseph Handcock, of the Bushveldt Carbineers, an
irregular unit consisting largely of Australians, by
the British, after the two soldiers had been found
guilty of charges relating to the deaths of some Boer
prisoners, has inspired controversy. A small group
of female Australian nurses served in the war.

'Boldrewood, Rolf': *Browne, Thomas Alexander

Bolte, Sir Henry Edward (1908-   ), politician, was
born at Ballarat, Victoria, and educated at Skipton
State School and Ballarat Grammar School. Bolte,
like his father, became a farmer. During the Second
World War he served in the *army, from 1940 to 1944.

He entered state politics, and was a Liberal Member of the Victorian Legislative Assembly from 1947 to 1972. Bolte was Premier and Treasurer, leading a Liberal Ministry, from 1955 to 1972.[1] He also held various other portfolios between 1948 and 1950, and from 1955 onwards. Bolte strongly supported states' rights, and his support for capital punishment aroused controversy. He retired in 1972.

Borovansky, Edouard (1902–59), ballet dancer, choreographer, and director, was born in Prerov (in present-day Czechoslovakia), and was educated at the Prague National Theatre Ballet School (and also belonged to its company for some time). He first visited Australia in 1929, with Anna Pavlova's company. Borovansky was a soloist with the Ballet Russe de Colonel de Basil from 1932 to 1939, when he left during an Australian tour. He began a ballet school in Melbourne in 1939, and an affiliated ballet club was formed the next year. His students performed as the Borovansky Australian Ballet in 1940. The Borovansky Ballet, as it became called, continued (with several breaks) until 1961, and then formed the basis for the Australian Ballet, established in 1962. The former's best-known dancers included Kathleen Gorham, Peggy Sager, Paul Hammond, Garth Welch and Marilyn Jones, and Dame Margot Fonteyn appeared with the company as a guest in 1957. Its repertoire covered classical works and some modern ballets, including Borovansky's *Terra Australis*. Borovansky, who has been described as 'the father of Australian ballet', died in Sydney.

Botany Bay: An inlet on the eastern coast of Australia, about eight kilometres south of present-day Sydney. James *Cook was the first white person to discover it. His first landing in Australia (or *New Holland, as it was then called) took place there on 29 April 1770, and he named it Stingray Bay. He stayed there for a week, during which time *Banks observed many new plants, hence its change of name

---

[1]The party in Victoria was known as the Liberal and Country Party for some of these years.

to Botany Bay. The British Government instructed
*Phillip and the *First Fleet to settle there, but on
his arrival at Botany Bay in 1788, Phillip decided
instead to establish the settlement at Port Jackson.
During the *transportation era the name Botany Bay
was often used as a synonym for New South Wales.

Bounty Mutiny: A mutiny that occurred near the
Tongan Islands in 1789. HMS *Bounty*, under *Bligh's
command, was carrying a cargo of bread-fruit trees
from Tahiti to the West Indies when the crew muti-
nied. Bligh and eighteen officers were cast off in a
small open boat, in which they sailed to Timor, a
distance of some 3618 miles, in about six weeks. Bligh
was exonerated at a court martial in England. Some
of the mutineers surrendered and others were captured in 1791. The frigate *Pandora*, taking them back
to England, sank in Torres Strait. The victims
included some of the mutineers. Ten of the mutineers
were eventually court-martialled in England; four
were acquitted and six were sentenced to death (but
only three were hanged). Fletcher Christian and
some of the other mutineers, with a number of Tahi-
tians, settled on Pitcairn Island in 1790. Their descendants moved to *Norfolk Island in 1856. Bligh's
account of the mutiny, *A Narrative of the Mutiny
on Board H.M.S. Bounty*, was published in London
in 1791. Marine archaeologists investigated the *Pandora* wreck in the 1980s.

Bourke, Sir Richard (1777–1855), *governor, was
born in Dublin, and educated at Westminster School
and Oxford, before pursuing a military career. From
1826 to 1828 he acted as Governor of Cape Colony,
where he was responsible for ending censorship of
the press, tried to reduce border conflict with the
Kaffirs, and legislated to improve conditions for free
coloured people, including the Hottentots. He was
appointed Governor of New South Wales in 1830, and
arrived in Sydney the following year. In New South
Wales, Bourke succeeded in extending financial
assistance beyond the Church of England to other
denominations, but his attempts to assist non-
Anglican schools were defeated. He introduced a
'bounty' system of *immigration. He also introduced

licences giving *squatters the right to use Crown lands. His conflict with *exclusives during his term of office reached a climax in an altercation with Campbell Riddell, the Colonial Treasurer, which led to Bourke's resignation in 1837.

Boxer Rising: A Chinese rebellion in 1900 against Europeans in China. A contingent of about 460 naval volunteers from Victoria and New South Wales went to China to assist Britain and other European countries in suppressing the rebellion. The men saw some fighting, but were mostly involved in non-combatant duties at Peking and Tientsin. They were withdrawn in 1901. Six Australian deaths occurred during the Boxer Rising.

Boyd, Benjamin (1803?-51), entrepreneur, was born in London, and became a stockbroker. Boyd sailed to Australia in 1842, having been promised some government assistance with his ventures, which were to be funded by the bank he had founded in 1839, the Royal Bank of Australia. He established a Sydney branch of the bank, ran a steamship service between Sydney, Twofold Bay and Hobart Town, became a *squatter, with properties in the Monaro district and the *Port Phillip District, and established a wool-cleaning establishment and stores at Neutral Bay. In 1847 he brought about 200 Pacific Islanders to Australia to use as cheap labour, a forerunner of *blackbirding, but the scheme failed within a year. Boyd founded two small towns at Twofold Bay, Boyd Town and East Boyd (which was the site of a whaling station), and represented the Port Phillip District in the Legislative Council of New South Wales from 1844 to 1845. In 1847 he was dismissed as director of the Royal Bank, which went into liquidation in 1849. Boyd sailed his yacht to California in 1849, but failed at the gold-fields, and in 1851 returned to the Pacific Islands, where he was apparently murdered in the Solomon Islands. A search for him in 1854 was unsuccessful.

Boyd Family: A well-known Australian artistic and literary family. Its members include **Arthur Merric Boyd** (1862-1940), painter, notably of water-colours;

Boyd Town

Arthur Merric Bloomfield Boyd (1920-), painter, whose paintings include the *Love, Marriage and Death of a Half-Caste* series, first exhibited in 1958; **David Fielding Gough Boyd** (1924-), potter and painter; **Guy Martin à Beckett Boyd** (1923-), sculptor; **Martin à Beckett Boyd** (who sometimes used the pseudonym 'Martin Mills') (1893-1972), writer, whose novels, some of which are based upon his own family, include *The Montforts* (1928), *Lucinda Brayford* (1946), *The Cardboard Crown* (1952), *A Difficult Young Man* (1955), *Outbreak of Love* (1957), *When Blackbirds Sing* (1962), and *The Tea-Time of Love* (1969); **Robin Gerard Penleigh Boyd** (1919-71), architect and writer, whose books include *Australia's Home* (1952), *The Australian Ugliness* (1960), and *The Great Australian Dream* (1972); **Theodore Penleigh Boyd** (1890-1923), painter and etcher; and **William Merric Boyd** (1888-1959), potter.

Boyd Town: *Boyd, Benjamin

Braddon's Blot: Derogatory term used to describe Section 87 of the *Constitution of the Commonwealth of Australia. It was named after Sir Edward Braddon, Premier of Tasmania from 1894 to 1899. Section 87 says:

During a period of ten years after the establishment of the Commonwealth and thereafter until the Parliament otherwise provides, of the net revenue of the Commonwealth from duties of customs and of excise not more than one-fourth shall be applied annually by the Commonwealth towards its expenditure.

The balance shall, in accordance with this Constitution, be paid to the several States, or applied towards the payment of interest on debts of the several States taken over by the Commonwealth.

A new financial arrangement, less favourable to the states, was made in 1910; it gave annual grants to the states of twenty-five shillings per head of population. But this was not in the Constitution, and could be repealed by Parliament at any time. It was repealed under the *Financial Agreement.

Bradfield, John Job Crew: *Sydney Harbour Bridge

Bradman, Sir Donald George (1908-), cricketer, was born at Cootamundra, New South Wales, and educated at Bowral Intermediate High School. Bradman played his first interstate match for New South Wales in 1927. He went on to play in many Sheffield Shield and Test matches (including the *bodyline series). He captained the Australian team in Test matches against England from 1936 to 1948. Bradman has often been described as the greatest batsman in the history of *cricket. He scored 8926 runs, averaging 110 runs, in Sheffield Shield cricket; 6996 runs, averaging 99.9 runs, in Test cricket; and 28,067 runs, averaging 95 runs, in all first-class cricket. He held the world's record score, in first-class cricket, of 452 not out. He chaired the Australian Board of Control for International Cricket from 1960 to 1963, and from 1969 to 1972. Bradman was also a stock and share broker. His publications include *Farewell to Cricket* (1950), *How to Play Cricket* (1955) and *The Art of Cricket* (1958).

Brennan, Christopher John (1870-1932), poet, was born to Irish parents in Sydney. His father was a brewer, later a publican. Brennan was educated at the Good Samaritan School and Convent, Sydney; St Aloysius's College; St Ignatius's College, Riverview; and the University of Sydney and the University of Berlin. He did not complete his doctorate. Before travelling to Berlin in 1892, Brennan taught at St Patrick's College, Goulburn, and St Ignatius's College, Riverview; after returning, he worked as a cataloguer, and later as an assistant librarian, in the Public Library of New South Wales (1895-1909). He pursued an academic career at the University of Sydney; he was a temporary lecturer in languages (1896-7, 1908-9) and in classics (1908) before being appointed to a permanent position in French and German in 1909; he became Associate Professor of German and Comparative Literature in 1921, but lost his position in 1925 because he had committed adultery. Brennan taught again in schools, at the Marist

'Brent of Bin Bin'

Brothers' High School, Darlinghurst (1927), and at St Vincent's College, Potts Point (1930–2). He died in Sydney. Brennan is best known for his poetry, which was influenced by the French Symbolists. His publications include *XVIII Poems, Being the First Collection of Verse and Prose* (1897), *XXI Poems: (1893–1897) Towards the Source* (1897), *Poems* (dated 1913, published 1914) and *A Chant of Doom and Other Verses* (1918).

'Brent of Bin Bin': *Franklin, Stella Maria(n) Sarah Miles

Bridges, Sir William Throsby (1861–1915), soldier, was born at Greenock, Scotland. His father was a naval officer. Bridges was educated at the Royal Naval School, New Cross, London, and at the Royal Military College of Canada, but did not complete his course at the latter. He followed his family to New South Wales in 1879, and he worked in the civil service there for some years before joining the New South Wales permanent forces in 1885. He served with the British cavalry in the *Boer War for a few months, but was invalided to England with enteric fever. He became the first Chief of the Australian General Staff in 1909. Some months later, he went to England, where he represented Australia on the Imperial General Staff. Bridges established the Royal Military College at Duntroon in 1911, and remained as its Commandant until 1914. As Inspector-General of the Australian Military Forces, he raised the *Australian Imperial Force at the outbreak of the First World War, and was appointed, with the rank of major-general, to command it. His division was the first to land at Anzac Cove on 25 April 1915, during the *Gallipoli campaign. Bridges was wounded in Monash Valley on 15 May 1915 and died three days later, while on the way to hospital in Egypt. He was knighted the day before his death. His remains were buried in the Australian Capital Territory.

Brisbane, the capital city of *Queensland, lies on both sides of the Brisbane River, about twenty

kilometres from the river mouth in *Moreton Bay.
A *penal settlement, named after the Governor of
New South Wales, was established there in 1824 and
operated until 1839. Free settlement was forbidden
until 1842, the year in which the first Brisbane land
sales occurred. Brisbane became a city in 1902. Its
population was about 5000 in 1859, 25,916 in 1871,
101,554 in 1891, and 942,836 in 1981.

Brisbane, Battle of: Popular name for one of the
most serious outbreaks of violence between Australian and American servicemen while the latter were
stationed in Australia during the Second World War.
A number of brawls occurred in Brisbane on 26
November 1942. Australian civilian and military
police and American military police were called in.
During the fighting, which lasted about three hours,
one Australian soldier was killed and at least eight
other Australians, including one civilian, were
wounded. Despite added police precautions, further
fighting broke out the following evening, lasting for
about four hours.

Brisbane Line: Popular name given to a supposed
plan to defend only the more populated areas of Australia (the settled areas south-east of Brisbane)
against Japanese attack during the Second World
War. E. J. Ward, the Minister for Labour and
National Service in the *Curtin Labor Government,
repeatedly alleged that previous non-Labor governments had made such a plan, and referred to it in
Parliament as the Brisbane Line in 1943. The allegations were denied. Curtin stated that the only such
plan was one prepared by military leaders, discussed
by the Advisory War Council in 1942, and rejected
by politicians from both sides. Ward then claimed
that an important document was missing from the
files. A Royal Commission was held into this claim,
during which time Ward was relieved of his portfolio;
it found that there was no missing document.

Brisbane, Sir Thomas (Makdougall from 1826)
(1773–1860), soldier, astronomer and *governor, was
born near Largs, in Ayrshire, Scotland, and was

educated by tutors, at the University of Edinburgh, and at the English Academy, Kensington. He then pursued a military career and fought in the Peninsular War, attaining the rank of general. Brisbane was in command of the Munster district in Ireland when he was appointed Governor of New South Wales in 1820. He relieved *Macquarie the following year. His instructions were based largely upon *Bigge's recommendations. A small nominated Legislative Council was established during his term of office. He faced problems because of the conflict between *emancipists and *exclusives in the colony, and he clashed with Frederick Goulburn, the Colonial Secretary. Brisbane protested to the Colonial Office over Goulburn's conduct, and both Brisbane and Goulburn were recalled in 1824. He left the colony in 1825, and was succeeded by *Darling. Brisbane was a keen astronomer; he built two observatories in Scotland and one in Australia (at *Parramatta).

Broken Hill: A mining centre situated in the Barrier Range, New South Wales, about 1100 kilometres west of Sydney. *Sturt explored the area and named it after its physical characteristics in 1844. Silver, lead and zinc were found in the area during the 1870s. Charles Rasp, a boundary rider, found the main lode in 1883. It was to become world-famous. The *Broken Hill Proprietary Company began there. Broken Hill, sometimes known as the Silver City, is significant because of the extent of its mineral deposits, and because of the strength of the Barrier Industrial Council, which has represented unions there since the Council's foundation in 1923. Mining continues in the area (which is known also for its wool-growing), but has been declining in recent years.

Broken Hill Proprietary Company Limited (BHP): Australia's largest company, BHP was formed in 1885 to mine silver, lead and zinc deposits found at *Broken Hill, New South Wales. It continued to mine there until 1939, while diversifying its activities elsewhere. It began steel-making at *Newcastle, New South Wales, in 1915. BHP's activities in the mid-1980s included steel-making, mining, oil production and manufacturing.

Broome, Sir Frederick Napier (1842-96), *governor, was born in Canada and educated in England. He farmed in New Zealand for a number of years, and held official positions in Natal and Mauritius, before his term of office as the Governor of Western Australia (1883-9). Broome supported the introduction of *responsible government for Western Australia, which was granted in 1890. After leaving Australia he acted as Governor of Barbados for some time, and was Governor of Trinidad from 1891 to 1896. His publications include *Poems from New Zealand* (1868) and *The Stranger of Seriphos* (1869).

Broughton, William Grant (1788-1853), Anglican clergyman, was born in England, worked as a clerk in the East India Company for some time, and was educated at Cambridge University. He was ordained as a deacon in 1818, and later as a priest. Broughton was appointed Archdeacon of New South Wales in 1828, arrived in Sydney the following year, and became Bishop of Australia (a new position) in 1836. He opposed *Bourke's religious and educational policies. Broughton built numerous churches and schools, began the building of St Andrew's Cathedral, and helped to found new dioceses in New Zealand and Australia. He became Bishop of Sydney, with authority over the other Australasian bishops, and organized a significant conference of these bishops in 1850. Broughton died in England, while on a trip to discuss church government.

Browne (né Brown), **Thomas Alexander** (1826-95), novelist, was born in London. His father, a shipmaster, brought his family to Australia about 1831. Browne was educated in Sydney at W. T. Cape's school and at Sydney College, and in Melbourne by the Reverend David Boyd. He was a *squatter from 1844 to 1869, at first near Portland, then near Swan Hill, and finally near Narrandera. He then became a government official, holding various positions at Gulgong, Dubbo, Armidale and Albury, in the years 1871-95. After retiring, he lived in Melbourne until his death. Browne wrote under the pseudonym 'Rolf Boldrewood', and is best known for his novel *Robbery Under Arms, A Story of Life and Adventure in the*

Bush and in the Goldfields of Australia (1888), much
of which was based upon actual events. It was first
published as a weekly serial in the *Sydney Mail*
(1882-3). At least one play and several films have
been based upon it. Browne wrote many other novels.

Bruce, Minnie (Mary) Grant (1878-1958), writer,
was born near Sale, Victoria. Her father, a surveyor,
was Irish; her mother was of Welsh descent. Mary
Grant Bruce was educated at Miss Estelle Beausire's
Ladies' High School in Sale. She then moved to Melbourne, where she worked as a secretary and then
as a journalist. She spent much of her life in Britain
and Europe. She is best known for her many children's books, particularly those in the Billabong series. The fifteen Billabong books, which relate the
saga of the Linton family and are set in Victoria,
were published between 1910 and 1942.

**Bruce of Melbourne, Stanley Melbourne, 1st
Viscount** (1883-1967), politician, was born in Melbourne, and educated at Melbourne Church of England Grammar School and Cambridge University.
He managed the London branch of his family's firm,
Paterson, Laing and Bruce, and practised at the Bar
for some time. During the First World War, Bruce
served in the British Army from 1914 to 1917; he
fought at Gallipoli, was wounded, and was invalided
to England in 1915. After returning to Australia, he
was a Member of the House of Representatives (1918-
29, 1931-3), representing the Nationalists, then the
*United Australia Party. He was Prime Minister and
Minister for External Affairs from 1923 to 1929, leading the Nationalist-Country Party coalition, sometimes known as the Bruce-*Page Government. Bruce
also held other portfolios. His main policies during
this period were summed up in the slogan *'Men,
Money and Markets'. The coalition was defeated, and
Bruce lost his own seat, in the 1929 federal elections.
Bruce was active in the *League of Nations; he represented Australia at the League (1921, 1932-9), was
on the Council (1933-6), and served as President
(1936). Bruce was Australia's High Commissioner in
London from 1933 to 1945. He played a particularly

significant role in representing Australia in London during the Second World War, serving on the British War Cabinet and Pacific War Council (1942-5). After retiring as High Commissioner, he remained in Britain, where he became director of a number of companies. He chaired the World Food Council (1947-51) and the British Finance Corporation for Industry (1947-57). He was the first Chancellor of the Australian National University (1951-61). Bruce died in London.

Bubonic Plague: An infectious disease caused by bacteria spread by flea-carrying rats. Cases of bubonic plague were found in Australia in January 1900, and about 1200 cases were recorded in the following ten years. Most of these occurred in New South Wales and Queensland, some in Western Australia, and a few in Victoria and South Australia; none were recorded in Tasmania. The worst year was 1900. The bubonic plague scare led to some improvements in hygiene, including the demolition of slums, the disposal of much rubbish, and the destruction of tens of thousands of rats.

Buckland River Riot: One of a number of anti-Chinese riots that occurred in Australia during the *gold-rushes (the worst being the *Lambing Flat Riots). On 4 July 1857 a mass meeting of white *diggers on the Buckland River gold-field, in north-eastern Victoria, resolved to expel the Chinese from the colony. At the time there were about 30,000 Chinese people in Victoria, about 2000 of whom were on the Buckland River gold-field. Shortly after the meeting, about 100 white diggers, allegedly led by Americans, drove the Chinese from that field, destroyed and stole their property, and attacked some of them. Some of the Chinese are believed to have been killed. Three whites were charged with rioting and one with theft; one was found guilty of 'unlawful assemblage' and the others were acquitted.

Buckley, William (1780-1856), so-called 'wild white man', was born in England. In 1802 he was sentenced to *transportation for life for having received stolen goods. In 1803 he and two companions escaped from a short-lived convict settlement near present-day *Sorrento, Victoria. His companions disappeared, but Buckley lived among *Aborigines until 1835, when he surrendered at Indented Head to a party of the newly arrived settlers in the *Port Phillip District. Buckley was pardoned, and acted as an interpreter with Aborigines for some time after Melbourne was founded in 1835.

Bulletin: A weekly journal. *Archibald and John Haynes founded the Sydney *Bulletin* in 1880. It became very popular, especially during the late nineteenth century, and was often fondly referred to as 'the Bushman's Bible'. By the late 1880s about 80,000 copies of each issue were being sold. Its early policies were nationalistic, radical and republican. Archibald edited the *Bulletin* from 1886 to 1902. A. G. Stephens edited the Red Page, a literary section on the inside front cover, from 1896 to 1906. The *Bulletin* promoted Australian writers and artists. Its writers included *Brennan, *Dennis, *Gilmore, *Lawson, 'Breaker' Morant, A. B. *Paterson and 'Steele Rudd' (*Davis); its artists included 'Hop' (Livingston Hopkins), *Lambert, Norman *Lindsay, David Low and David Souter. During the First World War, the *Bulletin* abandoned its Labor sympathies over the *conscription controversy and became a conservative journal. It continued to be published in the mid-1980s.

'Bunyip aristocracy': Derogatory term used to describe the hereditary peerage proposed by the Select Committee, chaired by *Wentworth, that drafted the New South Wales Constitution. Daniel Deniehy referred to 'Botany Bay aristocrats' and a 'bunyip aristocracy' in a speech on the Bill in 1853. The proposal was dropped. Bunyips are mythical Australian monsters, supposed to live in lakes and swamps.

Burke and Wills Expedition: Popular name for the Great Northern Exploration Expedition, a disastrous enterprise that cost seven lives. Robert

O'Hara Burke, an Irish-born policeman, led the expedition, organized by the Royal Society of Victoria and funded by that body, the Victorian Government and the public. The expedition's main purpose was to make the first crossing of Australia from south to north, which South Australians also were attempting. The well-equipped expedition left Melbourne in August 1860. William John Wills, an English-born surveyor and meteorologist, became second-in-charge during the expedition. Burke left a party at Menindie, which was to follow on, and established a base at Cooper's Creek in November 1860. William Brahe was left in charge there. Burke, Wills, John King and Charles Gray, with six camels, one horse and three months' provisions, left the Cooper's Creek base in December and reached the edge of the Gulf of Carpentaria in February 1861, thus becoming the first to make the crossing. (*Stuart, the South Australian, became the second in July 1862.) Gray died on the return to Cooper's Creek. The other three reached the base on 21 April 1861, only to discover that Brahe's party had left for Menindie that day. Burke decided, against Wills's advice, not to follow but to make for Mount Hopeless. Brahe returned to the base fifteen days after leaving it, but saw no signs of Burke, nor of the message Burke had left, and so left again. Several search parties were sent out, from Melbourne and elsewhere. One, led by A. W. Howitt, found King, who had been living with *Aborigines, in September 1861. Burke and Wills had died from malnutrition and exhaustion at the end of June. The public regarded them as heroes, but commissioners appointed by the Victorian Government to inquire into the expedition were very critical of Burke and several others.

Burrangong Riots: *Lambing Flat Riots

Bushfires: *Black Friday; *Black Thursday

'Bushman's Bible': *Bulletin

Bushrangers: Law-breakers who lived in the bush. The term came into use in the early nineteenth century. The first bushrangers were escaped *convicts, but the main period of bushranging, in the south-eastern colonies (where it was most common), was probably during the 1850s and 1860s. The best-known bushrangers include Martin Cash, John Donahoe, Frank Gardiner, Ben Hall, Michael Howe, *Kelly and his gang, Frank McCallum ('Captain Melville'), Dan Morgan, Andrew George Scott ('Captain Moonlite') and Frederick Ward ('Captain Thunderbolt').

Buvelot, Abram-Louis (1814–88), landscape painter, was born in Switzerland, and studied in Lausanne and Paris. He spent some eighteen years in Brazil, where he painted and was a photographer. He returned to Switzerland in 1852. Buvelot later visited the East Indies (present-day Indonesia) and India, and migrated to Victoria in 1865. He worked as a photographer in Melbourne for some months, before returning to painting and some teaching. Poor health forced him to stop painting in 1884, and he died in 1888. Bernard Smith wrote of him:

Louis Buvelot, through his teaching, wide influence and example may be said to have created a school. For this reason he has been rightly called the Father of Landscape Painting in Australia... He influenced... not only a number of artists who continued to supply the plein-air tradition of the Barbizon school to the Australian landscape, but also the men who were to create the Heidelberg School of Australian impressionist painting.[1]

Buvelot's paintings include *Summer Evening, Near Templestowe* (1866) and *Waterpool at Coleraine* (1869).

C

Calwell, Arthur Augustus (1896–1973), politician, was born in West Melbourne, and was educated at St Mary's, West Melbourne, and the Christian Broth-

---

[1]Bernard Smith, *Australian Painting, 1788–1970* (Oxford University Press, Melbourne, 1971), p. 64.

ers' College, North Melbourne. After working as a
public servant, he was a Labor Member of the House
of Representatives from 1940 until 1972. He was Minister for Information from 1943 until 1949, Australia's first Minister for Immigration from 1945 until
1949 (during which time he implemented an extensive European *immigration program), and Leader
of the Labor Opposition from 1960 to 1967. Calwell
was a strong supporter of the *White Australia Policy. He opposed Australia's involvement in the *Vietnam War. His publications include *Be Just and Fear
Not* (1972).

Campbell, Robert (1769–1846), merchant and pastoralist, was born in Scotland. In 1798 he became
a partner in the Calcutta firm of Campbell, Clarke
& Co. (Campbell & Co. from 1799 onwards). In 1796
the firm had sent a cargo to New South Wales aboard
the *Sydney Cove*, but the ship was wrecked during
the voyage. In 1798 Campbell visited the colony and
began trading operations. In 1800 he returned with
another cargo. He was largely responsible for founding the colony's sealing industry. Campbell eventually developed trading and importing interests in the
colony to such an extent that he became known as
the 'father of the mercantile community'. He also
became involved in colonial public affairs, and
served on the Legislative Council from 1825 until
1843. Campbell died at his property, Duntroon, which
later became the site of the Royal Military College.

Canadian Rebels: Political protesters who took
part in the rebellions of 1837 and 1838 in Upper
Canada (present-day Ontario) and Lower Canada
(present-day Quebec). Some of those involved were
executed, others were sent to Bermuda, and 153 were
transported to Australia. Ninety-five Upper Canadians (most of whom were American–Canadians)
were transported to Van Diemen's Land in 1839 and
1840. Three escaped and returned to Canada; the
others began to receive free pardons from 1843 onwards. Eventually almost all returned to Canada.
Fifty-eight Lower Canadians (most of whom were
French–Canadians) arrived in New South Wales in

1840. They also began to receive free pardons from 1843 onwards, and eventually fifty-four of them returned to Canada.

Canberra: Capital of the Commonwealth of Australia, situated in the *Australian Capital Territory, the site of which was chosen in 1908 and acquired from New South Wales in 1911. *Griffin was largely responsible for its design. Canberra was named and inaugurated in 1913, and the Commonwealth *Parliament transferred there from Melbourne in 1927. Canberra's population was 1150 in 1921, 56,449 in 1961, and 219,331 in 1981.

Canberra Pact: *Anzac Pact

Casey, Richard Gardiner, Baron (1890–1976), governor-general, was born in Brisbane, and educated at Melbourne Church of England Grammar School, the University of Melbourne and Cambridge University. During the First World War he served with the First AIF (1914–19). From 1919 to 1924 Casey worked for mining and engineering firms, and was then Australian External Affairs Liaison Officer in London for some years (1924–7, 1927–31). Casey was a Member of the House of Representatives, representing the *United Australia Party, from 1931 to 1940, holding various portfolios at different times. He resigned to become Minister to the United States of America, a position that he held from 1940 to 1942. He was a member of the British War Cabinet, and Minister of State resident in the Middle East, from 1942 to 1943. From 1944 to 1946 he was Governor of Bengal. He was a Liberal Member of the House of Representatives from 1949 to 1960, again holding various portfolios. Casey was granted a life peerage in 1960, and was Governor-General of Australia from 1965 to 1969. His publications include *An Australian in India* (1946), *Friends and Neighbours* (1954), *Personal Experiences, 1939–46* (1962) and *The Future of the Commonwealth* (1963).

Castle Hill Uprising: Convict rebellion in 1804 at Castle Hill, an agricultural settlement about eight kilometres north of *Parramatta, in New South Wales. Several hundred convicts captured Castle Hill on 4 March, as part of an unsuccessful plan to capture the Hawkesbury, Parramatta and Sydney settlements. George Johnston and a detachment of the *New South Wales Corps intercepted the convicts near Toongabbie on 5 March, captured Phillip Cunningham and William Johnston, two of the leaders, and then opened fire, killing nine convicts and wounding others, including Cunningham. Martial law, proclaimed by *King, was in force from 5 to 10 March. Cunningham and eight other convicts were hanged, others were flogged, about thirty were sent to *Newcastle, and some suspects were dispersed to *Norfolk Island and elsewhere. The event has been described as an Irish rebellion; Castle Hill had a large Irish population, most of those punished were Irish (Cunningham, for example, had been transported after the United Irishmen's rebellion of 1798) and many who took part apparently were Irish. The convict rebels also adopted the United Irishmen's slogan of 'Death or Liberty'.

Chaffey, George (1848–1932) and **William Benjamin** (1856–1926), Canadian-born irrigation pioneers, established successful irrigation settlements in California. In 1885 *Deakin met them there and discussed the possibilities of *irrigation for Victoria. The Chaffey brothers came to Australia in 1886, and with government assistance soon established Australia's first major irrigation settlements. Both were on the Murray River—one at Renmark in South Australia, the other at Mildura in Victoria—and they were to be primarily for fruit-growing. Both settlements suffered from numerous problems, the Chaffey brothers' practices were questioned, and their firm went into liquidation, the newly formed Renmark and Mildura Irrigation Trusts taking over. A Victorian Royal Commission largely blamed the Chaffey brothers for Mildura's problems. In 1897 George Chaffey returned to California, where he became involved in further irrigation projects. William Benjamin Chaffey spent the rest of his life in Mildura, where he farmed, founded the Mildura (later Mildara)

Winery Pty Ltd, was active in the Mildura and the Australian Dried Fruits Associations, and was involved in local government.

Chanak Crisis: Diplomatic crisis between Britain and Turkey in 1922, which strained Australia's diplomatic relations with Britain. Australia was a signatory to the Treaty of Sèvres (1920), which supposedly concluded the war (First World War) with Turkey. When the crisis occurred, the British Government's request for Dominion troops to reinforce British troops at Chanak was reported to Australian newspapers before the official request reached the Prime Minister, *Hughes. Hughes agreed to send troops if necessary, but complained to the British Prime Minister, Lloyd George, about the lack of consultation. The emergency passed and Australian troops were not sent. Hughes also complained when the British Government did not invite the Dominions to participate in the Lausanne Conference, at which the new treaty with Turkey was to be negotiated. In 1924 the Commonwealth Government approved the Treaty of Lausanne (1923), which finally concluded the war with Turkey.

Chartists were members of a British political movement formed in 1837. Their People's Charter of 1838, which gave rise to their name, contained six demands: universal male suffrage, voting by ballot, annual parliaments, payment of members of parliament, equal electoral districts, and abolition of the property qualification for members of parliament. In 1839, 1842 and 1848, Chartists made unsuccessful attempts to present petitions to parliament. The movement then declined, and ended about 1858. About 100 Chartists, including John Frost, were transported to Australia after events in 1839, 1842 and 1848. Their crimes included conspiracy, riot, sedition and treason. Most were transported as a result of the 'Plug-Plot' Riots of 1842, which were basically strikes against the reduction of wages. Virtually all of the transported Chartists went to Van Diemen's Land; three went to New South Wales. Chartist ideas had some influence in Australia—for example, in organizations such as the Ballarat Reform League, which was involved in the *Eureka Rebellion.

Chauvel, Sir Henry George (1865-1945), soldier, was born at Tabulam, New South Wales, and educated at the Sydney and Toowoomba Grammar Schools. His father was a grazier. Chauvel served in volunteer forces in New South Wales and Queensland before joining the Queensland permanent forces in 1896. He served in the *Boer War, and then held various military appointments, including that of adjutant-general of the Australian forces (1911-14), before the First World War. During the war he commanded the 1st Light Horse Brigade, in Egypt and Gallipoli, in 1914 and 1915; the 1st Division, in Gallipoli and Egypt, for several months in 1915 and 1916; the Australian and New Zealand Mounted Division, in the Sinai campaign, in 1916 and 1917; the Desert Column in 1917; and the Desert Mounted Corps, in Palestine, from 1917 to 1919. Chauvel has often been described as a hero of the Palestine campaign in particular, and was mentioned in dispatches numerous times during the war. His honours and decorations included the Croix de Guerre and the Order of the Nile (which he was awarded twice). After the war he was Inspector-General of the Australian Military Forces from 1919 to 1930, and also Chief of the General Staff from 1923 to 1930, becoming the first Australian general in 1929. During the Second World War, Chauvel was Inspector-in-Chief of the Volunteer Defence.

Chifley, Joseph Benedict (1885-1951), politician, was born at Bathurst, New South Wales, was educated at the local school and the Patrician Brothers' School, Bathurst, and held various jobs, mostly in the New South Wales Railways, before becoming an engine-driver. He was active in union affairs, was dismissed during the *Wartime Transport Strike of 1917, and was demoted on his re-employment. Chifley was a Labor Member of the House of Representatives from 1928 to 1931, and from 1940 to 1951, and held various positions, including those of Treasurer (1941-9), Minister for Post-War Reconstruction (1942-5) and

Prime Minister (1945-9). He introduced *uniform taxation in 1942. His government supported a policy of full employment, increased social services, encouraged large-scale *immigration, established the *Snowy Mountains Hydro-Electric Scheme and *Trans Australia Airlines, nationalized *Qantas (its attempt to nationalize domestic airlines failed), attempted unsuccessfully to introduce *bank nationalization (which Chifley had recommended some years before in a minority report written when he was a member of the Royal Commission on Monetary and Banking Reform (1935-6)) and in a controversial move used troops to work open-cut mines during the *Coalfields Strike of 1949. Chifley's description of the goal of the labour movement as the 'light on the hill' has become famous. He declared, in a speech to the New South Wales state conference of the *Australian Labor Party in June 1949: 'We have a great objective—the light on the hill—which we aim to reach by working for the betterment of mankind not only here but anywhere we may give a helping hand.'[1] Chifley led the Opposition from 1949 until his death.

Chisholm (née Jones)**, Caroline** (1808-77), philanthropist, was born in England. At the age of twenty-two she married Archibald Chisholm of the East India Company, and converted to Roman Catholicism at about this time. In 1832 she founded the Female School of Industry for the Daughters of European Soldiers, in Madras. From 1838 to 1846 she lived in Australia. She founded a Female Immigrants' Home in Sydney in 1841; she accompanied immigrants to country areas, where she arranged accommodation and employment for them; she organized a settlement for about twenty-three families during the *depression of the 1840s; and she and her husband travelled throughout New South Wales and collected about 600 statements from immigrants about their lives in Australia. From 1846 to 1854 Caroline Chisholm lived in England. She gave evi-

---

dence before two House of Lords Committees, one
on the administration of the criminal law, the other
on colonization from Ireland; she disseminated much
information about Australia; and in 1849 she founded
the Family Colonization Loan Society, which
initially chartered ships to bring settlers to Australia.
From 1854 to 1866 she again lived in Australia, and
was active in public life until ill health curtailed her
activities. In 1854 she toured the Victorian gold-
fields, after which she arranged for the construction
of shelter sheds on the roads to the diggings. She
campaigned against the *squatters' hold on the land.
In 1862, because of financial difficulties, she opened
a girls' school in Sydney. In 1866 she returned to
England, and lived there until her death. She wrote
a number of pamphlets.

Church and School Corporation: A body established in New South Wales in 1826, under instructions from the British Government, which was to
be given one-seventh of the colony's lands, with
which it was to maintain the Church of England's
churches and schools. Other religious denominations
opposed its existence. The Corporation received some
lands and financial support, but its operations were
suspended in 1829, and it was finally dissolved in
1833.

Clark, Andrew Inglis (1848-1907), lawyer and politician, was born and educated in Hobart. He worked
in his family's engineering firm before studying law,
and was admitted to the Bar in 1877. Clark was a
Member of the Tasmanian House of Assembly for
some years (1878-82, 1887-98), during which time he
was Attorney-General twice (1887-92, 1894-7), and
initiated much legislation, including that of 1896
introducing the Hare–Clark voting system (as it was
later called) in Tasmania. He attended the Federal
Council several times, the Australasian Federation
Conference of 1890, and the National Australasian
Convention of 1891 (during which he helped *Griffith, *Barton and *Kingston to produce the draft
constitution adopted by the convention, having
already written his own draft constitution before the

convention). His knowledge of, and admiration for, the American system were evident. Clark was appointed to the Tasmanian Supreme Court in 1898. He helped to found the University of Tasmania, and was its Vice-Chancellor from 1901 to 1903. His publications include *The Federal Financial Problem and Its Solution* (1900) and *Studies in Australian Constitutional Law* (1901).

Clarke, Marcus Andrew Hislop (1846-81), journalist and novelist, was born in London. His father was a lawyer. Clarke migrated to Australia in 1863, and held various jobs. He worked for the Bank of Australasia; he worked on a station in Victoria; he contributed to various journals and newspapers, including the Melbourne *Argus* (on whose staff he worked for a time), the Melbourne *Herald*, the London *Daily Telegraph* and the Melbourne *Age*; he owned and edited the *Colonial Monthly* (previously the *Australian Monthly Magazine*) for some time; he edited the *Humbug* and the *Australian Journal*; and he was secretary to the trustees (1870-3), and assistant librarian (1873-81), of the Public Library of Victoria. Clarke is best known for his novel *His Natural Life* (1874), usually called by its later title, *For the Term of His Natural Life.* It was first published in the *Australian Journal* (1870-2) and tells the story of a convict's life in Van Diemen's Land. Clarke's other publications include *Long Odds* (1869), *Old Tales of a Young Country* (1871), *Holiday Peak and Other Tales* (1873), *'Twixt Shadow and Shine, An Australian Story of Christmas* (1875), *Four Stories High* (1877), *The Future Australian Race* (1877), *The Man with the Oblong Box* (1878), *The Mystery of Major Molineux and Human Repetends* (1881), *The Conscientious Stranger, A Bullocktown Idyll* (1881), *Sensational Tales* (1886), *Chidiock Tichbourne, or the Catholic Conspiracy* (1893), *Australian Tales* (1896) and *Stories of Australia in the Early Days* (1897). He also wrote essays and drama.

Clarke, William John Turner (1801?-74), pastoralist, was born in England, where he worked as a drover for some time, before migrating to *Van

Diemen's Land in 1829. He worked as a butcher and government meat contractor, and began to acquire land in Van Diemen's Land, and later in the *Port Phillip District. Clarke built up large flocks of sheep, and introduced the Leicester breed to Australia. He was a Member of the Victorian Legislative Council (1856-61, 1863-70), and a director of the Colonial Bank. 'Big' Clarke, as he came to be called, 'acquired the reputation of being the wealthiest man in the country',[1] and left approximately £2,500,000 and much property in Tasmania, Victoria, South Australia and New Zealand. Other members of Clarke's family, notably his son Sir William John Clarke (1831-97), a pastoralist and philanthropist, have also been prominent in Victoria's history.

Closer Settlement: Land policy pursued throughout Australia for many years, especially during the period from the 1880s to the 1920s. Its main aim was to establish small settlers on farms in specific areas. The Darling Downs in Queensland and Gippsland in Victoria are examples. The reasons for closer settlement included the failure of many *selectors; the need for more agricultural production because of Australia's increased population; improved agricultural, transport, and refrigeration methods; and the interest in land policy stimulated by the theory propounded by Henry George, an American economist, that there should be a single tax on land. Governments opened up new areas of Crown land, introduced land taxes, compulsorily acquired land from large land-owners and made it available for smaller settlers, expanded railways, supported irrigation schemes such as those begun by the *Chaffey brothers, and provided credit and other assistance. Closer settlement was sometimes linked with migration schemes. Group settlement, involving groups of settlers working together, and *soldier settlement were specialized forms of closer settlement. Closer settlement proved to be very expensive.

---

[1]Hugh Anderson, 'William John Turner Clarke', in Douglas Pike (ed.), *Australian Dictionary of Biography*, volume 1 (Melbourne University Press, Melbourne, 1966), p. 229.

Coalfields Lock-out: A lock-out (that is, 'a refusal on the part of an employer, or employers acting in concert, to furnish work to their operatives, except on conditions to be accepted by the latter collectively') by mine-owners on the northern coalfields of New South Wales from March 1929 to June 1930. Mine-owners locked out some 10,000 miners after the miners refused to accept reduced wages. The New South Wales Government attempted to reopen the Rothbury mine in December 1930; one miner, Norman Brown, was killed and nine others were wounded in a violent clash between miners and police. The miners returned to work, basically on the mine-owners' terms.

Coalfields Strike: A major industrial dispute in 1949. Some 23,000 black-coal miners throughout Australia went on strike on 27 June. The Communist-led Miners' Federation was demanding long-service leave, a 35-hour week and increased wages. The effects of the strike were widespread; heavy restrictions on the use of coal and gas were imposed, industry almost ceased, and unemployment soared. The *Chifley Labor Government legislated quickly to freeze union funds, and eight union officials were jailed under this legislation. Australian Railways Union members, under heavy police protection, shifted coal from some coalfields. Chifley announced that troops would be used to work open-cut mines; some 2500 troops began to do so on 1 August. The demands had not been met when the miners returned to work on 15 August. There has been much debate about the causes and handling of the strike.

Cobb & Co.: Famous Australian coaching firm. Four Americans (Freeman Cobb, John B. Lamber, John Murray Peck and James Swanton) founded a carrying firm, known as Cobb & Co., in 1853. Its wagons ran from Melbourne to Liardet's Beach (present-day Port Melbourne). Cobb & Co. began taking passengers to the Victorian gold-fields in 1854. The syndicate sold the business in 1856, and several different owners followed. James Rutherford, an American who was to play an important role in running Cobb & Co. over the next fifty years, headed a syndicate that bought the business in 1861. Cobb & Co. expanded to New South Wales in 1862 and Queensland in 1865. Bathurst, New South Wales, became the company's headquarters in 1862. Cobb & Co. is best known for its coaching activities; in 1870 it used 6000 horses daily, its coaches covered 28,000 miles weekly, and its mail subsidies were £95,000 yearly.[1] The company also had manufacturing and pastoral interests. The last Cobb & Co. coach ran in Queensland in 1924. The name Cobb & Co. has become part of Australian folklore.

Coles, Sir George James (1885–1977), was born at Jung, Victoria, and educated at Beechworth College. He opened a variety shop in Collingwood, the slogan of which was 'Nothing over a shilling', in 1914, but sold it in 1916, and served in the First AIF until 1918. (His brother James, who partnered him in the business, was killed during the First World War.) George and another brother, Arthur (later Sir Arthur) William Coles, opened another variety shop in Collingwood in 1919. Its slogan, 'Nothing over half-a-crown' (two shillings and sixpence), remained in force until 1938. A company was established in 1921, with George as its managing director until 1931, followed by Arthur from 1931 to 1940. Sir Kenneth Frank Coles, Sir Edgar Barton Coles and Sir Norman Cameron Coles, all brothers of George and Arthur, also became involved in the business. G. J. Coles & Coy Ltd developed into a very large retail business, and merged with the Myer organization (which had been founded by *Myer) in 1985.

Collins, David (1756–1810), colonial administrator, was born in England. Like his father, he pursued a career in the marines. Collins came to New South Wales, as the colony's Deputy-Judge-Advocate, with the *First Fleet. He remained in the colony in that position until 1796, when he returned to England. Collins was commissioned as the Lieutenant-Governor of a proposed new British convict settlement

---

[1]Cited in A. G. L. Shaw, *The Economic Development of Australia* (Longman, Australia, fifth edition, 1966), p. 82.

in the Bass Strait area in 1803, unsuccessfully attempted to establish such a settlement near present-day *Sorrento later that year, and finally transferred the settlement to *Van Diemen's Land in 1804. He was Lieutenant-Governor of Van Diemen's Land (the colony's first) from then until his death. His publications include *An Account of the English Colony in New South Wales* (two volumes, 1798, 1802).

'Collins, Tom': *Furphy, Joseph

Colombo Plan: A plan designed to foster economic development within the South and South-East Asian region. It originated from discussions at a conference of foreign ministers of the *Commonwealth of Nations held in Colombo in 1950. Donor countries provide financial, technical and educational assistance. Members include Australia, Canada, Japan, *New Zealand, the United Kingdom, the United States of America and twenty-one countries within the region.

Colonial Sugar Refining Company Limited (CSR): One of Australia's largest companies. It was formed in Sydney in 1855, its original purpose to refine raw sugar. It began to manufacture raw sugar in New South Wales in 1870, and eventually operated a large number of mills and plantations, many of which were in Queensland. It also operated in Fiji and New Zealand. From the late 1930s it diversified into other industries, and its activities in the 1980s included mining. It became known as CSR Limited in 1973.

Common Market: *European Economic Community

Commonwealth Banking Corporation: Statutory organization, comprising savings, trading and development banks. The *Fisher Labor Government introduced legislation to establish the Commonwealth Bank, sometimes referred to as the 'people's bank', in 1911. It was to be a savings and trading bank, to be capitalized by the Commonwealth Government, and to compete with other banks. Its savings-bank functions began in 1912 (the Commonwealth Savings Bank of Australia being created in 1927); its trading bank functions began in 1913 (the Commonwealth Trading Bank being created in 1953). The Commonwealth Bank began to operate as a central bank from about 1930. *Chifley increased its powers in 1945, but his attempt to introduce *bank nationalization in 1947 failed. Legislation to establish the *Reserve Bank of Australia, which was to take over central banking functions, and the Commonwealth Banking Corporation, which was to comprise the Commonwealth Savings Bank, the Commonwealth Trading Bank and the new Commonwealth Development Bank of Australia, was passed in 1959. The Commonwealth Banking Corporation came into being in 1960.

Commonwealth Conciliation and Arbitration Court: Federal body established under the *Commonwealth Conciliation and Arbitration Act* 1904 to settle interstate industrial disputes. The so-called *Harvester Judgement of 1907 was one of the Court's best-known decisions. In 1956, following a *High Court decision, the Court was replaced by two new bodies, the Commonwealth Conciliation and Arbitration Commission and the Commonwealth Industrial Court. The Federal Court of Australia, established in 1976, has taken over the latter body's work.

Commonwealth Grants Commission: Statutory body established in 1933 to give advice on applications by the states to the Commonwealth for special financial assistance. The original claimant states were South Australia (until 1959, and again between 1970 and 1975), Tasmania (until 1974) and Western Australia (until 1968), the original standard (non-claimant) states being Victoria, New South Wales and Queensland (which many years later became a claimant state). A proposal in 1936 to abolish the Commission was abandoned in 1938. Following the introduction of *uniform taxation in 1942, the Commission gave advice on additional tax reimbursement grants (as well as special grants) until 1946, after which it continued to advise on special grants. Tax reimbursement grants were replaced by financial assistance grants in 1959, which in turn were replaced by a system of personal income tax sharing in 1976, the Commission continuing throughout to give advice on special grants. It gained some powers (later changed) to give advice about financial assistance to local government in 1973, and powers to advise on matters relating to the Northern Territory in 1978 and the Australian Capital Territory in 1980. It began reviews of tax-sharing relativities in 1978. The Commission was located in Melbourne until 1972, when it was moved to Canberra.

Commonwealth of Australia: Official title of the Australian nation. It comprises the six states that were formerly colonies—*New South Wales, *Queensland, *South Australia, *Tasmania, *Victoria and *Western Australia—and the *Australian Capital Territory and the *Northern Territory. The *federation movement mainly occurred during the 1880s and 1890s. The *Federal Convention (1897-8) produced a draft federal constitution, which was put to the people at two referendums. The first failed; the second, which was held after amendments were made, passed in all of the colonies. This constitution formed the basis of the British *Commonwealth of Australia Constitution Act* (1900). The Commonwealth of Australia was inaugurated on 1 January 1901. Powers were distributed between the Commonwealth and state parliaments; the former consists of the House of Representatives and the Senate. The Northern Territory was transferred from South Australia to the Commonwealth in 1911. Land was transferred from New South Wales to the Commonwealth for the creation of the Australian Capital Territory in 1911. The Commonwealth of Australia is not to be confused with the *Commonwealth of Nations, to which Australia belongs.

Commonwealth of Nations: An association of nations, including Australia, that were formerly part of the British Empire. The term 'British Common-

wealth' began to replace 'British Empire' during the
*First World War. The word 'British' was dropped
in the late 1940s. Queen Elizabeth II is the Head
of the Commonwealth. Commonwealth Heads of
Government meet regularly, and a Commonwealth
Secretariat was established in London in 1965.

**Commonwealth Scientific and Industrial
Research Organization (CSIRO):** A statutory
body, which replaced the Council for Scientific and
Industrial Research in 1949. The latter body, which
had replaced the Institute of Science and Industry
in 1926, had devoted most of its research to primary
industries, but it also assisted secondary industries
from 1936 onwards. CSIRO's many functions include
research, training of research workers, liaison with
research institutions in Australia and other countries, and publication of scientific and technical
material. Its achievements have included the introduction of myxomatosis to reduce rabbit numbers,
developments in the control of diseases affecting
livestock, advances in the processing of textiles, and
significant research on soils.

Communist Party of Australia: An Australian
political party, founded at a meeting of twenty-six
socialists in Sydney in 1920. J. S. Garden and
W. P. Earsman were largely responsible for founding
it. It affiliated with the Comintern in 1922. During
the Second World War it was banned, under wartime
powers, from 1940 to 1942. Its peak, in terms of membership and influence in the trade union movement,
occurred during the 1940s. F. W. Paterson, its only
parliamentarian, was a Member of the Queensland
Legislative Assembly from 1944 to 1950. *Menzies's
attempts to dissolve the Communist Party in the
early 1950s failed; the *Communist Party Dissolution
Act* 1950 was found to be invalid by the *High Court
in 1951, and a referendum that would have given
the Commonwealth Government the power to ban
communism was narrowly defeated on 22 September
1951. The party has suffered two major splits; the
first led to the formation of the Peking-oriented Communist Party of Australia (Marxist-Leninist) in 1963,

and the second to the formation of the Moscow-oriented Socialist Party of Australia in 1971.

Compulsory Voting: The obligation to vote at political elections. The principle of compulsory voting was introduced in Queensland in 1915, Victoria in 1926, New South Wales in 1928, Tasmania in 1928, Western Australia in 1936 and South Australia in 1942. The same principle was introduced for Commonwealth elections in 1924. It is now compulsory to vote in elections for all Australian houses of parliament, except the South Australian Legislative Council.

Conder, Charles Edward (1868–1909), painter, was born and educated in England. His father was a railway engineer. Conder arrived in New South Wales in 1884. He worked in the office of the Lands Department in Sydney for about eight months, in trigonometrical survey camps in New South Wales for about two years, and then as an illustrator for the *Illustrated Sydney News.* He attended night classes at the Royal Art Society of New South Wales. From 1888 to 1890 Conder lived in Melbourne, where he attended night classes at the Melbourne National Gallery School. Conder became one of the leading painters in the group that became known as the *Heidelberg School, and contributed more than forty works to the controversial Exhibition of 9 × 5 Impressions. In 1890 Conder moved to Paris, where he studied at the Atelier Cormon for some time, and in 1894 he moved to London. He became famous for his watercolours on silk fans. He died in England. His Australian paintings include *The Departure of the S.S. Orient—Circular Quay* (1888), *A Holiday at Mentone* (1888) and *Cove on the Hawkesbury* (c. 1888).

Conscription: Compulsory enlistment for military service. The *Defence Act* 1903 introduced the principle of conscription of men for service within Australia during wartime, but not for overseas service during either wartime or peacetime. The *Defence Act* 1909 introduced the principle of conscription of men for service within Australia during peacetime. Compulsory military training for boys and men, aged between 12 and 25, was introduced in 1911. It was conducted on a part-time basis, and was restricted to home service. This continued during the First World War. During the war, intensely bitter conscription debates occurred. The Commonwealth Government, led by *Hughes, made two unsuccessful attempts to introduce conscription of men for overseas service. Two referendums (or plebiscites) on the subject were held, the first in 1916, the second in 1917. Both failed. After the First World War, compulsory military training continued, although on a diminishing scale during the 1920s. The *Scullin Labor Government abolished it in 1929. The *Menzies *United Australia Party Government reintroduced conscription of men for service within Australia in 1939. The *Curtin Labor Government introduced a limited form of conscription of men for overseas service in 1943. Conscripts could be sent to a prescribed area, the 'South-Western Pacific Zone', outside Australia. (A form of industrial conscription for men and woman had also been introduced in Australia during the Second World War.) The Menzies Liberal–Country Party Government reintroduced conscription of men in 1951. This became known as the National Service scheme. Eighteen-year-olds were required to complete a period of training (part of which was full-time), and then to remain in the Reserve for some years. Until 1957 they could choose to serve in the navy, the army or the air force. Those who chose the services other than the army had to be prepared to serve overseas. From early 1957 conscripts served in the army, and were selected by ballot. This scheme was abolished in 1959. The Menzies Liberal–Country Party Government introduced another National Service scheme in 1965. Twenty-year-old men were selected by ballot. Those selected were obliged to serve in the army for two years on a full-time basis, and they could be sent overseas. This scheme was in operation when the *Holt Liberal–Country Party Government decided to send conscripts to the *Vietnam War in 1966. Almost 64,000 men were conscripted under this scheme (some others chose alternatives, such as part-time service in the citizen forces) from 1965 to 1972; of these some 15,500 served in Vietnam. Intensely bitter conscription debates occurred again. The period of service was reduced to eighteen months in late 1972. The newly elected *Whitlam Labor Government abolished conscription in December 1972.

Constitution of the Commonwealth of Australia: Australia's written constitution. It is the ninth clause of the British *Commonwealth of Australia Constitution Act* (1900). This Act created a federation, of which the colonies became states. The Constitution consists of 128 sections, divided into eight chapters: The Parliament, The Executive Government, The Judicature, Finance and Trade, The States, New States, Miscellaneous, and Alteration of the Constitution. A referendum must be carried to alter the Constitution.

Convicts: *Transportation

Cook, James (1728–79), navigator and cartographer, was born in England. He was educated at a village school, was apprenticed to a shopkeeper for about eighteen months, and then worked for a coal-shipper for about three years. In 1755 he joined the British navy. Cook is best known for three expeditions. As lieutenant, he commanded HM Bark *Endeavour* on an expedition to observe the transit of Venus and to explore the South Pacific (1768–71). *Banks accompanied him on this expedition. After observations were made at Tahiti (1769) Cook circumnavigated New Zealand, charted its coast, and claimed possession of some areas for Britain. In 1770 he sailed north along the eastern coast of *New Holland, made several landings, including one at *Botany Bay, and claimed possession of the eastern part of the continent (an area he later named *New South Wales) for Britain on 22 August 1770. He confirmed the existence of Torres Strait. From 1772 to 1775 Cook was in charge of an expedition to discover whether there was another southern continent. He sailed in the *Resolution*, with Tobias Furneaux in the *Adventure*. Cook circumnavigated the world in high southern latitudes, but did not find another continent. He discovered New Caledonia and *Norfolk Island. Furneaux sailed along the southern and eastern coasts of *Van Diemen's Land during this voyage. As post-captain, and a Fellow of the Royal Society, Cook commanded an expedition to search for a passage between the North Pacific and the North Atlantic; he set sail in the *Resolution*, with Charles Clerke in the *Discovery*, in 1777. During the voyage Cook visited Van Diemen's Land. He explored the Pacific coasts of North America and Siberia, but failed to find a passage. In 1779 Cook was killed by islanders in the Sandwich Islands (present-day Hawaii). The *Resolution* and the *Discovery* returned to England in 1780.

Cook, Sir Joseph (1860–1947), politician, was born in Staffordshire, England. After leaving school at about nine, he worked in the mines. In 1885 he migrated to New South Wales. He worked as a miner, and later as an auditor, and continued his trade union involvement, begun in England. He was a Member of the New South Wales Legislative Assembly from 1891 to 1901. He was first elected to represent Labor, but stood as an Independent Labor candidate after refusing to sign the solidarity pledge in 1894. Cook was a Member of the House of Representatives from 1901 to 1921, becoming Leader of the Free Traders in 1908. He became Deputy Leader and Minister for Defence in the *Deakin Fusion Government (1909–10). Cook was largely responsible for the defence legislation changes providing for a compulsory military training scheme for males within Australia and the establishment of a military college, concluded naval arrangements with Britain, and also played a large part in arranging Kitchener's visit to Australia. He led the Liberals (formerly the Fusionists) at the 1913 federal elections, in which they narrowly won control of the House of Representatives, but not of the Senate, and Cook was Prime Minister from June 1913 to September 1914. Labor won the 1914 elections, following a double dissolution. When the

Nationalist Party emerged in 1917, Cook became Deputy Leader. He was Australian High Commissioner in London from 1921 to 1927.

Copland, Sir Douglas Berry (1894–1971), economist and diplomat, was born at Timaru, New Zealand, and graduated from the University of New Zealand. He was Professor of Economics at the University of Tasmania from 1920 to 1924, then Sidney Myer Professor of Commerce and Dean of the Commerce Faculty at the University of Melbourne from 1924 to 1944. During the *Great Depression of the 1930s he chaired the committee that was largely responsible for formulating the so-called Premiers' Plan. During the Second World War, Copland was Commonwealth Prices Commissioner (1939–45), and also an economic consultant to the Prime Minister (1941–5). He then served as Australian Minister in China (1946–8), the first Vice-Chancellor of the Australian National University (1948–53), Australian High Commissioner to Canada (1953–6), and the first principal of the Australian Administrative Staff College at Mount Eliza (1956–9). He also chaired the newly formed Committee for the Economic Development of Australia from 1960 to 1966. His numerous publications include *Australia in the World Crisis, 1929–1933* (1934), *W. E. Hearn, First Australian Economist* (1935) and *The Changing Structure of the Western Economy* (1961).

Coppin, George Selth (1819–1906), comic actor and entrepreneur, was born in Sussex, England, the son of strolling players, and became involved in the theatre at an early age. He arrived in Sydney in 1843. Coppin, who has frequently been described as 'the father of Australian theatre', acted in most of the Australian colonies and New Zealand at various times; he founded several theatre companies; he brought more than 200 overseas entertainers, including *Williamson and Maggie Moore, to Australia; and he built a number of theatres, the best-known being the prefabricated Olympic Theatre (the so-called 'Iron Pot') in Melbourne. His other business interests included hotel-keeping, mining and racing.

Coppin also had a political career in Victoria; he was a Member of the Legislative Council (1858-63, 1889-95), and of the Legislative Assembly (1874-7, 1883-8), and was responsible for introducing the *Real Property Act* 1862, based on the *Torrens system. His philanthropic work included helping to found the Victorian Humane Society, and he was an active Freemason.

Cosme: *New Australia

Council for Scientific and Industrial Research: *Commonwealth Scientific and Industrial Research Organization

Country Party: *National Party

Country Women's Association (CWA): A non-political, non-sectarian, voluntary organization. Open to all women, the CWA was founded in New South Wales and Queensland in 1922, Western Australia in 1924, Victoria in 1928, South Australia in 1929, Tasmania in 1936 and the Northern Territory in 1960. The national organization was founded in Melbourne in 1945. The CWA provides educational, cultural, health and other services, and has links with the Associated Country Women of the World. It had some 55,000 members in 1983.

Cowper, Sir Charles (1807-75), politician, was born in England, and brought to Australia in 1809. His father was a clergyman. Cowper was educated privately. He worked in the Commissariat Department for some time; was the secretary of the *Church and School Corporation from 1826; became a pastoralist; and managed the Sydney Tramway and Railway Company for some years from 1849. He was a Member of the Legislative Council of New South Wales for several periods (1843-50, 1851-6, 1860), and played a leading role in the movement against *transportation in the late 1840s and early 1850s. Cowper also was a Member of Legislative Assembly of New South Wales for most of the time from 1856 to 1870. He was Premier five times (1856, 1857-9, 1861-3,

1865-6, 1870) and Colonial Secretary six times (1856, 1857-9, 1860-1, 1861-3, 1865-6, 1870). He played a large part in steps leading to New South Wales' adoption of manhood *suffrage in 1858, introduction of land reforms in 1861, abolition of state grants to religion in 1862, and adoption of the *Torrens system in 1862. After resigning from politics in 1870, he became the Agent-General for New South Wales in London, a position he held until his death.

Cowra Outbreak: An attempted escape in 1944 by about 1100 Japanese prisoners-of-war from a camp at Cowra, New South Wales, during the Second World War. They used makeshift weapons, such as baseball bats. Several hundred prisoners escaped, but were killed or recaptured. Four guards and more than 230 prisoners were killed; three guards and more than 100 prisoners were wounded.

Cresswell, Sir William Rooke (1852-1933), vice-admiral, was born at Gibraltar, where his father was deputy postmaster-general. He was educated at Aitken's Private School, Gibraltar, and Eastman's Naval Academy, Southsea, England, and entered the Royal Navy as a cadet in 1865. He served in various parts of the world before resigning in 1878. Cresswell arrived in Australia in 1879, and engaged in droving and other activities in the Northern Territory until 1885, when he entered the South Australian defence forces, becoming naval commandant in 1893, and being promoted captain in 1895. He became the commandant of the Queensland naval forces in May 1900. During the *Boxer Rising, he commanded the *Protector* (his former ship from South Australia) from August 1900 to January 1901. A strong advocate of the creation of an Australian navy, Cresswell became director of the Commonwealth naval forces in 1904 (during which year he had also become naval commandant of Victoria), and a member of the Council of Defence, and of the Australian Naval Board, in 1905. He became rear-admiral, and first naval member of the Commonwealth Naval Board, in 1911. Cresswell played a large role in the development of the *Royal Australian Navy before and during the

First World War. He retired in 1919, and was promoted vice-admiral in 1922.

Cricket was introduced to New South Wales at least as early as 1803, and has since become one of Australia's most popular sports, played mainly by men. The Melbourne Cricket Club, which was to play a significant role in the development of Australian cricket, was founded in 1838. Test matches have been played against England since 1876-7, the first being held in Australia. (An Aboriginal team had earlier toured England, in 1868.) After an Australian team won a match in London in 1882, the London *Sporting Times* published a notice that English cricket had died, that the body was to be cremated and the ashes taken to Australia. When an English team won a series held in Australia in 1882-3, the English captain was given an urn of ashes, which was taken to Lord's Cricket Ground in London, where it remains, regardless of which team 'wins the Ashes', that is, wins the greater number of matches in a Test series. The Australian Board of Control for International Cricket was founded in 1905. The *bodyline series of 1932-3 was particularly controversial. Australia has also played Test matches against South Africa (from 1902-3 to 1969-70), the West Indies (from 1930-1), New Zealand (from 1945-6), India (1947-8) and Pakistan (from 1956-7). The establishment of World Series Cricket by Kerry Packer in 1977 was controversial. Australia's domestic first-class competition, played for the Sheffield Shield Trophy, began in 1892-3. Notable Australian cricketers have included members of the famous Gregory family, Frederick Robert Spofforth (1853-1926), Montague Alfred Noble (1873-1940), Victor Trumper (1877-1915), Warwick Windridge Armstrong (1879-1947), Charles George Macartney (1886-1958), *Bradman (1908-), Keith Miller (1919-) and Richard Benaud (1930-).

'Crimson thread of kinship': A now-famous phrase used by *Parkes, the Premier of New South Wales, in a speech advocating the federation of the Australian colonies. He gave the speech at a dinner held during a conference (known at the time as the Australasian Federation Conference) in Melbourne in 1890. The full sentence read: 'The crimson thread of kinship runs through us all.'[1]

CSIRO: *Commonwealth Scientific and Industrial Research Organization

CSR: *Colonial Sugar Refining Company Limited

Currency Lads and Lasses: The name given in the early nineteenth century to people of European descent born in Australia, especially those of convict parentage. British-born settlers were known as 'sterling'. The names came from the distinction made between 'currency', coins or promissory notes valid for local use only, and 'sterling', British coins or treasury bills. 'Currency' was worth less than 'sterling'.

Curtin, John Joseph (1885–1945), politician, was born at Creswick, Victoria, where his father was a policeman. Curtin spent most of his early years in the Melbourne suburb of Brunswick. After leaving school at 13 he worked in various jobs, mostly in the printing trade. He joined the Socialist Party in 1906, and later joined the Labor Party. He was secretary of the Timber Workers' Union from 1911 to 1915. He then moved to Perth, where he edited the *West Australian Worker* from 1917 to 1928. He entered federal politics, and was a Labor Member of the House of Representatives (1928–31, 1934–45). During the *Great Depression, Curtin opposed both the Premiers' Plan and J. T. *Lang's plan. After losing his seat in 1931 he worked as a freelance journalist and as an advocate for Western Australia before the *Commonwealth Grants Commission. He led the Labor Opposition from 1935 to 1941, when he became Prime Minister. He held office until his death in July 1945, shortly before the end of the Second World War. Curtin insisted, in the face of opposition from Churchill and Roosevelt, on the return of Australian troops from the Middle East to defend Australia,

---

[1] *Argus*, 7 February 1890.

rather than their diversion to defend Burma. He appealed to the United States, not Britain, for support, issuing a public statement (which appeared under his name, but was apparently written by his publicity officer) that included the following words: 'Without any inhibitions of any kind, I make it quite clear that Australia looks to America, free of any pangs as to our traditional links or kinship with the United Kingdom.'[1] He strongly supported the American General Douglas MacArthur, Supreme Commander of the Allied forces in the south-west Pacific, and in 1943 extended the area in which Australia conscripts could be used to include a number of places overseas (although he had been an anti-conscriptionist during the First World War).

CWA: *Country Women's Association

Cyclone Tracy: *Darwin

D

Daintree, Richard (1831–78), geologist and photographer, was born and educated in England, and arrived in Victoria in 1852, during the *gold-rushes. He was an assistant geologist in the Victorian Geological Survey from 1854 to 1856, went back to England and studied at the Royal School of Mines Laboratory for some time, and returned to Victoria in 1857. After working in the Geological Survey from 1859 to 1864, he settled on the land in northern Queensland. Daintree was responsible for the opening of several Queensland gold-fields in the 1860s, before and during his term as government geologist in northern Queensland (1868–70). His photographs 'present a vivid picture of early settlement in Queensland'.[2] He was a commissioner in charge of Queensland's display at the Exhibition of Art and Industry

---

[1]Melbourne *Herald*, 27 December 1941.

[2]G. C. Bolton, 'Richard Daintree', in Douglas Pike (ed.), *Australian Dictionary of Biography*, volume 4 (Melbourne University Press, Melbourne, 1972), p. 1.

in London in 1871, and was then Queensland Agent-General in London from 1872 to 1876. He died in England. His publications include *Queensland, Australia, Its Territory, Climate, and Products* (c. 1872).

Dampier, William (1652?-1715), mariner and writer, was born in England. He engaged in various trading, naval and privateering ventures. He and other buccaneers from the *Cygnet* spent about three months on the western coast of *New Holland (now Australia) in 1688. After returning to England in 1691 he wrote of his experiences in the South Seas. He was appointed to command an expedition to explore the eastern coasts of New Holland and New Guinea, and sailed from England in HMS *Roebuck* in 1699. He explored part of the western coast of New Holland and discovered New Britain (which he named), but the *Roebuck*'s poor state precluded exploration of the eastern coasts. The *Roebuck* sank off Ascension Island on the return voyage. In 1702 Dampier was court-martialled over his conduct during the expedition and was found to be unfit to command naval vessels. In 1703 he led a disastrous privateering expedition to the South Seas in the *St George*. In 1707 he returned to England. He then sailed around the world between 1708 and 1711 as pilot on Captain Woodes Rogers' privateer, the *Duke*. Dampier's publications, which led to much interest in New Holland (even though they contained unfavourable comments), include *A New Voyage Round the World* (1697).

Darling, Sir Ralph (1775-1858), *governor, was born to English parents in Ireland. He followed his father and pursued a military career. Darling succeeded *Brisbane as Governor of New South Wales in 1825, and was also nominally Governor of Van Diemen's Land, whose separate government he proclaimed in 1825, and which was administered by a lieutenant-governor. Darling's powers in New South Wales were limited by the Executive Council, which was established in 1825, and the Legislative Council, which was increased in size and authority in 1828. He was responsible for tightening up the convict system (as he had been instructed), and for improvements in the general administration of the colony. Like his predecessors, he faced problems because of the conflict between *emancipists and *exclusives in the colony. Darling's governorship ended in 1831. A British parliamentary inquiry into Darling's actions in the *Sudds and Thompson affair was held in 1835; Darling was exonerated. He died in Brighton, England.

Darwin, the administrative capital of the *Northern Territory, lies on the shores of Port Darwin. Officers of HMS *Beagle* discovered the harbour, and named it after Charles Darwin, in 1839. The settlement of Palmerston, on the site of present-day Darwin, began in 1862. It soon became known as Darwin, and its name was officially changed in 1911. Darwin was the northern base for the *Overland Telegraph Line. Troops were stationed there during the Second World War, and it became the target for repeated Japanese air attacks. The first, and most severe, of these occurred on 19 February 1942. The town was rebuilt after the war. Cyclone Tracy damaged or destroyed most of the city on 25 December 1974. The city has since been rebuilt. The population in 1981 was 56,482.

Darwin, Bombing of: *Darwin; *Second World War

Davis, Arthur Hoey (1868-1935), writer, was born at Drayton, Queensland. He is better known as 'Steele Rudd'. His father was a blacksmith and *selector. Davis attended the Emu Creek school until he was about twelve years old. He worked as a public servant in Brisbane from 1885 to 1904. Davis was a regular contributor to the *Bulletin* from 1895 onwards. He made several attempts to run his own journal; the results were *Steele Rudd's Magazine* (1903-7), *Steele Rudd's Annual* (1917-23), *Steele Rudd's* (1924-5) and *Steele Rudd's and the Shop Assistant's Magazine* (1926-7). He also farmed from 1909 to 1917. Davis died in Brisbane. He is best known for his humorous descriptions of selection life, based partly on his own family's experiences, in books such as *On Our Selection* (1899). *On Our Selection* has been adapted for stage, film (silent and sound) and radio (under the title of *Dad and Dave*). His many publications include *Our New Selection* (1903), *Sandy's Selection* (1904), *Back at Our Selection* (1906), *Dad in Politics and Other Stories* (1908), *Stocking Our Selection* (1909), *From Selection to City* (1909), *On Emu Creek* (1923) and *The Rudd Family* (1926).

Davis Cup: *Tennis

Dawson, Andrew (Anderson) (1863-1910), politician, was born in Rockhampton, Queensland. He left school at 12 and held various jobs, including that of miner, mostly in Charters Towers. He also became involved in the trade union movement and journalism. Dawson was a Labor Member of the Queensland Legislative Assembly from 1893 to 1901. He was Premier and Chief Secretary in a minority Labor Government, which formally lasted from 1 December to 7 December 1899; it was the first Labor Government in any of the Australian colonies, and reputedly the first in the world. Dawson, who had supported federation, was a Labor Senator from 1901 to 1906. He was Minister for Defence in the *Watson Labor Government of 1904. He was defeated, while standing as an Independent, in the federal elections of 1906. He died in Brisbane.

Deakin, Alfred (1856-1919), politician, was born in Melbourne, and educated at the Melbourne Church of England Grammar School and the University of Melbourne. He practised as a lawyer. After meeting David *Syme in 1878 he wrote for the Melbourne *Age*. He edited the *Leader* (the *Age*'s weekly) in 1880. Later, in a secret arrangement, he was the special correspondent for the English *Morning Post* from 1901 to 1914. He also wrote a number of books. Deakin was elected as a Liberal Member of the Legislative Assembly in Victoria in 1879, but lost his seat in a by-election held because of doubts about the earlier poll. After another unsuccessful attempt, he won a seat in 1880. He held office in coalition governments from 1883 to 1890, and he was Chief Secretary from

1886 to 1890. Deakin chaired a Royal Commission inquiring into *irrigation in 1884, visited California and met the *Chaffey brothers, and introduced the first legislation in Australia to promote an irrigation scheme. He remained on the back-benches for ten years from 1890 and also practised law again. He was active in various public organizations, such as the *Australian Natives' Association and the Imperial Federation League. Deakin played a significant role in the *federation movement; he served on the Federal Council, attended the *Federal Convention, chaired the Federation League of Victoria, and took part in the delegation that went to London in 1900 to explain the Commonwealth of Australia Constitution Bill. He was a Member of the House of Representatives from 1901 to 1913. He was Attorney-General in the *Barton Protectionist Government from 1901 to 1903, and succeeded Barton as Prime Minister and Minister for External Affairs in 1903, remaining in these positions until 1904. He was again Prime Minister, and Minister for External Affairs, at the head of the Protectionists, from 1905 to 1908. He was Prime Minister again, leading the so-called *Fusion Party, in 1909-10. After its defeat by Labor, he led the Opposition (by then known as the Liberals) from 1910 to 1913. Deakin retired in 1913. His health had deteriorated, especially his memory, before his death in 1919. Deakin's publications include *Quentin Massys, A Drama in Five Acts* (1875), *A New Pilgrim's Progress* (1877), *Irrigated India* (1893) and *Temple and Tomb in India* (1893). His *The Federal Story* (1944) and *The Crisis in Victorian Politics, 1879-1881* (1957) were published posthumously.

Democratic Labor Party (DLP): A minor Australian political party formed after the *Australian Labor Party split during the mid-1950s. The Catholic Social Movement and the Industrial Groups within the Australian Labor Party worked together to oppose community influence in the trade union movement. *Evatt publicly attacked both groups in 1954, and members were expelled from the Australian Labor Party in 1955. The expelled members formed the Australian Labor Party (Anti-Communist) in 1955, which became the Democratic Labor Party in 1957. The Movement, as it was called, became the National Civic Council in 1957. The Democratic Labor Party was represented in the Senate until 1974, at times holding the balance of power. A conference of the party in 1978 voted narrowly in favour of its disbandment, but it was soon reconstituted, and continued to field candidates in the mid-1980s.

Denison, Sir William Thomas (1804–71), governor-general, was born in London, was educated at Eton, and graduated from the Royal Military Academy in 1826, after which his work included serving as an engineer officer in Canada and England. He was Lieutenant-Governor of *Van Diemen's Land from 1847 to 1855, during which time he had to resolve the situation involving the *Patriotic Six, was censured following his conflict with the Supreme Court, and took a keen interest in education. Although Denison advocated the continuation of *transportation to the colony, it ended during his term of office. He became *Governor of New South Wales in 1855, also becoming the nominal Governor-General of all the Australian colonies. *Responsible government began in New South Wales in 1856. Denison strengthened New South Wales's defences, attempted to improve the administration of public works, controlled the transfer of Pitcairn Islanders to *Norfolk Island, and shortly before his term ended in January 1861 became involved in controversy with *Cowper over control of the great seal of New South Wales. He was then Governor of Madras from 1861 to 1866. He died in England. His publications include *Varieties of Vice-Regal Life* (1870).

Dennis, Clarence Michael James (1876–1938), journalist and poet, was born to Irish parents at Auburn in South Australia. His father was a hotel-keeper. Dennis was educated at Gladstone Primary School, St Aloysius's College at Sevenhill, and the Christian Brothers' College in Adelaide. He worked first as a clerk, then pursued a journalistic and literary career, interrupted by several brief periods of other employment, including work for the Commonwealth Government during the First World War. He wrote prose and poetry for numerous newspapers and journals, such as the *Bulletin*; he and others founded the Adelaide *Gadfly*, which he edited for about eighteen months; and he wrote a daily column for the Melbourne *Herald* from 1922 to 1938. He died in Melbourne. C. J. Dennis is best known for *The Songs of a Sentimental Bloke* (1915). It is written in vernacular verse, and tells the story of the 'Sentimental Bloke', a *larrikin named Bill, and his sweetheart Doreen. Numerous adaptations have been made for film, stage, radio, record and television. His other publications include *Backblock Ballads and Other Verses by Den* (1913), *The Australaise, A Marching Song* (1915), *The Battle of the Wazzir* (1916), *The Moods of Ginger Mick* (1916) (a sequel to *The Songs of a Sentimental Bloke*), *The Glugs of Gosh* (1917), *Doreen* (1917), *Digger Smith* (1918), *Jim of the Hills, A Story in Rhyme* (1919), *A Book for Kids* (1921), *Rose of Spadgers, A Sequel to Ginger Mick* (1924), *I Dips Me Lid to the Sydney Harbour Bridge* (1932) and *The Singing Garden* (1935).

Depression (1840s): Australia's first economic depression. The worst years were 1841, 1842 and 1843, and New South Wales and Van Diemen's Land were hardest hit. Insolvencies, unemployment and poverty were widespread. Several banks failed, including the Bank of Australia, the Sydney Banking Company and the Port Phillip Bank. Historians have suggested various factors that helped either to cause or to exacerbate the depression. They include a serious drought in New South Wales during the late 1830s; declining wool prices overseas and wheat prices locally; a diminished flow of English capital to the colonies; too much borrowing on limited security; the withdrawal of colonial government funds from banks in New South Wales (necessitated largely because land revenue had fallen) to pay for *immigration; and the reduction of commissariat expenditure to New South Wales as a result of the cessation of *transportation to that colony. Most historians stress internal, rather than external, factors as causes. Various measures were implemented in an

attempt to cope with the depression. Assorted legislation in New South Wales introduced more generous
provisions for insolvents, abolished imprisonment
for debtors and allowed borrowers to use stock and
prospective wool-clips as security for advances. Some
*squatters resorted to the boiling-down of sheep for
tallow. The depression lasted until about the mid-
1840s.

Depression (1890s): An economic depression experienced by the eastern colonies, Victoria being the
most severely affected. The depression lasted from
about 1890 to 1894. Many financial institutions collapsed, including building societies, land banks and
trading banks. The main bank crashes occurred in
1893. Unemployment was high. *Immigration virtually ceased. Historians have suggested various factors that helped either to cause or to exacerbate the
depression. They include the decline in overseas
prices for wool and wheat; the cessation of overseas
capital flow; speculation in real estate, especially in
Melbourne and Sydney, during the boom years of
the 1880s; over-expansion in both the public and
private sectors, especially in the pastoral industry;
industrial unrest; and the effects of drought conditions. There is debate as to whether the depression
was caused by external or internal factors. Gold discoveries in Western Australia, notably at *Kalgoorlie
and Coolgardie, and changes and improvements in
Australian primary industries assisted subsequent
recovery.

Depression (1930s): *Great Depression

Dictation Test: *White Australia Policy

Digger: A term with several Australian meanings.
During the *gold-rushes of the 1850s, miners became
known as diggers. During the First World War, Australian and New Zealand soldiers were called diggers,
and the word continued to be used during the Second
World War. The word is used also as an informal
mode of address among Australian men.

Dismissal of the Whitlam Government

Discovery of Australia: Ancestors of the *Aborigines are believed to have settled in Australia more than 40,000 years ago. There is some speculation that the Portuguese were the first Europeans to discover Australia, but the first known European landing was made by *Janssen (or Jansz), a Dutch navigator, in 1606. Numerous Dutch contacts followed, including *Hartog's visit in 1616, the wrecking of the *Batavia* in 1629, and *Tasman's voyages in 1642 and 1644. English contacts began with the wrecking of the *Tryal* off the islands now called the Monte Bello Islands in 1622, the sighting of the coast by the *London* in 1681, *Dampier's visits in 1688 and 1699, and James *Cook's survey of the east coast in 1770. Following the settlement of *New South Wales in 1788, notable British exploration by sea included George Vancouver's survey of part of the south coast in 1791; the voyages of *Bass and *Flinders, together and individually, between 1795 and 1803; James Grant's exploration of parts of the coast of present-day *Victoria in 1800 and 1801; and John Murray's exploration of Western Port, part of King Island, Port Phillip and Corio Bay in 1801 and 1802. Phillip Parker King, the son of Philip Gidley *King, surveyed a considerable part of the Australian coast between 1817 and 1822. Early French contact included Marion du Fresne's visit to *Van Diemen's Land in 1772; François Alesne de St Allouarn's visit to the west coast in 1772; *La Pérouse's visit in 1785; Joseph-Antoine Raymond Bruny d'Entrecasteaux's visit to Van Diemen's Land and the south coast of the mainland in 1792; and *Baudin's exploration between 1801 and 1803.

Dismissal of the Whitlam Government (1975): A political and constitutional crisis. The House of Representatives, which had a Labor majority, and the Senate, which had a non-Labor majority, reached a deadlock following the so-called Loans Affair, which involved attempts by several Labor ministers to raise overseas loans without consulting Cabinet. The Prime Minister, *Whitlam, would not agree to a dissolution, which the Senate was demanding

79

before it would pass the Appropriation Bills (popularly known as Supply). The Governor-General, Sir John Kerr, having obtained advice from the Chief Justice of the *High Court, *Barwick, a former Liberal minister, withdrew Whitlam's commission as Prime Minister, and instead commissioned *Fraser, the Leader of the Opposition, on 11 November. Fraser advised Kerr to dissolve both houses, and the Appropriation Bills were passed. Fraser's Liberal–National Country Party coalition secured majorities in both houses at the elections held on 13 December. The dismissal of the Whitlam Government continues to be the cause of controversy.

Dixon, Sir Owen (1886–1972), lawyer, was born in Hawthorn, Victoria. His father was a solicitor. He was educated at Hawthorn College and the University of Melbourne, was admitted to the Bar in 1910, and was appointed King's Counsel in 1922. He acted as a Justice of the Supreme Court of Victoria in 1926. Dixon became a Justice of the *High Court in 1929, was appointed to the Privy Council in 1957, and was Chief Justice of the High Court from 1952 to 1964. He attempted to establish a consistent interpretation of Section 92 of the *Constitution of the Commonwealth (the section that reads, in part: 'On the imposition of uniform duties of customs, trade, commerce, and intercourse among the States, whether by means of internal carriage or ocean navigation, shall be absolutely free.') During the Second World War, he chaired the Central Wool Committee (1940–2), the Australian Shipping Control Board (1941–2), the Marine War Risks Insurance Board (1941–2), and the Allied Consultative Shipping Council of Australia (1942). He was the Australian Minister in Washington from 1942 to 1944. In 1950 he was the United Nations mediator in the Kashmir dispute between India and Pakistan. Sir Owen Dixon died in Hawthorn. His publications include *Jesting Pilate, and Other Papers and Addresses* (1965).

DLP: *Democratic Labor Party

Dobell, Sir William Smith (1899–1970), painter, was born in Newcastle, New South Wales. His father was a building contractor. Critics have described Dobell as 'a myth in his country and a legend in his hometown'[1] and 'from 1944 Australia's most celebrated portrait and genre painter'.[2] Dobell was an apprentice architect in Newcastle from 1916 onwards. He studied at Julian Ashton's School, Sydney, between 1924 and 1929; at the Slade School, London, in 1929 and 1930; and in Holland in 1930. Dobell remained abroad, in Europe and England, until 1939, when he returned to Sydney. He taught part-time at the East Sydney Technical College. During the Second World War, he served in a camouflage unit and as an official artist in the Civil Construction Corps. In 1944, Dobell became involved in controversy when his *Portrait of an Artist* (1943), a portrait of Joshua Smith, won the Archibald Prize for 1943. Two artists challenged the validity of the award, on the grounds that the painting was a caricature, not a portrait. Dobell won the court case. He went on to win two more Archibald Prizes and numerous other awards. He also painted four portraits for covers of *Time* magazine. He died at Lake Macquarie. His best-known paintings include *The Cypriot* (1940), *Portrait of a Strapper* (1941), *Portrait of an Artist* (1943), *The Billy Boy* (1943) and *Dame Mary Gilmore, O.B.E.* (1955-7).

Donahoe (or Donohoe), **John:** *Bushrangers

Dorchester Labourers: *Tolpuddle Martyrs

Droughts can be described, in general terms, as lengthy periods of rainfall deficiency. The most severe and widespread droughts occurring in Australia between 1860 (when reliable records were established) and 1975 include those of 1864-6, 1880-6, 1888, 1895-1903, 1911-16, 1918-20, 1939-45 and 1964-8, the worst being that of 1895-1903 (sometimes called the

[1]Bernard Smith, *Australian Painting, 1788-1970* (Oxford University Press, Melbourne, 1971), p. 405.
[2]Alan McCulloch, *Encyclopedia of Australian Art* (Hutchinson of Australia, Melbourne, 1968), p. 168.

1902 drought), during which sheep numbers, which had exceeded 106 million in 1892, were halved, cattle numbers fell from more than 12 million in 1895 to 7 million in early 1903, and the average wheat yield for the Commonwealth dropped to 2.4 bushels per acre in 1902.

Drysdale, Sir George Russell (1912–81), painter, was born in England. He settled in Australia with his family in 1923, and was educated at Geelong Grammar School. He later studied art in Melbourne, London and Paris. Russell Drysdale, who spent most of his life in Australia, probably is best known for his outback landscapes. He has been described as 'a kind of twentieth-century [Henry] Lawson of painting'.[1] His paintings won numerous awards. Drysdale became a member of the Commonwealth Art Advisory Board in 1962, and a member of the Board of Trustees, Art Gallery of New South Wales, in 1963. His paintings include *The Rabbiter and His Family* (1938), *Sunday Evening* (1941), *The Drover's Wife* (1945), *Two Children* (1946) and *Sofala* (1947).

Duffy, Sir Charles Gavan (1816–1903), Irish nationalist and Victorian politician, was born in Monaghan, Ireland. His father was a shopkeeper. Duffy was educated at a Presbyterian school. He founded the *Nation*, a weekly journal, in Dublin in 1842, and was admitted to the Bar in Ireland in 1845. As one of the leaders of the Young Irelanders (members of an Irish nationalist movement), Duffy was tried for treason in 1848, but was released after five trials. He was a Member of the British House of Commons from 1852 to 1855. Duffy arrived in Melbourne in 1856, and worked as a barrister, before entering colonial politics. He was a Member of the Victorian Legislative Assembly for several periods (1856–64, 1867–74, 1876–80), was Premier and Chief Secretary in 1871–2, and held various portfolios at different times. He introduced legislation that abolished the property qualification for members of the

---

[1] Bernard Smith, *Australian Painting, 1788–1970* (Oxford University Press, Melbourne, 1971), p. 247.

Legislative Assembly, and was responsible for land legislation in 1862 that was designed to help *selectors, but which failed, and helped *squatters more than selectors. Duffy, a liberal, also supported *protection and federation. He was one of the founders of the *Advocate*, a Catholic journal, which began in 1868. Duffy lived in Nice, France, from 1880 until his death. His publications include *Ballad Poetry of Ireland* (1845), which he edited, *Young Ireland* (1880), *Four Years of Irish History* (1883), *The League of North and South* (1886), *Life of Thomas Davis* (1890), *Conversations with Carlyle* (1892), *Bird's Eye View of Irish History* (1892) and *My Life In Two Hemispheres* (1898).

Duntroon: *Army; *Bridges, Sir William Throsby; *Campbell, Robert

Dyson Family: A well-known Australian artistic and literary family. Its best-known member is **William (Will) Henry Dyson** (1880–1938), artist and writer, who was born at Alfredton, near Ballarat. His father worked on the gold-fields as a miner and hawker. The family moved to Melbourne when Dyson was a child, and he was educated at Albert Park State School. Dyson drew cartoons for the *Bulletin* and other journals, became friendly with the *Lindsay family, and played a leading role in Melbourne's bohemian society. He married Ruby Lindsay in 1909; shortly after their marriage, they sailed for England. Dyson was an extremely successful radical cartoonist on the London *Daily Herald* from 1912 to 1916. He then became an Australian war artist, and was wounded twice. He again worked on the *Daily Herald* from 1918 to 1921. He was greatly affected by his wife's death, in 1919, during the *'Spanish' Influenza Pandemic. Dyson did not regain his pre-war force as a cartoonist, although his most famous cartoon, 'Peace and Future Cannon Fodder', was published in 1919. In 1925 he returned to Australia, where he drew for the Melbourne *Herald*. He also drew for *Punch*, and later for *Table Talk*. He took up etching, which later brought him further fame in England and the United States of America. He returned to

England, via America, in 1930. He again worked as a cartoonist on the *Daily Herald* from 1931 until his death. Dyson's publications include *Cartoons* (1913), *Cartoons* (1914), *Kultur Cartoons* (1915), *Conscript 'Em* (1915), *Will Dyson's War Cartoons* (1916), *Australia at War* (1918), *Poems in Memory of a Wife* (1919) and *Artist Among the Bankers* (1933). Other well-known members of the family include **Ambrose (Amb) Arthur Dyson** (1876–1913), Will's elder brother, cartoonist and illustrator, whose subjects include *larrikins; **Edward Ambrose (Amby) Dyson** (1908–53), Ambrose's son, cartoonist; and **Edward George Dyson** (1856–1931), Will's eldest brother, writer, whose publications include *Rhymes from the Mines* (1896), *Below and On Top* (1898), *The Gold-stealers* (1901), *In the Roaring Fifties* (1906), *Fact'ry 'Ands* (1906), *Benno and Some of the Push* (1911) and *Spats' Fact'ry* (1914).

E

Eardley-Wilmot, Sir John Eardley (1783–1847), colonial administrator, was born in London and educated at Harrow. His father was a master in chancery. Eardley-Wilmot, who was created a baronet in 1821, was called to the Bar in 1806, chaired the Warwickshire Quarter Sessions from 1830 to 1843, and was a Member of the House of Commons from 1832 to 1843. During his term of office as Lieutenant-Governor of *Van Diemen's Land, which began in 1843, he was faced with the *depression of the 1840s; had to implement the unpopular new probation system; was involved in various conflicts with the Anglican Bishop Nixon; and was a central figure in the constitutional crisis involving the *Patriotic Six. Eardley-Wilmot was recalled in 1846, allegedly for neglecting the convict system. He was informed privately that he would not be employed in an official position again because of alleged rumours about his personal life. He died in Van Diemen's Land the following year. His publications include *An Abridgement of Blackstone's Com-*

mentaries (1822) and *A Letter to the Magistrates of England* (1827).

EEC: *European Economic Community

Eight-hour Day Movement: Nineteenth-century campaign for shorter working hours. Unionists campaigned for the reduction of the working week (which then comprised six days) from sixty to forty-eight hours. Sydney stonemasons and Melbourne building workers, the latter having formed an Eight Hours League, became the first to gain the reduction in 1856. Annual celebrations were introduced in Melbourne and later elsewhere. Many unions were first formed for the purpose of fighting for the eight-hour day. Most Australian workers had gained it by the end of the nineteenth century. All of the states, the Australian Capital Territory and the Northern Territory now commemorate the movement with an annual public holiday, held on various dates and known by various names (such as Labour Day and Eight Hour Day).

Emancipists: A term used during the period of *transportation. It had several different meanings. In a narrow sense, it referred only to those convicts who had been pardoned, conditionally or absolutely, by the governor. In a broader sense, it was applied to all ex-convicts, and this usage was more common. The term was also applied to members of a political group, consisting of emancipists and liberals, that campaigned for legal and political reforms in New South Wales during the 1820s, 1830s and early 1840s. *Wentworth was the acknowledged leader of this group for many years. In 1835 this group founded the *Australian Patriotic Association. Emancipists and *exclusives came into conflict over various issues relating to the former's position in colonial society.

Equal Pay: The right of women to receive the same wages and salaries as men. The principle of equal pay was introduced in Australia in a series of stages. Queensland legislated for equal pay as early as 1916, but the legislation proved to be ineffective. New

South Wales legislated for 'equal pay for equal work', to be phased in over five years, in 1958. This legislation differentiated between men's and women's work. Women performing 'men's work' were to receive equal pay; women performing 'women's work' (such as that performed by typists) were not. Other states had introduced similar legislation by the late 1960s. The Commonwealth Conciliation and Arbitration Commission accepted the principle of 'equal pay for equal work', to be phased in over three years, in 1969. Equal pay was not to be provided 'where the work in question is essentially or usually performed by females'. In 1972 the Commission accepted the principle of 'equal pay for work of equal value', to be gradually introduced by mid-1975, but rejected a claim for the introduction of an equal minimum wage for men and women. The Commission introduced the principle of the same minimum wage for men and women in 1974. Acceptance of equal pay in theory has not led to equal incomes in practice.

Escape Cliffs: *Northern Territory; *Port Essington

Eureka Flag: Flag flown by *diggers during the *Eureka Rebellion, and later by other groups, including striking shearers at *Barcaldine and, more recently, members of the Builders' Labourers' Federation. The flag has a white cross and five white stars, one in the centre and one at each of the four ends of the cross, representing the constellation of the Southern Cross, on a blue background.

Eureka Rebellion: An armed conflict in 1854 between *diggers and government authorities on the gold-fields at Ballarat, Victoria. The diggers' grievances included the licence system and its administration (under which diggers were forced to pay thirty shillings a month, had to carry their licences at all times, and had to face licence hunts, which were deeply resented), corruption among officials, lack of political representation and limited access to land. A digger named Scobie was kicked to death near the Eureka Hotel on 7 October. Bentley, the hotel licensee, and three others were charged with Scobie's murder. Magistrates discharged them on 12 October, strengthening the diggers' suspicions of corruption. Diggers held a mass protest meeting on 17 October, after which the Eureka Hotel was burnt down. As a result, three diggers were charged on 21 October with riot. At another mass meeting on 11 November, diggers formed the Ballarat Reform League. Bentley was eventually convicted of Scobie's murder on 23 November. Ballarat Reform League representatives demanded the release of the three charged with riot. *Hotham, the Lieutenant-Governor (later Governor) of Victoria, refused, and sent more troops to Ballarat. Diggers and soldiers scuffled when the latter entered Ballarat on 28 November, and at a mass meeting the next day, displaying the Southern Cross flag (now usually called the *Eureka flag), diggers resolved to burn their licences. The authorities conducted another licence hunt the following day. About 1000 diggers, led by *Lalor, built a stockade ('breastwork or enclosure of upright stakes') on the Eureka lead. About 280 soldiers and police attacked the stockade on 3 December, rapidly overpowering the 150 or so diggers inside at the time. They took more than 100 prisoners. About thirty diggers and five soldiers and police were killed. Martial law was proclaimed and remained in force for several days. Thirteen diggers were charged with high treason; the prosecution against one was dropped and juries acquitted the others. Rewards were offered for information leading to the capture of Lalor and two others, but were later withdrawn. A Royal Commission was appointed in 1854 to inquire into the gold-fields. Its recommendations, most of which were adopted, included the abolition of the licence fee, the introduction of an export duty on gold, and the introduction of a miner's right, which conferred legal and political rights, to cost £1 a year.

European Economic Community (EEC): An organization of European countries that aims to bring about the economic union of its members. The EEC, often known as the Common Market, was officially established in 1958, following the signing of a treaty in Rome in 1957. The original members were

Belgium, France, Italy, Luxembourg, the Netherlands and West Germany. Britain, Denmark and the
Irish Republic joined in 1973. Other countries have
since joined. The entry of Britain (which had always
been one of Australia's main markets) into the Common Market has had serious implications for Australia.

Evatt, Herbert Vere (1894-1965), lawyer and politician, was born at Maitland, New South Wales. His
father was a publican. He was educated at Fort Street
High School and the University of Sydney, admitted
to the Bar in 1918, and appointed King's Counsel
in 1929. Evatt was a Justice of the *High Court from
1930 to 1940, and Chief Justice of New South Wales
from 1960 to 1962. He was a Member of the Legislative Assembly of New South Wales from 1925 to
1930, serving as a Labor Member to 1927, then as
an Independent Labor Member. Evatt was a Labor
Member of the House of Representatives from 1940
to 1960, and held various offices, including those of
Attorney-General (1941-9) and Leader of the Opposition (1951-60). The split in the Labor Party that
resulted in the formation of the *Democratic Labor
Party occurred during the period of Evatt's leadership of the federal parliamentary party. He was prominent in the early development of the *United Nations
Organization; he presided over the United Nations
General Assembly (1948-9), and chaired the United
Nations Atomic Energy Commission (1947) and the
United Nations Palestine Commission (1947). Evatt,
who was a Doctor of Laws and a Doctor of Letters,
wrote a number of books including *The King and
His Dominion Governors* (1936), *Rum Rebellion*
(1938) and *Australian Labour Leader, W. A. Holman
and the Labor Movement* (1940).

Exclusionists: *Exclusives

Exclusives: The name applied in New South Wales,
during the *transportation period (especially the
1820s and 1830s), to those people who opposed the
restoration of complete civil rights to *emancipists.
They were sometimes known as exclusionists.

Exiles: Convicts who had served a prison term in England, and in some cases had laboured on public works, before undergoing *transportation to Australia, where they were given conditional pardons or *tickets-of-leave. A large proportion of the exiles were sent to the *Port Phillip District.

Exploration of Australia by land mostly took place in the nineteenth century. Early exploration in eastern Australia included the crossing of the *Blue Mountains, John Oxley's expedition to Port Macquarie in 1818, the *Hume and Hovell expedition to the south in the mid-1820s, and Allan Cunningham's discovery of the Darling Downs in 1827. *Sturt solved the 'riddle of the rivers' in the 1820s and 1830s, and also explored in the centre of Australia in the mid-1840s. *Mitchell explored in the south-east in the 1830s, and in the north in the mid-1840s. Paul Edmund de Strzelecki discovered and named Mount Kosciusko in 1840, and then crossed Gippsland (which Angus McMillan had already explored). *Grey undertook expeditions in Western Australia in the 1830s. *Eyre explored parts of South Australia from 1839 onwards, and became the first European to cross the desert now known as the Nullarbor Plain. *Leichhardt explored in the north-east and north in the 1840s, finally disappearing during an expedition. Edmund Kennedy led a disastrous expedition in the north-east in 1848. Augustus Charles Gregory explored in the west in the 1840s, in the north and north-east in the 1850s, and from central Queensland to Adelaide in 1858. In 1861, some members of the *Burke and Wills expedition crossed the continent from south to north, but died on the way back. *Stuart, after two unsuccessful attempts in 1860 and 1861, also crossed from south to north in 1862. John *Forrest explored in Western Australia and South Australia in the 1860s, 1870s and 1880s; in 1870 he crossed the Nullarbor Plain area from west to east. *Warburton's party became the first to cross Australia from the centre to the west (1873-4). Ernest Giles explored in the centre of the continent in the 1870s and crossed much of the continent from east to west, and back again, in 1875 and 1876. Many other explorers and *overlanders also opened up parts of the continent. Much of Van Diemen's Land was explored in the first few decades of white settlement.

Eyre, Edward John (1815-1901), explorer, was born in England. His father was a vicar. Eyre migrated to New South Wales in 1833, became a *squatter, and later overlanded stock to the *Port Phillip District and South Australia. After moving to Adelaide, he undertook expeditions to the Flinders Ranges and the Eyre Peninsula in 1839. He took stock by sea to *Albany, and overlanded them to Perth, in 1840. Later that year he made unsuccessful attempts to find a route from Adelaide to the west. However, in 1841, he became the first white person to cross the area now known as the Nullarbor Plain. Eyre, John Baxter and three Aborigines left Fowler's Bay in February; two of the Aborigines killed Baxter, and fled, in April; Eyre and the other Aborigine, Wylie, having been helped by French *whalers near present-day Esperance, finally reached Albany in July. Eyre was the resident magistrate and protector of Aborigines at Moorundie, in South Australia, from 1841 to 1844. In 1846 he was appointed Lieutenant-Governor of New Zealand, a position he held until 1853. In 1854 he was appointed Lieutenant-Governor of St Vincent (in the West Indies), held that position until 1860, was acting Governor of the Leeward Islands for some time, and became acting Governor of Jamaica in 1864. His controversial handling of a Negro uprising there in 1865 led to his recall. Eyre died in England. He published *Journals of Expeditions of Discovery into Central Australia and Overland from Adelaide to King George's Sound in the Years 1840-1* (1845).

F

Fadden, Sir Arthur William (1895-1973), was born in Queensland. He was educated at Walkerston State School, and was assistant Town Clerk (1913-18) and

Town Clerk (1918) at Mackay before practising as a chartered accountant in Townsville. Fadden was a Country Party Member of the Queensland Legislative Assembly from 1932 to 1935, then a Country Party Member of the House of Representatives from 1936 to 1958, becoming Leader of the Country Party in 1941. He held various portfolios at different times. After *Menzies resigned as Prime Minister, Fadden replaced him, leading a *United Australia Party-Country Party Government. His Prime Ministership was short-lived (29 August–7 October 1941). Labor and the Independents defeated Fadden's budget, and *Curtin became the next Prime Minister. Fadden was Leader of the Opposition until 1943, and continued to lead the Country Party until his retirement from Parliament in 1958. From 1949 to 1958 he was Deputy Prime Minister and Treasurer in the Menzies Government. He pursued business interests after leaving politics.

Fairfax, John (1804–77), newspaper proprietor, was born in Warwick, England. In 1836, while running a newspaper in England, he went bankrupt. He later paid his creditors. Fairfax migrated to Sydney in 1838, and became the Librarian of the Australian Subscription Library in 1839. He and Charles Kemp bought the daily *Sydney Herald* in 1841, a paper that had been founded as a weekly in 1831. Its name was changed to *Sydney Morning Herald* in 1842. Fairfax bought Kemp's interest in 1853, and his sons joined him in the business. The *Sydney Morning Herald* became the major daily newspaper in New South Wales. Fairfax also became a foundation director of the Australian Mutual Provident Society, a director of the Sydney Insurance Company and various other institutions, a trustee of the Savings Bank of New South Wales, and president of the Young Men's Christian Association. He was actively involved in the Congregational Church. He was nominated to the Legislative Council in 1874. Fairfax died in Sydney. His sons continued to run the newspaper after his death. In the 1980s, Fairfax's descendants are major shareholders in John Fairfax and Sons Ltd, which has extensive media interests. The *Sydney Morning*

Herald continues to be one of Australia's major daily newspapers.

Farrer, William James (1845-1906), wheat-breeder, was born in England. His father was a tenant-farmer. Farrer was educated at Christ's Hospital, London, and Pembroke College, Cambridge. Ill health forced him to abandon his medical studies. In 1870 he migrated to Australia, where he worked as a tutor on a sheep station. Farrer qualified as a surveyor in 1875 and worked in that capacity with the Department of Lands in New South Wales from 1875 to 1886. He then settled on the Murrumbidgee River, near present-day Canberra, and experimented with wheat-breeding from 1886 to 1898, when he was appointed wheat experimentalist with the Department of Agriculture, a position he held until his death. Farrer's work contributed greatly to the development, in Australia and other countries, of the wheat industry. His best-known wheat, 'Federation' (named in 1901), was the most widely grown wheat in Australia from 1910 to 1925.

Fawkner, John Pascoe: *Melbourne; *Strutt, William

Federal Convention (1897-8): A significant event in the *federation movement leading to the creation of the *Commonwealth of Australia. The Convention, which had been proposed at the Corowa Conference, had as its purpose the drafting of a federal constitution to be put to the people at a referendum. It comprised ten delegates each from New South Wales, Victoria, South Australia, Tasmania and Western Australia (the delegates being elected by voters in each colony, except in Western Australia, where they were elected by Members of Parliament). Queensland did not send delegates. Notable delegates included *Barton, *Deakin, *Kingston and *Reid. The Convention met in Adelaide and Sydney in 1897, and in Melbourne in 1898. A federal constitution was drafted. The first federal referendum (held in four colonies in 1898) failed; the second (held in five colonies in 1899, and one in 1900), after amendments were made, passed in all of the Australian colonies.

Federal Court of Australia: *Commonwealth Conciliation and Arbitration Court

Federation Cup: *Tennis

Federation Movement: The movement that led to the federation of the Australian colonies in 1901. Politicians and others had proposed federation as early as the 1840s, but serious attempts were not made to introduce it until the 1880s and 1890s. The Federal Council, which was formed in 1885 and met regularly for the rest of the nineteenth century, was weakened by the absences of South Australia (except for two years) and New South Wales. *Parkes publicly supported federation in his *Tenterfield Oration in 1889. Those in favour of federation argued that uniform policies with regard to matters such as defence, *immigration and tariffs would be advantageous. Federation was discussed at various conferences. They included the Australasian Federation Conference, held in Melbourne in 1890; the National Australasian Convention, held in Sydney in 1891, at which a draft constitution was produced; the so-called Corowa Conference in 1893, attended by representatives of the Australasian Federation League, the *Australian Natives' Association, and other organizations; the Premiers' Conference held in Hobart in 1895; the *Federal Convention, held in Adelaide and Sydney in 1897 and Melbourne in 1898, at which another draft constitution was produced; and the Premiers' Conference held in Melbourne in 1899. Two federal referendums were held, based on the draft constitution produced at the Federal Convention. The first was held in New South Wales, Victoria, Tasmania and South Australia in 1898. 'Yes' majorities were recorded in each of these colonies, but the 'Yes' majority in New South Wales was insufficient to carry the referendum there. The draft constitution was amended and a second referendum was held in those colonies in 1899. Increased 'Yes' majorities were recorded in each of them. A

'Federation' Wheat

'Yes' majority was also recorded in Queensland, when the referendum was held there later in 1899. Western Australia voted in favour of federation at the referendum held there in 1900, shortly after the British Parliament had passed the *Commonwealth of Australia Constitution Act*. Federation occurred on 1 January 1901. The six colonies became states of the *Commonwealth of Australia, which was part of the British Empire. Fiji and New Zealand had shown interest in the early stages of the movement, but ultimately did not join the Australian colonies in federation.

'Federation' Wheat: *Farrer, William James

Felton, Alfred (1831–1904), businessman and philanthropist, was born in England, where he is believed to have been apprenticed to a chemist. His father was a tanner. Felton migrated to Victoria in 1853, transported goods during the *gold-rushes, and then became a merchant, and later a pharmaceutical chemist, in Melbourne. He and Frederick Sheppard Grimwade bought a drug-house, which they renamed Felton, Grimwade & Co., in 1867; it became the largest in Victoria, with some interests elsewhere. They also founded various other businesses during the 1870s and 1880s, and Felton bought two large rural properties in partnership with Charles Campbell. Felton died in 1904, and left money to establish a trust fund, originally of approximately £380,000; half of the income was to be used for charities, especially those helping women and children, the other half to buy art works for the Melbourne National Gallery. The Felton Bequest has been, and continues to be, of great importance to the gallery.

Female Factory: A name that usually refers to an institution that existed, during the *transportation period, at *Parramatta, New South Wales. *King established it in 1804. The Female Factory provided asylum, punishment, and sometimes employment (such as cloth-making), for convict and other women. A new building was erected near Parramatta in 1821. It was extended in 1828 and again in 1839. It housed female convicts who had been sent there on arrival,

who were unable to be assigned, or who had been
returned from assignment. It also housed convict and
other women who had committed crimes within the
colony. The largest numbers housed there were 1203
women and 263 children in 1842. It was closed in
1848. There was a similar institution at the Cascades,
near Hobart.

Financial Agreement (1927): An agreement between the Commonwealth and State Governments.
The Australian people approved it at a referendum
in 1928, and the *Constitution of the Commonwealth
of Australia was amended accordingly in 1929. Sawer
describes the changes brought about by the Financial
Agreement in the following way.

*Firstly, the Commonwealth took over all existing
debts of the States. Secondly, an Australian Loan
Council was established, consisting of representatives of the Commonwealth and the States, with con-
clusive authority to raise loans for non-defence
purposes for all Australian governments. Thirdly,
the Commonwealth ceased making per capita payments to the States, and instead undertook to make
a regular contribution to the interest and sinking
funds on the State indebtedness which it took over,
the States remaining liable to the Commonwealth
for the principal and remainder of the interest...*[1]

The Financial Agreement helped to transfer power
from the states to the Commonwealth.

First Fleet: The eleven ships that carried the first
white settlers (convicts, marines and civilians) to
Australia. The First Fleet, under the command of
*Phillip, sailed from England in 1787. The ships were
HMS *Sirius*, HMS *Supply*, the *Alexander*, the *Char-
lotte*, the *Friendship*, the *Lady Penrhyn*, the *Prince
of Wales*, the *Scarborough*, the *Borrowdale*, the *Fish-
burn* and the *Golden Grove*. The Fleet arrived at
*Botany Bay, but the site was considered unsuitable.
Instead, the landing was made at Sydney Cove in
Port Jackson on 26 January 1788. One thousand and

---

[1]Geoffrey Sawer, *Australian Federal Politics and Law, 1901–1929* (Melbourne University Press, Melbourne, 1956), p. 262.

thirty people went ashore; of these 548 men and 188 women were convicts. The colony of New South Wales was formally proclaimed on 7 February.

First World War (1914-18): A major war, also known as the Great War, in which many countries, including Australia, were involved. It was fought between the Allied and Associated Powers and the Central Powers. The Allied and Associated Powers included Serbia, Britain, Belgium, Russia, France, Japan, Canada, New Zealand, Australia, Italy (from 1915), Rumania (from 1916), the United States of America (from 1917), Montenegro, Greece and Portugal. The Central Powers included Germany, Austria-Hungary, Turkey (from 1914) and Bulgaria (from 1915). The long-term causes, complex and numerous, included international tensions over naval, trade and colonial matters, exacerbated by the existence of various international alliances. The immediate cause was the assassination of Archduke Franz Ferdinand, the Austro-Hungarian heir, by a Serbian nationalist, at Sarajevo, in June 1914. Fighting began in August. The main areas of fighting during the war were on the Western, Eastern, Balkan and Italian Fronts, and in Palestine, Mesopotamia and Africa. The main naval operations occurred in the Pacific and South Atlantic Oceans, and the Adriatic and North Seas. The Central Powers were defeated. The armistice with Germany, which marked the end of fighting, was signed on 11 November 1918. After the war the provisions of various treaties, including the Treaty of *Versailles, were determined at the *Paris Peace Conference. An estimated ten million people died directly because of the First World War. The *'Spanish' Influenza Pandemic, which began in the war's latter stages, is believed to have claimed an even greater number of lives. Australia, as a member of the British Empire, automatically followed Britain to war in August 1914. The *Australian Imperial Force, raised by *Bridges, was Australia's main expeditionary force during the war. An Australian Naval and Military Expeditionary Force was also raised. The *Royal Australian Navy and the Australian Flying Corps, the predecessor of the *Royal Australian Air Force, took part. All members of the Australian forces who served overseas were volunteers. At the beginning of the war, Australian forces quickly captured German *New Guinea. During the war, the main areas in which they fought were the Dardanelles, during the *Gallipoli campaign, which led to the creation of the *Anzac Legend; France and Belgium, where Australian soldiers were particularly prominent in the attacks at Pozières (July-September 1916), Bullecourt (April-May 1917), Third Ypres (September-November 1917), the counter-attack at Villers-Bretonneux (April 1918) and the assault at Amiens (August 1918); and Egypt and Palestine, where the Australian Light Horse played a notable role. They were also involved in minor engagements elsewhere. Prominent Australian soldiers included *Chauvel, *Gellibrand and *Monash. The Australian forces, whose members were often used as shock troops, suffered extremely high casualty rates. Australia's population in 1916 was 4,875,325. During the war, the Australian troops raised (excluding naval forces) numbered 416,809; of these 331,789 took the field. The battle casualties numbered 215,045; of these, 59,342 were killed or died of wounds. There were also naval casualties, including 170 deaths. It should be noted that many of the other countries involved in the war relied upon *conscription. Two attempts to introduce conscription for overseas service, led by *Hughes and opposed by people such as *Mannix, failed. The conscription issue was a major factor leading to the split that occurred in the *Australian Labor Party during the war. The Commonwealth Government, whose powers increased during the war, introduced wartime legislation such as the *War Precautions Act. The *Industrial Workers of the World became the subject of controversy. The Returned Sailors' and Soldiers' Imperial League of Australia, later the *Returned Services League of Australia, was founded during the war years.

Fisher, Andrew (1862-1928), politician, was born in Scotland and educated at a local school. He began to work in mines when he was about 10, and became involved in the Ayrshire Miners' Union. He migrated to Queensland in 1885 and held various jobs, including those of manager and engine-driver, in mining areas. His union involvement continued; he became secretary and president of the Gympie branch of the Amalgamated Miners' Association. He was also involved in the newly formed Labor Party; he was president of the Gympie branch, and was elected to the Queensland Legislative Assembly in 1893. After losing his seat in 1896, Fisher returned to engine-driving, acted as auditor for the municipal council, and helped other Labor supporters to establish the Gympie *Truth*. He was re-elected in 1899 (without formal Labor endorsement), and was Secretary for Railways and Public Works in the *Dawson Government, the first Labor Government in the Australian colonies, which lasted for only a few days in December 1899. Fisher campaigned for federation, and was a Member of the House of Representatives from 1901 to 1915. He was Minister for Trade and Customs in the *Watson Labor Government (April–August 1904). He became Labor Leader on Watson's resignation in 1907, and Prime Minister and Treasurer in a minority Labor Government in November 1908. His Government was defeated by the newly formed *Fusion Party in May 1909. Fisher was again Prime Minister and Treasurer following Labor's win in the 1910 elections. This Government's achievements included the provision of maternity allowances, the extension of old age and invalid pensions, and the establishment of the Commonwealth Bank (later the *Commonwealth Banking Corporation). Following Labor's loss in the 1913 elections, Fisher became Leader of the Opposition. The Liberals controlled the House of Representatives, but not the Senate. A double dissolution occurred in 1914. Labor won the elections, and Fisher again became Prime Minister and Treasurer. He resigned in 1915, and served as Australian High Commissioner in London from 1916 to 1921. He died in England.

Flags: *Aboriginal Flag; *Australian National Flag; *Eureka Flag

Flinders, Matthew (1774–1814), navigator, was born in England. His father was a surgeon. In 1789

Flinders joined the navy; he sailed to the South Seas
with *Bligh (1791-3), took part in the battle of the
'Glorious First of June', a British naval victory
against the French in 1794, and sailed to New South
Wales in HMS *Reliance* in 1795. He and *Bass
explored parts of *Botany Bay in 1795. After visiting
*Norfolk Island in the *Reliance*, he and Bass explored
from Port Jackson to present-day Lake Illawarra in
1796. Both sailed to Cape Town in the *Reliance* (1796-
7). Flinders (as lieutenant) sailed in the *Francis* to
the Furneaux Islands in 1798. He became convinced
of the existence of a strait between New South Wales
and *Van Diemen's Land. He (in command) and Bass
sailed south from Port Jackson in the *Norfolk*, confirmed the existence of the strait (now known as Bass
Strait), discovered Port Dalrymple, and circumnavigated Van Diemen's Land (1798-9). Flinders then
sailed the *Norfolk* north from Port Jackson to near
present-day Bundaberg, charting part of the coast.
He returned to England in the *Reliance* in 1800. He
was promoted commander and placed in charge of
HMS *Investigator*, with instructions to survey the
coast of *New Holland. Despite the *Investigator*'s
poor condition, Flinders circumnavigated the continent between 1801 and 1803, charting large sections
of the coast. He met *Baudin at Encounter Bay in
early April 1802. Shortly afterwards he entered Port
Phillip, and climbed the highest peak (later named
Flinders Peak) in the You Yangs. Sailing to England
to request the use of another vessel, Flinders was
aboard HMS *Porpoise* when it was wrecked in 1803.
He navigated the cutter back to Port Jackson, a distance of some 1200 kilometres, to seek help. He sailed
for England once again that year, this time in charge
of the schooner *Cumberland*. As the schooner was
leaking badly, he sought aid in Mauritius. However,
Britain and France were at war, and the French
confined him on Mauritius until 1810. He then
returned to England, where he was promoted post-
captain. He died in London. His publications include
*Observations on the Coasts of Van Diemen's Land,
on Bass's Strait and its Islands, and on part of the
Coasts of New South Wales* (1801) and *A Voyage
to Terra Australis* (1814).

Flinders Island: *Furneaux Islands; *Robinson, George Augustus

Flying Doctor Service: *Royal Flying Doctor Service

Flynn, John: *Royal Flying Doctor Service

Football has been played throughout Australia for many years. Rugby Union (an amateur game), Rugby League (a professional game) and Soccer have been particularly strong in New South Wales and Queensland, Australian Rules in Victoria, South Australia, Western Australia and Tasmania. The game that became known as Rugby Union was first played in Australia in 1864, Rugby League in 1907 and Soccer in 1880. Australian Rules was first played in the 1850s. The latter is a fast, free-flowing sport, characterized by aerial contests, physical contact and long kicking. It is played on an oval field, with an oval ball. Each side now has twenty players, including two interchange players. A game is played over four quarters, each twenty-five minutes long, with time added to compensate for delays in play. The Melbourne Football Club was formed in 1858; soon after, several other Victorian clubs were formed, and the rules of the new game evolved over the next few years. Henry Colden Antill Harrison, the 'father of Australian Rules football', drafted a code that was adopted in 1866. The new game differed from the Rugby football then being played in Australia in that it 'did away with scrimmaging..., touchdowns, heavy tackling, off and on side, and cross bars on the goals, and introduced free kicks for marking the ball, as well as for penalties, and allowing running only for the distance required to get rid of the ball ...'[1] The game spread to the other colonies (and briefly to New Zealand and elsewhere). Developments included the introduction of umpires in 1872, uniforms for players in 1873, 'behind' posts on either side of the goal posts (a 'behind' being worth one

---

[1]Frank Crowley, *A Documentary History of Australia*, volume 2, *Colonial Australia, 1841–1874* (Nelson, Melbourne, 1980), p. 629.

point, a goal six points) in 1897, and boundary
umpires in 1903. Eight clubs left the Victorian Football Association, which had been founded in 1877,
and founded the Victorian Football League (which
became the sport's major organization) in 1896.

Forde, Francis Michael (1890-1983), politician,
was born in Queensland. He was educated at a local
state school, and at the Christian Brothers' College
at Toowoomba, and worked variously as a teacher,
a telegraphist and an electrical engineer. Forde was
a Labor Member of the Queensland Legislative
Assembly from 1917 to 1922, and then a Queensland
Member of the House of Representatives from 1922
to 1946. He held various portfolios at different times,
and was Deputy Prime Minister from 1941 to 1946.
After *Curtin's death, Forde was Prime Minister, as
a short-term measure in July 1945, until *Chifley was
elected to that position. Forde served as High Commissioner in Ottawa from 1946 to 1953, after which
he returned to state politics, first as a Labor organizer
(1953-5), and then as a Member of the Legislative
Assembly from 1955 to 1957.

Forrest of Bunbury, John, 1st Baron (1847-
1918), politician and explorer, was born in Bunbury,
Western Australia, was educated at Bishop Hale's
School, Perth, and became a surveyor. He worked
in the Surveyor-General's Office from 1865 to 1890.
During this time he led several major expeditions,
including one to search for *Leichhardt in 1869, and
another from Perth to Adelaide in 1870. Forrest was
a Member of the Western Australian Legislative
Council (1883-90), then a Member of the Legislative
Assembly (1890-1901), and was Western Australia's
first Premier (1890-1901). He was largely responsible
for the construction of the Goldfields Water Supply,
which took water to the *Kalgoorlie area, and the
development of the harbour at *Fremantle. Forrest
was active in the *federation movement; he attended
the National Australasian Convention, several meetings of the Federal Council, and the *Federal Convention. He entered federal politics, was variously
a Protectionist, Fusion, Liberal and Nationalist

Fort Dundas

Member of the House of Representatives from 1901 to 1918, and held various portfolios at different times. In 1918 he became the first Australian to be granted a peerage. He died, while in office, at sea off Sierra Leone. His publications include *Explorations in Australia* (1875), *Notes on Western Australia* (1884) and *The Present and Future of Western Australia* (1897).

Fort Dundas: *Northern Territory; *Port Essington

Fort Wellington: *Northern Territory; *Port Essington

'Fourteen Powers' Referendum: Popular name given to a referendum in 1944 to alter the *Constitution of the Commonwealth. The subject was postwar reconstruction and democratic rights. It was introduced by the *Curtin Labor Government, the proposals having been drafted by *Evatt, during the Second World War. Voters were asked whether they would give the Commonwealth Parliament the exclusive right to legislate in fourteen specific areas for a period of five years after the war ended. State Parliaments had previously been responsible for these areas; the Commonwealth Parliament could deal with them during the war. The powers related to the reinstatement of returned service personnel; employment and unemployment; organized marketing of commodities; companies; trust, combines and monopolies; profiteering and prices; production and distribution of goods; control of overseas exchange and investment, and raising of money in accordance with Loan Council plans; air transport; uniformity of railway gauges; national works; national health; family allowances; and Aborigines. Voters had to accept or reject all of the powers. The referendum, held on 19 August 1944, was not carried. There were 2,305,418 'No' votes and 1,963,400 'Yes' votes. New South Wales, Victoria, Queensland and Tasmania voted 'No'; South Australia and Western Australia voted 'Yes'.

Foveaux, Joseph (1765–1846), colonial administrator, pursued a military career. He joined the *New

South Wales Corps in 1789, and arrived in New South Wales in 1792. He commanded the Corps, during William *Paterson's absence, from 1796 to 1799. Foveaux was acting Lieutenant-Governor (1800-1), and then Lieutenant-Governor (1801-4), at *Norfolk Island. He returned to England, partly because of ill health, in 1804. On his return to New South Wales, he found the aftermath of the *Rum Rebellion; *Bligh was under arrest and George Johnston was in control. Foveaux took control from Johnston in mid-1808, and remained in charge until Paterson arrived from Van Diemen's Land in early 1809. Foveaux sailed for England in 1810. His military career continued, and he was promoted lieutenant-general in 1830. He died in London.

Franklin, Sir John (1786-1847), Arctic explorer and colonial administrator, was born and educated in England. His naval career included service in the Battle of Copenhagen (1801), in the Battle of Trafalgar (1805) and off the Greek coast (1830-3). He served on the *Investigator* during *Flinder's *New Holland expedition (1801-3), was second-in-charge of an unsuccessful expedition to find the North-West Passage (1818), and led two expeditions to Arctic America (1819-22, 1824-8). Franklin was Lieutenant-Governor of *Van Diemen's Land from 1837 to 1843, when he was recalled. He then led a naval expedition that discovered the North-West Passage, but he and the rest of the expedition's members died. Relics of the expedition were not found for some years. Franklin's publications include *Narrative of a Journey to the Shores of the Polar Sea, in the Years 1819-22* (1823) and *A Narrative of Some Passages in the History of Van Diemen's Land during the last three years of Sir John Franklin's Administration in the Colony* (1845).

Franklin, Stella Maria(n) Sarah Miles (1879-1954), novelist, was born to Australian parents at Talbingo, New South Wales. She was educated privately and at Thornford Public School. While also writing, she worked as a governess near Yea, Victoria, and as a maid in Sydney and Melbourne. Miles

Franklin sailed to the United States of America in 1906. She lived in Chicago, and worked in secretarial and editorial positions for the National Women's Trade Union League of America, between 1907 and 1915. During this time she worked with Alice *Henry. In 1915 she sailed to England, where she held various jobs before engaging in voluntary war work with the Scottish Women's Hospitals in Macedonia in 1917 and 1918. She lived in London between 1918 and 1926, and for most of this time held a secretarial position with the National Housing and Town Planning Council. She also visited the United States of America and Australia in 1923 and 1924. She returned to live permanently in Australia in 1927. She visited the United States of America and England again in 1930–32. During the Second World War she did some voluntary work in Australia. Miles Franklin joined the Fellowship of Australian Writers in 1933 and the Sydney PEN Club in 1935, encouraged other writers, gave lectures on Australian literature, and provided in her will for an annual Miles Franklin award for Australian literature. She died in Sydney. Miles Franklin is best known for her novel *My Brilliant Career* (1901), upon which a later film was based. She wrote a number of novels under the pseudonym 'Brent of Bin Bin'; her authorship of these was not definitely established until 1966. These novels are *Up the Country* (1928), *Ten Creeks Run* (1930), *Back to Bool Bool* (1931), *Prelude to Waking* (1950), *Cockatoos* (1954) and *Gentleman at Gyang Gyang* (1956). Miles Franklin's other novels include *Some Everyday Folk and Dawn* (1909), *The Net of Circumstance* (1915), which was published pseudonymously, *Old Blastus of Bandicoot* (1931), *Bring the Monkey* (1933), *All That Swagger* (1936), (with Dymphna Cusack) *Pioneers on Parade* (1939) and *My Career Goes Bung* (1946), which is a sequel to *My Brilliant Career*. She also wrote *Sydney Royal* (1947), a children's story, *Laughter, Not for a Cage* (1956), based upon some of her lectures on Australian literature, *Childhood at Brindabella* (1963), which is autobiographical, and (with Kate Baker) *Joseph Furphy, The Legend of a Man and His Book* (1944).

Fraser, John Malcolm (1930-), politician, was born in Melbourne, was educated at Melbourne Church of England Grammar School and Oxford University, and became a grazier. He was a Victorian Liberal Member of the House of Representatives from 1955 to 1983, and held various portfolios. Malcolm Fraser became Leader of the Liberal Party in 1975, and was appointed caretaker Prime Minister following the *dismissal of the Whitlam Government in 1975. He was Prime Minister from 1975 to 1983, when his Government was defeated by the Labor Party, led by *Hawke. He then resigned as Leader of the Liberal Party, and from Parliament.

Free, Compulsory and Secular: A popular term used to describe the system of education introduced in the Australian colonies during the latter part of the nineteenth century. All of the colonies 'passed education Acts which committed them to the establishment of national systems of education entirely supported by central government funds, and under Ministerial control'.[1] These Acts were passed in Victoria in 1872, South Australia and Queensland in 1875, New South Wales in 1880, Tasmania in 1885, and Western Australia in 1893 and 1895. The term is somewhat misleading; some fees were charged, some absences were accepted, and some religion was taught.

Free Trade: A fiscal policy under which governments theoretically do not intervene directly in the flow of goods and services between, or within, countries. The tariff question was one of the most controversial issues in Australian politics in the late nineteenth and early twentieth centuries. The two most populous colonies, Victoria and New South Wales, adopted different policies—Victoria protectionist and New South Wales free trade. The other

---

[1]A. G. Austin, *Australian Education, 1788-1900, Church, State and Public Education in Colonial Australia* (Pitman, Melbourne, third edition, 1972), p. 173.

colonies adopted various policies. Following Federation in 1901, the Constitution of the Commonwealth guaranteed free trade between the states (formerly colonies), but *protection was gradually adopted as a national policy. The *Free Trade Party and the *Protection Party were absorbed into the *Fusion Party in 1909.

Free Trade Party: One of the two main non-Labor political parties (the other being the *Protectionist Party) in the newly formed Commonwealth Parliament in 1901. Many members of the Free Trade Party accepted the inevitability of some degree of *protection and the Free Trade Party governed federally, in coalition with some Protectionists, in the Reid–McLean Government, from 1904 until 1905. In 1906, some of the Free Traders joined with some of the Protectionists and became known as the Tariff Reformers. The Free Trade Party was led by *Reid (1901–8) and Joseph *Cook (1908–9). The Free Traders merged with the Protectionists and the Tariff Reformers to form the *Fusion Party in 1909. There had also been Free Traders in colonial parliaments.

Fremantle, a city within the Perth metropolitan area, and Western Australia's main port, is situated on the mouth of the Swan River, where Charles Fremantle took British possession of the western part of Australia in 1829. A settlement was established there later that year. Fremantle was connected by rail with Perth, 19 kilometres away, in 1881, became a municipality in 1883 and a city in 1929. Its inner harbour, designed by Charles O'Connor, was completed in 1897. Fremantle's population in 1981 was about 30,000.

Furneaux Islands: A group of islands in Bass Strait, lying north-east of Tasmania, of which they form a part. The larger islands are, in order, Flinders Island (measuring approximately 64 by 29 kilometres), Cape Barren Island and Clarke Island. The smaller ones include Preservation, Chappell and Babel Islands. Aborigines are believed to have lived in the area some 8000 years ago. Tobias Furneaux (after whom James *Cook named the group), commanding one of Cook's ships during the latter's second voyage, sailed along the eastern side of the islands in 1773. The *Sydney Cove* was beached on Preservation Island in 1797, and the following year *Flinders visited the islands twice (once with *Bass). *Sealers began to use these and other Bass Strait islands in the 1790s and early 1800s. Muttonbirding also began on the Furneaux Islands during this period. A settlement for the so-called last Van Diemen's Land Aborigines was founded at Wybalenna (or Settlement Point) on Flinders Island in 1832, and continued until 1847, when most of the survivors were moved to Oyster Cove, near Hobart. Other settlers gradually arrived on the islands, including *soldier settlers on Flinders Island after the Second World War. The islands' main industries in the early 1980s were pastoral, fishing and muttonbirding.

Furphy, Joseph (1843–1912), writer, was born to Irish parents at Yering (present-day Yarra Glen) in the *Port Phillip District. He is more commonly known as 'Tom Collins'. His father was a tenant-farmer. Furphy was educated at home and at schools at Kangaroo Ground and Kyneton. His various jobs included operating a threshing plant in the Kyneton district; working a selection in the Colbinabbin district for about six years; owning and driving bullocks in the Riverina district for seven or eight years; and working in his family's iron foundry at Shepparton for about twenty years. He moved to Western Australia in 1904 and died there in 1912. Furphy is best known for his novel *Such is Life, Being Certain Extracts from the Life of Tom Collins* (1903). Written in diary form, it is set in the Riverina in the 1880s, and based largely upon his own experiences of bush life. His other publications include *Rigby's Romance* (1921) and *The Buln-Buln and the Brolga* (1948).

Fusion Party: The Protectionists led by *Deakin, the Free Traders led by Joseph *Cook, and the Tariff Reformers (or Corner Group) led by *Forrest, merged to become the Fusion Party in the Commonwealth

Parliament in 1909. Deakin became the leader, Cook his deputy, and the party governed for a short time in 1909-10. It had become known as the *Liberal Party by 1913.

Fuzzy-Wuzzy Angels: A name given by Australians to the Papuans and New Guineans who carried Australian supplies and wounded servicemen, especially along the *Kokoda Trail, during the Second World War.

G

Gallipoli Campaign: An unsuccessful Allied attempt to force the Dardanelles during the First World War. Its main aims were to force Turkey out of the war and to open a safe sea route to Russia. A naval expedition, launched in February and March 1915, failed. A military expedition (relying mainly upon British, Australian, New Zealand and French troops), with some naval support, was then attempted. The first landings, on the Gallipoli peninsula and the Asian mainland, were made on 25 April 1915. The Anzac landing, on a beach later renamed Anzac Cove, is commemorated on *Anzac Day. Turkish resistance was strong. Further landings were made, but fighting on the peninsula reached a stalemate. The Allied troops were withdrawn in December 1915 and January 1916. The Australian casualties on Gallipoli were 8587 killed and 19,367 wounded.

Game, Sir Philip Woolcott: *Lang, John Thomas; *New Guard

Gardiner (Christie), Francis: *Bushrangers

Gawler, George (1795-1869), *governor, was born in England, and like his father, pursued a military career. Gawler took office as the Governor of South Australia in 1838; he was also the Resident Commissioner. (The two positions had formerly been separate, and held by *Hindmarsh and James Hurtle Fisher.) Gawler had much land surveyed, undertook extensive public works, and established a police force. South Australia experienced severe financial difficulties. Gawler was recalled in 1841, returned to England, and did not hold public office again. *Grey's dispatches criticized him, but historians have criticized the dispatches. Gawler's publications include *The Close and Crisis of Waterloo* (1813), *The Essentials of Good Skirmishing* (1837), *The Tranquil-lization of Syria and the East* (1845) and *The Emancipation of the Jews* (1847).

Gellibrand, Sir John (1872–1945), soldier and farmer, was born at Ouse, Tasmania. His father was a grazier and politician. Gellibrand was educated in England at the King's School, Canterbury, and the Royal Military College, Sandhurst, and pursued a career in the British Army, serving in various places, including South Africa (during the *Boer War) and Ceylon. Soon after retiring, he returned to Tasmania and settled on an orchard at Risdon. Gellibrand served with the First *Australian Imperial Force from 1914 to 1919, rising to become the commander of the 3rd Division, with the rank of major-general, in May 1918. He was wounded several times during the First World War, received numerous honours and decorations, including the Distinguished Service Order and Bar, the Croix de Guerre and Legion d'Honneur, and the American Distinguished Service Medal, and is remembered particularly for his contribution to the fighting at Second Bullecourt (May 1917). After the war, Gellibrand was the Tasmanian Public Service Commissioner (1919–20), then the Victorian Chief Commissioner of Police (1920–2), and also commanded the 3rd Division of the Australian Military Forces (1921–2). In 1922 he established the Remembrance Club in Hobart, which led to the formation of the Legacy movement (the main aim of which came to be to care for the dependants of deceased ex-servicemen). He was a Nationalist Member of the House of Representatives, for the Tasmanian seat of Denison, from 1925 to 1928. He then farmed in Tasmania for some years, and died at his property near Yea, Victoria, on which he had settled in 1937.

Giblin, Lyndhurst Falkiner (1872–1951), political economist, was born in Hobart, the son of William

Robert *Giblin. He was educated at the Hutchins
School, Hobart; University College, London; and
King's College, Cambridge. (He became an honorary
fellow of the latter in 1938, and a Giblin studentship
was established there after his death.) He also represented England at Rugby Union. Giblin worked at
various jobs, including those of gold-prospector and
sailor, in different parts of the world, before settling
in Tasmania in about 1906. He was a Labor Member
of the Tasmanian House of Assembly from 1913 to
1916, then served in the First *Australian Imperial
Force (having served earlier in the citizen forces).
He was wounded several times, was mentioned in
dispatches and awarded the Military Cross and Distinguished Service Order, and rose to the rank of
major. After the war, he was the Tasmanian government statistician from 1919 to 1928, then Ritchie
Professor of Economics, at the University of Melbourne from 1929 to 1939. During the *Great Depression, he was one of the economists who were largely
responsible for the so-called Premiers' Plan. He acted
as the Commonwealth statistician in 1931 and 1932,
was a member of the newly formed *Commonwealth
Grants Commission from 1933 to 1936, and of the
Commonwealth Bank Board from 1935 to 1942. He
chaired an advisory committee on financial and economic policy from 1939 to 1947. Giblin has been
described as having 'won professional renown in the
fields of Federal finance, tariff policy, employment
analysis, Depression diagnosis, and post-war economic management'.[1] He died in Hobart. His publications include *Growth of a Central Bank* (1951),
which was published posthumously.

Giblin, William Robert (1840–87), lawyer and politician, was born in Hobart, and educated at Hobart
High School. He became a barrister in 1864, the year
in which he also founded the Hobart Working Men's
Club. Giblin was a Member of the Tasmanian House
of Assembly from 1869 to 1884, was Premier twice

[1] Neville Cain, 'Lyndhurst Falkiner Giblin', in Bede Nairn and Geoffrey
Serle (eds), *Australian Dictionary of Biography*, volume 8 (Melbourne
University Press, Melbourne, 1981), p. 647.

(1878, 1879–84), and held other portfolios. He 'reorganized the colony's finances, secured the adoption of an equitable taxation policy and initiated an active programme of public works'.[1] He was appointed to the Tasmanian Supreme Court in 1885. Lyndhurst Falkiner *Giblin was one of his sons.

Gill, Samuel Thomas (1818–80), artist, was born in England and educated at a school run by his parents. His father was a Baptist minister. The family arrived in Adelaide in 1839. Gill established a studio there in 1840, and gained a reputation for his drawings and lithographs. His subjects included rural scenes, views of Adelaide, and local people. In 1846 he was a draughtsman with J. A. Horrocks's expedition to the area north of Spencer Gulf, during which Horrocks died. In 1852, during the *gold-rushes, Gill moved to Victoria, and his drawings and lithographs of life on the gold-fields became popular in England and Australia. In 1869 the trustees of the Public Library of Victoria commissioned Gill, who has been called the 'Artist of the Gold-fields', to paint forty water-colours of life on the Victorian diggings in the early 1850s. Gill also did some work in New South Wales. Bernard Smith has said of him:

Gill is the first artist whose work expresses a distinctly Australian attitude to life; the sardonic humour, the nonchalance and the irreverent attitude to all forms of authority, so frequently remarked upon by the students of Australian behaviour, are all present in his work.[2]

Gilmore (née Cameron), **Dame Mary Jean** (1865–1962), writer, was born near Goulburn, New South Wales. Her father, who held farming and other jobs, was Scottish, her mother Australian. She was educated at schools at Brucedale, Wagga Wagga and Downside, before becoming a pupil-teacher. She

[1]E. M. Dollery, 'William Robert Giblin', in Douglas Pike (ed.), *Australian Dictionary of Biography*, volume 4 (Melbourne University Press, Melbourne, 1972), p. 243.

[2]Bernard Smith, *Australian Painting, 1788–1970* (Oxford University Press, Melbourne, 1971), p. 50.

taught at schools in New South Wales from 1877 to
1895. She claimed that, although listed under her
brother's name, she was the first female member of
the *Australian Workers' Union. She was involved
in William *Lane's *New Australia movement, and
lived at the Cosme settlement in Paraguay from 1896
to 1899, during which time she taught, edited the
colony's newspaper, married William Alexander Gilmore in 1897, and bore a son in 1898. Mary Gilmore
then taught English in Patagonia, before returning
to Australia, via London, with her husband and son.
She lived near and in Casterton, Victoria, from 1902
to 1912, when she moved to Sydney, where she
remained for the rest of her life. Mary Gilmore wrote
for local newspapers while living in the country; her
life and poems were featured in the *Bulletin's Red
Page on 3 October 1903; she began the *Australian
Worker's* women's page in 1908 and edited it until
1931; she had books of poetry and prose published;
she wrote a regular column entitled 'Arrows' for the
Tribune, a Communist newspaper, from 1952 to 1962;
and she was a foundation member of the Fellowship
of Australian Writers in 1928, and did much to encourage other writers. Dame Mary Gilmore died in 1962.
She had been created a Dame in 1937. Her publications include many volumes of poetry, *Hound of
the Road* (1922), *Old Days, Old Ways, A Book of
Recollections* (1934) and *More Recollections* (1935).

Gipps, Sir George (1791–1847), *governor, was born
in Kent, England, the son of a clergyman, and educated at the King's School, Canterbury, and the
Royal Military Academy, Woolwich. He pursued a
military career. He was appointed Governor of New
South Wales in 1837, arriving in Sydney the following year. The land proposals of 1844 (the main feature
of which were that *squatters would pay an annual
licence fee of £10 per run, would be able to buy a
320 acre homestead for £1 per acre after five years'
occupation, ensuring tenure of the entire run for eight
years, and then would have to buy another 320 acres
every eight years to maintain security over the run)
were vehemently opposed by the squatters (especially
W. C. *Wentworth), whose demands were eventually

largely met when the Order-in-Council of 1847 brought the British *Waste Lands Occupation Act* (1846) into operation. Gipps insisted, in the face of much public opposition, upon the prosecution of those involved in the outbreak of violence against Aborigines at *Myall Creek. As instructed, he established the unsuccessful *Port Phillip Protectorate, designed to control and protect Aborigines. He favoured the introduction of a national system of government schools, but ultimately allowed the subsidized denominational system to continue. Gipps's governorship ended in 1846, and he was in very poor health when he left the colony that year.

Gladstone Colony: *North Australia

Glover, John (1767–1849), landscape painter, was born in England. His father was a farmer. Glover became a writing-master at Appleby in about 1789, and a drawing-master at Lichfield in 1794. He studied under William Payne, and perhaps John 'Warwick' Smith, in London. In 1805 Glover moved to London, where he taught painting. He was a founding member of the Society of Painters in Water-Colours in 1804, president of it in 1807, and a founding member of the Society of British Artists in 1823. He also painted in oils. Glover lived in the Lake District for two years from about 1817. He opened a gallery for his own works, in London's Old Bond Street, in 1820. In 1831 Glover settled in *Van Diemen's Land, three of his sons having already done so. He continued to paint landscapes, and in 1835 he exhibited more than sixty pictures, said to be 'descriptive of the Scenery and Customs of Van Diemen's Land',[1] in London. Glover died at his property, near Launceston, in Van Diemen's Land. His paintings include *Australian Landscape with Cattle* (c. 1835).

Gold-rushes, rushes of people to newly discovered gold-fields, occurred in several parts of Australia

---

[1]Cited in Bernard Smith, 'John Glover', in Douglas Pike (ed.), *Australian Dictionary of Biography*, volume 1 (Melbourne University Press, Melbourne, 1966), p. 456.

during the nineteenth century. Although gold was discovered earlier, the first rushes did not begin until gold was discovered in payable quantities near Bathurst, New South Wales, in 1851. John Lister and the Tom brothers made the discoveries; Edward Hammond Hargraves publicized them and received official rewards. The richer Victorian gold-fields, near Ballarat and Bendigo, were discovered shortly afterwards. Continuing discoveries attracted many people from other countries and other colonies. New South Wales's population increased from 187,000 to 350,000, and Victoria's from 77,000 to 540,000, between 1850 and 1860. A third of the world's gold output between 1851 and 1861 came from Victoria. Queensland gold discoveries began in the 1860s. Queensland's main rush, to the Palmer River, occurred during the 1870s. Western Australian gold discoveries began in the 1880s. Discoveries at Coolgardie in 1892, and *Kalgoorlie in 1893, led to rushes.

Goldstein, Vida Mary Jane (1869–1949), feminist and suffragist, was born in Victoria, and educated privately and at the Melbourne Presbyterian Ladies' College. She and her sisters ran a preparatory school for part of the 1890s. She became involved in organizations such as the National Anti-Sweating League, helped to organize the Queen Victoria Hospital Appeal for the Queen's Diamond Jubilee in 1897, and campaigned for reformist legislation such as the Victorian *Children's Court Act* (1926). She helped to collect signatures for a female suffrage petition (later presented to the Victorian Parliament) in 1890; spoke publicly in favour of female suffrage from 1899; visited the United States of America in 1902, attending conferences, giving evidence in support of female suffrage to a Congress committee, and making speeches; helped to found, and was president of, the Women's Political Association, which existed from 1903 to 1919; founded, owned and edited the *Woman's Sphere*, a monthly journal; was active in many other women's organizations; founded, owned and edited the *Woman Voter*, a weekly journal, which existed from 1909 to 1919; went to Britain (invited by the Women's Social and Political Union), where she

wrote and spoke advocating female suffrage, and
formed the Australian and New Zealand Women's
Voters' Association in London in 1911. Goldstein,
one of the first women in the British Empire to stand
for election to parliament, was unsuccessful as an
Independent candidate for the Senate in 1903. She
stood again for parliament, unsuccessfully, four more
times. During the First World War, she chaired the
newly formed Peace Alliance; founded, and was president of, the Women's Peace Army, which lasted from
1915 to 1919; and helped to organize a Women's
Unemployed Bureau and the Women's Rural Industries Company Limited. She and Cecilia John
attended a Women's Peace Conference in Switzerland in 1919. Goldstein returned to Australia about
three years later, but did not resume an active public
life.

Golf has been played in Australia for many years.
The first golf course in the Australian colonies was
established in Melbourne in 1847. A golf club was
founded in Sydney in the 1880s, and others were
established there and elsewhere in the 1890s and
later. The Australian Golf Union was established in
1898, and the Australian Ladies' Golf Union in 1921.
Golf has become a popular sport in Australia, especially since the Second World War, and there were
more than 1200 golf courses in the country by the
early 1980s. Peter William Thomson (1929–), one
of Australia's best-known golfers, won the British
Open five times, the Australian Open three times,
the New Zealand Open nine times, and numerous
other championships.

Gordon, Adam Lindsay (1833–70), poet, was born
in the Azores. His father was a retired army officer.
Gordon was educated in England at Cheltenham
College, the Royal Military Academy at Woolwich,
and the Royal Worcester Grammar School. He
migrated to South Australia in 1853, and belonged
to the South Australian Mounted Police from 1853
to 1855. In the remaining years of his life he held
various jobs, including those of horsebreaker and
steeplechase rider, mostly in South Australia and

Victoria. He was a Member of the South Australian
House of Assembly in 1865-6. Gordon wrote prose,
but is best known for his poetry. He shot himself
at Brighton Beach, Victoria, on 24 June 1870, the
day after his *Bush Ballads and Galloping Rhymes*
was published. Financial difficulties, ill health
caused by riding accidents, and the death of his only
child apparently were factors leading to his suicide.
Gordon's poetry was very popular in the years following his death. His publications include *The Feud,
A Ballad* (1864), *Ashtaroth, A Dramatic Lyric* (1867)
and *Sea Spray and Smoke Drift* (1867).

Gorton, Sir John Grey (1911-), politician, was
born in Melbourne, was educated at Sydney Church
of England Grammar School, Geelong Grammar
School and Oxford University, and worked for some
time on his family's orchard at Mystic Park, Victoria.
During the Second World War, he was a fighter pilot
in the Royal Australian Air Force from 1940 to 1944,
and was badly wounded. He was a Victorian Liberal
Senator from 1949 to 1968, and then a Liberal
Member of the House of Representatives from 1968
to 1975, holding various portfolios. Gorton was Prime
Minister from 1968 to 1971, but lost the confidence
of his party, using his casting vote to decide the issue,
and was replaced by *McMahon. Gorton stood unsuccessfully as an Independent Senate candidate for the
Australian Capital Territory in 1975.

Government Men: A popular name given to convicts during the period of *transportation.

Governors administered New South Wales from
1788, South Australia from 1836, and Queensland
from 1859. Lieutenant-Governors administered some
of New South Wales's dependencies (which included
Van Diemen's Land until 1825) at various times.
Those appointed to administer some colonies were
also originally designated lieutenant-governors; this
happened in Western Australia until 1832, and in
Van Diemen's Land and Victoria until 1855. Their
administrators were then designated governors.
Early colonial administrators held very wide powers,
but these diminished as other political institutions

developed. Two administrators of New South Wales
were designated governors-general in the years
between 1855 and 1861. Since Federation, there have
been governors-general and state governors. The
Governors-General of the Commonwealth of Australia (up to the mid-1980s) have been the Earl of Hopetoun (1901-3), Baron Tennyson (1903-4), Baron
Northcote (1904-8), the Earl of Dudley (1908-11),
Baron Denman (1911-14), Sir Ronald Craufurd
Munro-Ferguson (later Viscount *Novar) (1914-20),
Baron Forster (1920-5), Baron Stonehaven (1925-31),
Sir Isaac *Isaacs (1931-6), Baron Gowrie (1936-45),
the Duke of Gloucester (1945-7), Sir William *McKell
(1947-53), Sir William Slim (1953-60), Viscount Dun-
rossil (1960-1), Viscount De L'Isle (1961-5), Baron
*Casey (1965-9), Sir Paul *Hasluck (1969-74), Sir
John Kerr (1974-7), Sir Zelman Cowen (1977-82) and
Sir Ninian Stephen (1982-   ). The governor-general
represents the Crown in the Commonwealth of Australia, and the governors represent the Crown in
the states. Some have deputies, called lieutenant-
governors.

Goyder's Line: Popular name given to a rainfall
line dividing *South Australia. George Woodroofe
Goyder, the Surveyor-General, was instructed in 1865
to show 'the line of demarcation between that portion
of the country where the rainfall has extended, and
that where the drought prevailed'.[1] Goyder's Line
stretched from Swan Reach to Mount Remarkable,
south to the Broughton, and north-west to the Gawler
Ranges. The area to the north of it, which comprised
most of South Australia, was considered to be arid.
In theory, Goyder's Line was to be used in the review
of pastoral leases; in practice, it was used to show
which areas were thought to be suitable for agriculture.

Grainger, George Percy (from 1911, Percy
Aldridge) (1882-1961), pianist and composer, was
born in Melbourne, where he was taught piano by

---

[1]Cited in 'George Woodroofe Goyder', an unsigned article, in Douglas
Pike (ed.), *Australian Dictionary of Biography*, volume 4 (Melbourne
University Press, Melbourne, 1972), p. 279.

his mother, and also studied with Louis Pabst (1892-4). He studied at the Hoch Conservatory, Frankfurt-am-Main, Germany, where his teachers included Iwan Knorr and James Kwast, from 1895 to 1899, and later studied with Ferruccio Busoni in Berlin. From 1901 to 1914 Grainger lived mostly in London, where his concert career began. He then settled in New York in 1914, served in a United States Army band from 1917 to 1919, became an American citizen in 1918, taught piano at the Chicago Musical College from 1919 to 1928, and chaired the New York University music department in 1932 and 1933. He founded the Grainger Museum, at the University of Melbourne, in 1935. Grainger toured widely in Europe, Scandinavia, Australasia and elsewhere. His reputation as a composer was firmly established before the First World War. His compositions, many of which can be described as experimental, include choral, orchestral and chamber works, military band music and piano pieces (including his best-known work, *Country Gardens* (1908)). He composed many settings of British and Danish folk-songs, and more than thirty settings of Kipling's poems. Grainger died in New York.

Grants Commission: *Commonwealth Grants Commission

Great Depression (1930s): A world-wide economic depression, which began in 1929. Australia was badly affected. The main causes of Australia's depression were external—the collapse of wool and wheat prices, and the cessation of overseas loans. Internal factors, including an existing recession and drought, exacerbated the situation. National income fell markedly between 1929 and 1932; unemployment rose to about 30 per cent in 1932, and many other people were only partly employed; and wages, prices, company profits, dividends and interest rates fell. The *Australian Labor Party split, the *United Australia Party superseded the *Nationalist Party, and the *Communist Party prospered. Unemployed workers formed many organizations, often associated with Trades Halls or the Communist Party, and other organizations such as the *New Guard were founded. A *secession movement developed in Western Australia, and new states movements flourished in New South Wales. Some government unemployment relief was made available. Thousands of evictions occurred, sometimes leading to violence, as on *Bloody Friday. Shanty settlements were established. Thousands of people went to the country in a futile search for work. Various possible solutions were suggested, resulting in what is sometimes described as the 'Battle of the Plans'. Sir Otto Niemeyer, a representative of the English banks who visited Australia in 1930 at the Prime Minister's invitation, proposed a deflationary plan involving balanced budgets, and cuts in wages and government expenditure. The Labor Federal Treasurer, *Theodore, and the left wing of the Labor Party proposed a mildly inflationary plan involving the creation of credit. The Labor Premier of New South Wales, J. T. *Lang, proposed an inflationary plan involving repudiation of overseas debts and reduced interest rates. All Australian governments eventually adopted the so-called Premiers' Plan, for which the economists *Copland, L. F. *Giblin, L. G. Melville and E. O. G. Shann were largely responsible. It was a partly deflationary plan, the aim of which supposedly was 'equality of sacrifice', involving reduced government expenditure, wages, pensions, and interest rates, and increased taxation. It also involved a substantial currency depreciation and some limited borrowing. There has been, and continues to be, debate as to whether it improved or worsened the situation. Recovery began in late 1932. Income, investment and employment returned to pre-depression levels by 1937. Unemployment was finally nearly eliminated during the Second World War.

Great War: *First World War

Great White Fleet: Popular name given to the United States Pacific Fleet, which visited Australia in 1908, at *Deakin's invitation, during its worldwide tour. The fleet, consisting of sixteen battleships, which were painted white, visited Sydney, Melbourne and *Albany. It attracted very large crowds, said to have been the largest in Australia's history to that time.

Greenway, Francis (1777-1837), architect, was born near Bristol in England. While practising as an architect, he was convicted of forgery; he was sentenced to death, but the sentence was commuted to fourteen years' *transportation, and he arrived in Sydney in 1814. Greenway soon received a *ticket-of-leave, and practised as an architect in the colony. He advised on public works, and *Macquarie appointed him civil architect and assistant engineer in 1816, positions he held until 1822. Greenway received a conditional pardon in 1818 and a free pardon in 1819. He designed numerous notable buildings, some of which still exist, albeit in altered form. His buildings included a lighthouse on the south head of Port Jackson, a *Female Factory at Parramatta, convict barracks in Sydney, St Matthew's Church at Windsor, St Luke's Church at Liverpool, St James's Church in Sydney, and the Supreme Court in Sydney. After his dismissal in 1822, he did little further work, one notable exception being a house in Sydney for *Campbell. Greenway died at his property in the Hunter River Valley.

Grey, Sir George (1812-98), explorer, *governor and politician, was born in Portugal, and educated in England. He attended the Royal Military College, Sandhurst, joined the British army, and served in Ireland for some years. He sailed to Western Australia in 1837, conducted two expeditions in the northwest, and was the resident magistrate at Albany in 1839-40. He was the Governor of South Australia from 1841 to 1845 (following *Gawler). Grey was then Governor of New Zealand from 1845 to 1853, Governor of Cape Colony (part of present-day South Africa) from 1854 to 1861, and Governor of New Zealand again from 1861 to 1868. He returned to England, but in 1870 went back to New Zealand, where he was a Member of the House of Representatives from 1874 to 1894. He was Prime Minister from 1877 to 1879. Grey was one of New Zealand's representatives at the National Australasian Convention (a significant event in the *federation movement) in 1891. He returned to England in 1894, and died there. His publications include *Vocabulary of the Dialects Spoken by the Aboriginal Races of South-Western Australia* (1839) and *Journal of Two Expeditions of Discovery in North-West and Western Australia during the years 1837, 38, and 39* (1841).

Griffin, Walter Burley (1876–1937), architect and landscape architect, was born near Chicago in the United States of America. His father was an insurance agent. Griffin studied architecture at the University of Illinois, and was an associate of Frank Lloyd Wright for some years before establishing his own practice. In 1912 he won an international competition for a design for Australia's federal capital, later named *Canberra. From 1913 to 1920 Griffin was the Federal Capital Director of Design and Construction. His term of office was marked by controversy, and various amendments were made, by Griffin and others, to his original plan. In 1920 he refused a place on the Federal Capital Advisory Committee, which took over his role. Griffin also practised privately in Australia, his designs including those for the towns of Griffith and Leeton; housing estates such as Summit and Glenard (both at Eaglemont) in Melbourne and Castlecrag (the construction of which was never completed) in Sydney; Newman College, at the University of Melbourne, Melbourne's Capitol Theatre, and numerous municipal incinerator buildings. In 1935 Griffin left Australia to work in India, where he later died.

Griffith, Sir Samuel Walker (1845–1920), politician and lawyer, was born in Wales, educated at schools in Ipswich, Woolloomooloo and Maitland, and at the University of Sydney, and was admitted to the Bar in Brisbane in 1867 (and was appointed Queen's Counsel in 1876 and a Privy Counsellor in 1901). Griffith was a Member of the Legislative Assembly of Queensland from 1872 to 1893. He was Premier twice (1883-6, 1890-3) and held numerous other portfolios. His first government passed legislation aimed at allowing small settlers, rather than *squatters, greater access to the land. It passed legislation banning the importation of Pacific Islanders (brought to Australia under the *blackbirding practice) after the end of 1890, but Griffith lifted the ban in 1892. During the *Shearers Strike of 1891, Griffith, who previously had received some support from the labour movement, used soldiers to defeat the strikers, and imprisoned some of the latter. A strong advocate of federation, Griffith drafted the bill for the constitution of the Federal Council of Australasia; presided over the Federal Council three times; attended the Australasian Federation Conference in 1890; and was largely responsible for the draft constitution (much of which later became part of the *Constitution of the Commonwealth of Australia) produced by the National Australasian Convention of 1891. He was the Chief Justice of Queensland from 1893 to 1903, and was then the first Chief Justice of the *High Court of Australia from 1903 to 1919. Griffith strongly defended states' rights while on the High Court.

Grose, Francis (1758?-1814), soldier and colonial administrator, was born in England. He pursued a military career, and helped to raise, and commanded, the *New South Wales Corps. He was appointed Lieutenant-Governor of New South Wales in 1789, and arrived there in 1792. When ill health forced *Phillip to leave the colony later in that year, Grose took over. He controlled the colony for much of the interregnum. In 1794 ill health also forced him to leave; William *Paterson then took control. Grose's military career continued, and he died in England.

Guérard, Johann Joseph Eugen von (1812?-1901), artist, was born in Vienna, and studied art in Italy and Germany for a number of years. His father was a court painter. After leaving Germany in 1848, he may have visited the Californian goldfields. He arrived in Victoria in late 1852, and spent about a year on the gold-fields, where he made numerous sketches. In the following years he travelled and sketched extensively (sometimes with scientific expe-

ditions, such as A. W. Howitt's of 1860) in Australia
and New Zealand. He was the curator of the Melbourne National Gallery, and the first master of its
art school, from 1870 to 1881, when he resigned for
health reasons. His landscape paintings, said to have
been influenced by the Austrian Biedermeier School,
were exhibited widely in Australia, Europe and elsewhere. He illustrated S. D. Bird's *On Australasian
Climates* (1863), and published a collection of lithographs of Western District scenes entitled *Australian
Landscapes* (1867). His paintings include *Valley of
the Mitta Mitta, with the Bogong Ranges* (1866).

H

Hall, Benjamin: *Bushrangers

Hampton, John Stephen (1810?-69), *governor,
served as a British naval surgeon before becoming
the comptroller-general of convicts in *Van Diemen's
Land in 1846, a position that he held until he left
the colony in 1855. He was involved in controversy
when he would not give evidence to a Legislative
Council Select Committee inquiring into convict
administration in 1855. During Hampton's term of
office as Governor of Western Australia, which lasted
from 1862 to 1868, he treated convicts strictly; he
used convict labour extensively for public works,
such as the building of Government House in Perth,
the Perth Town Hall, and numerous roads and
bridges, including a bridge over the river at Fremantle; and he helped to improve the colony's financial position. He died in England.

Hancock, Sir William Keith (1898-   ), historian,
was born in Melbourne, and educated at the Universities of Melbourne and Oxford. He was Professor
of History at Adelaide University (1924-33), Professor of History at Birmingham University (1934-44),
Professor of Economic History at Oxford (1944-9),
Director of the Institute of Commonwealth Studies
at London University (1949-57), and Professor of

History and Director of the Research School of Social Sciences at the Australian National University (1957-61). He edited the British official histories (civil series) for the Second World War, and wrote *British War Economy* (1949) with M. M. Gowing. Sir Keith Hancock's other publications include *Australia* (1930), *Survey of British Commonwealth Affairs* (1937-42), *Country and Calling* (1954), *Smuts, The Sanguine Years 1870-1919* (1962), *Smuts, The Fields of Force 1919-1950* (1968), *Discovering Monaro* (1972), *Professing History* (1976) and *Perspective in History* (1982).

Hargrave, Lawrence (1850-1915), aeronautical pioneer, was born and educated in England. After migrating to Sydney in 1865 he worked in engineering jobs, took part in several expeditions to New Guinea and elsewhere, and was an assistant astronomical observer at the Sydney Observatory for some years. From 1883 onwards he worked full-time on aeronautical and other research. His aeronautical research included construction of model aeroplanes, experimentation with box-kites (with which he lifted himself from the ground in 1894), and development of aeronautical engines. His research had some influence in other countries.

Hargraves, Edward Hammond: *Gold-rushes

Harney, William Edward (1895-1962), author, received little formal education. He worked in the bush until his enlistment in the *Australian Imperial Force in 1915. After returning to Australia after the First World War, Harney worked as a drover and cattleman. He came into close contact with Aborigines in remote parts of northern Australia, and was a native affairs officer for some time; later, he was curator of Ayers Rock. Bill Harney's radio talks and books about bush life became well known. His books include *Taboo* (1943), *North of 23°* (1946), *Brimming Billabongs* (1947) and (with A. P. Elkin) *Songs of the Songman* (1949).

Harpur, Charles (1813-68), poet, was born at Windsor, New South Wales, where his father was a schoolmaster and parish clerk. Both of Harpur's parents had been transported to Australia as convicts. Harpur held various jobs, including those of clerk, farmer and assistant gold commissioner. Harpur is best known for his poetry. His publications include *Thoughts, A Series of Sonnets* (1845), *Songs of Australia* (1851), *The Bushrangers, A Play in Five Acts, and Other Poems* (1853), *A Poet's Home* (1862), *A Rhyme* (c. 1864) and *The Tower of the Dream* (1865). He also wrote literary and political criticism.

Harris, Alexander[1] (1805–74), writer, was born in London. His father was a Nonconformist minister and schoolmaster. Harris worked as a compositor in London, before coming to Australia in 1825. He held various jobs in Australia. After some fifteen years, he returned to England, where he was a missioner in London for some time. In 1851 Harris migrated to the United States of America, where he taught, wrote and preached. He died in Canada. Harris is best known in Australia for *Settlers and Convicts, or Recollections of Sixteen Years' Labour in the Australian Backwoods, by an Emigrant Mechanic* (1847), which is a partly factual, partly fictitious account of life in New South Wales, during the 1820s and 1830s. His other publications include *A Guide to Port Stephens in New South Wales, the Colony of the Australian Agricultural Company*[2] (1849) and *The Emigrant Family, or The Story of an Australian Settler, by the Author of "Settlers and Convicts"* (1849). The latter book, a novel, was later published as *Martin Beck, or The Story of an Australian Settler* (1852).

Hartog (or Hartooch or Hartichs), **Dirck** (or Dirk) (dates unknown), Dutch mariner, is the first European known to have landed on the western coast of Australia. He did so in October 1616, while commanding the *Eendracht*, a Dutch East India Company ship, on a voyage from Holland to Batavia (present-day Jakarta). He examined part of the coast,

---

[1]For many years this name was thought to be a pseudonym, but it is now accepted as genuine.
[2]Harris's authorship of this has been questioned.

landed on an island (now named Dirk Hartog Island) near Shark Bay, and left behind an inscribed pewter plate. The area near by became known as Eendracht Land. William de Vlamingh, another Dutch mariner, replaced the plate with another (now known as the Vlamingh Plate) in 1697.

Harvester Judgement: Popular name given to the judgement of 1907 that introduced the principle of the *basic wage for men (also known as the family, living, or minimum wage). A Victorian manufacturer, Hugh Victor *McKay, applied for exemption from excise duties on agricultural machinery made by his Harvesting Machine Company, on the grounds that he paid his employees 'fair and reasonable' wages. Such exemption was possible under the *Excise Tariff (Agricultural Machinery) Act* 1906, which was part of the *New Protection legislation. The President of the *Commonwealth Conciliation and Arbitration Court, Henry Bournes *Higgins, ruled that McKay was not paying 'fair and reasonable' wages. Higgins calculated that a male employee maintaining a household of 'about five persons' (that is, two adults and three children) required wages of seven shillings per day, or forty-two shillings per week, to cover such costs as food, clothing and shelter. McKay was paying unskilled male labourers six shillings per day.

Hasluck, Sir Paul Meernaa Caedwalla (1905–   ), governor-general, was born in Fremantle, Western Australia, and educated at the Perth Modern School and the University of Western Australia. He worked as a journalist with the *West Australian* newspaper from 1922 to 1938, and as a lecturer (later, reader) in the History Department of the University of Western Australia (1939–40, 1948–9). He worked in the Commonwealth Department of External Affairs from 1941 to 1947. Hasluck also entered federal politics; he was a Liberal Member of the House of Representatives from 1949 to 1969, serving as Minister for Territories (1951–63), Minister for Defence (1963–4) and Minister for External Affairs (1964–9). His term of office as Minister for External Affairs, during which he encouraged local participation in the administration of *Papua New Guinea, was particularly noteworthy. He was Governor-General of the Commonwealth of Australia from 1969 to 1974. Hasluck's publications include *Our Southern Half-castes* (1938), *Black Australians* (1942), *Workshop of Security* (1948), *Native Welfare in Australia* (1953), *The Government and the People, 1939–45* (two volumes, 1951, 1970), part of the Australian official war history, and *The Office of Governor-General* (1979).

Hawke, Robert James Lee (1928–), politician, was born in Bordertown, South Australia, the son of a Congregational minister. He attended Perth Modern School, graduated BA and LLB from the University of Western Australia, and was Western Australia's Rhodes Scholar of 1952. Hawke was a research officer and industrial advocate for the *Australian Council of Trade Unions from 1958 to 1969, president of that organization from 1970 to 1980, and national president of the *Australian Labor Party from 1973 to 1978. He became a Labor Member of the House of Representatives in 1980, and Prime Minister in 1983.

Haynes, John: *Archibald, Jules François; *Bulletin*

Heidelberg School: A term that refers to a group of Australian impressionist painters, since described as 'the first distinctive Australian school of painting',[1] that flourished during the late 1880s. The group's name came from Heidelberg, the area of Melbourne that inspired many of their paintings. *Conder, *McCubbin, *Roberts and *Streeton were the leading painters of the Heidelberg School. The most famous exhibition of Heidelberg School paintings was the Exhibition of 9×5 Impressions (painted on cigar-box lids measuring nine inches by five), which was held in Melbourne in 1889. Examples of Heidelberg School paintings include Conder's *The Departure of the S.S. Orient—Circular Quay* (1888) and

---

[1]Bernard Smith, *Australian Painting, 1788–1970* (Oxford University Press, Melbourne, 1971), p. 82.

Streeton's *Still Glides the Stream and Shall Forever Glide* (1889). Many were of distinctive, sometimes historical, Australian subjects; examples include McCubbin's *Down on His Luck* (1889) and Roberts's *Shearing the Rams* (1889-90).

Heinze, Sir Bernard Thomas (1894-1982), music scholar and conductor, was born at Shepparton, Victoria, and studied at the Conservatorium attached to the University of Melbourne, the Royal College of Music (of which he was later made a Fellow), London, and the Schola Cantorum, Paris. He served in the Royal Artillery from 1915 to 1920. Heinze was the Ormond Professor of Music at the University of Melbourne from 1925 to 1956, then director of the New South Wales Conservatorium, Sydney, from 1956 to 1966. He became conductor of the Melbourne University Symphony Orchestra in the mid-1920s, was appointed life conductor of the Melbourne Philharmonic Society in 1928, was conductor of the Victorian Symphony Orchestra from 1933 to 1956, and also appeared as guest conductor in various other countries. He inaugurated 'Young People's Concerts' (a forerunner of the Australian Broadcasting Commission Youth Concerts, introduced in 1947, for which he was also largely responsible) in 1925. Heinze, who became musical adviser to the Australian Broadcasting Company in 1929, and to its successor, the *Australian Broadcasting Commission, in 1934, did much to develop the presentation of orchestral concerts in Australia.

Henry, Alice (1857-1943), journalist and feminist, was born at Richmond, Melbourne. Her parents were Scottish, her father an accountant, her mother a seamstress. Alice Henry attended various Melbourne schools, including Richard Hale Budd's Educational Institute for Young Ladies. She taught for some time, before becoming a journalist in 1884. She wrote for journals and newspapers, such as the *Argus* and the *Australasian*, for some twenty years. She campaigned for social reforms, such as the introduction of female *suffrage in Australia (and later in America). After visiting England in 1905, Alice Henry

settled in the United States of America. She lectured,
wrote, and organized for the National Women's
Trade Union League of America in Chicago; she
edited the woman's page of the *Union Labor Advocate* (1908-19), and the League's journal, *Life and Labor* (1911-15); she ran the League's Educational
Department (1920-2); and under the League's auspices, she visited England, Europe and Australia
(1924-6). After returning to live in Melbourne in 1933,
she was active in such organizations as the *National
Council of Women. Alice Henry died at Malvern,
Melbourne. Her publications include *The Trade
Union Woman* (1915) and *Women and the Labor
Movement* (1923). In 1937 she compiled a bibliography of Australian women writers.

Henty, Edward (1810-78), pastoralist and politician, was born in Sussex, England. His father was
a farmer and banker. In 1832 he went to Launceston,
in Van Diemen's Land, with his parents and some
other members of the family. In November 1834,
Edward, accompanied by Henry Camfield and four
indentured servants, began to establish a settlement
at Portland Bay (on the coast of present-day Victoria), which both he and his father had previously
visited. Edward, who has generally been considered
to be the first permanent white settler in the *Port
Phillip District, was soon joined by several of his
brothers. The Hentys farmed, were involved in whaling, and also took up runs inland. The British Government refused their requests, which began before
Edward settled at Portland Bay, to buy land on the
mainland. After the proposed town of Portland was
surveyed in 1839, the Hentys had to buy land at
auction and to remove some of their improvements.
They later reached a settlement with the authorities.
Edward Henty moved to Muntham, one of the family's stations on the Wannon River, in the early 1840s,
and was a Member of the Victorian Legislative
Assembly from 1856 to 1861. He died in Melbourne.

Herbert, Sir Robert George Wyndham (1831-1905), politician, was born in Brighton, England, and
educated at Eton and Balliol College, Oxford. His

father was a barrister. Herbert was private secretary
to W. E. Gladstone (then Chancellor of the Exche-
quer) in 1855, and was called to the Bar of the Inner
Temple in 1858. He arrived in the newly separated
colony of Queensland as private secretary to Governor Bowen, and as Queensland's first Colonial Secretary, in 1859. Herbert was Queensland's first
Premier, from 1860 to February 1866 (and again
briefly in July and August 1866), during which time
his main aims were 'to extend settlement especially
on the north coast, encourage immigration, diversify
the economy and establish a firm basis for government'.[1] Herbert returned to England in 1866, and
became assistant secretary to the Board of Trade
(1868–70), assistant under-secretary (1870–1) and permanent under-secretary (1871–92, and for a brief
period some years later) in the Colonial Office. He
was Agent-General for Tasmania from 1893 to 1896,
and chaired the Tariff Reform Commission in 1903.
He died in England.

Higgins, Henry Bournes (1851–1929), lawyer and
politician, was born and educated in Ireland, and
arrived in Melbourne with his family in 1870. His
father was a Methodist minister. Higgins taught in
schools and privately, and studied Arts and Law at
the University of Melbourne (on the council of which
he later served from 1887 to 1923). He became a
leading equity lawyer, and was appointed King's
Counsel in 1903. He was a Member of the Victorian
Legislative Assembly from 1894 to 1900, when he
was defeated, partly because of his opposition to
Australia's involvement in the *Boer War. Higgins
represented Victoria at the *Federal Convention
(1897-8), and opposed the subsequent bill. He was
a Member of the House of Representatives from 1901
to 1906, and served as Attorney-General in the short-
lived *Watson Government of 1904, although he was
not a member of the Labor Party. Higgins was
appointed to the *High Court in 1906, and became

[1]B. A. Knox, 'Sir Robert George Wyndham Herbert', in Bede Nairn,
Geoffrey Serle and Russel Ward (eds), *Australian Dictionary of Biography*, volume 4 (Melbourne University Press, Melbourne, 1972),
p. 383.

the President of the *Commonwealth Conciliation
and Arbitration Court the following year. His best-
known decision was the *Harvester Judgement. He
resigned as President in 1920, but remained on the
High Court until his death. He was a strong advocate
of Irish Home Rule. His publications include *Essays
and Addresses on the Australian Commonwealth
Bill* (1900) and *A New Province for Law and Order*
(1922).

High Court: Australia's federal supreme court. Its
main functions are that 'it interprets the Constitution; it is a court of appeal from decisions of State
courts; and it has an original jurisdiction'.[1] It was
created by Section 71 of the *Constitution of the
Commonwealth, and its first members were appointed in 1903; they were the Chief Justice, Sir
Samuel *Griffith, and the two puisne judges, Sir
Edmund *Barton and Richard Edward O'Connor.
The size of the Court was increased to five in 1907,
and to its present size of seven in 1912. The Chief
Justices of the High Court (to the mid-1980s) have
been Sir Samuel Griffith (1903-19), Sir Adrian Knox
(1919-30), Sir Isaac *Isaacs (1930-1), Sir Frank
Gavan Duffy (1931-5), Sir John *Latham (1935-52),
Sir Owen *Dixon (1952-64), Sir Garfield *Barwick
(1964-81) and Sir Harry Gibbs (1981-   ).

Higinbotham, George (1826-92), politician and
lawyer, was born in Dublin. After migrating to Australia in 1854 he pursued careers in the law, journalism and politics. Higinbotham edited the Melbourne *Argus* from 1856 to 1859. He was then a
Member of the Victorian Legislative Assembly (1861-
71, 1873-6). From 1863 to 1868, he was Attorney-
General; he has been described as being 'unquestion-
ably the leading radical in Victoria'[2] at that time.
In 1866 he chaired a Royal Commission inquiring

---

[1]J. M. Bennett, 'Law Courts', in *The Australian Encyclopaedia*, volume
3 (The Grolier Society of Australia, Sydney, third edition, 1977),
p. 503.

[2]Gwyneth M. Dow, 'George Higinbotham', in Douglas Pike (ed.), *Australian Dictionary of Biography*, volume 4 (Melbourne University
Press, Melbourne, 1972), p. 391.

into public education. Higinbotham was appointed to the Victorian Supreme Court in 1880, becoming Chief Justice in 1886. Parliament publicly thanked him for his work in consolidating the Victorian statutes.

Hindmarsh, Sir John (1785–1860), *governor, pursued a career in the British navy before becoming the first Governor of South Australia in 1836. He disagreed with *Light's choice of site for the capital, Adelaide. He and James Hurtle Fisher, the Resident Commissioner (who represented the Colonization Commission), also clashed over various issues, and Hindmarsh was recalled in 1838. *Gawler took office as both Governor and Resident Commissioner later that year. In 1840 Hindmarsh was appointed Governor of Heligoland, a position he held until 1856. He died in London.

Hinkler, Herbert John Louis (1892–1933), aviator, was born and educated in Bundaberg, Queensland. His father was a German stockman. While young, Hinkler studied mechanics, built gliders, and worked as a mechanic for an American aviator in Australia and New Zealand. He also worked in the Sopwith factory in England for some time. During the First World War he enlisted with the British Royal Naval Air Service, served variously as mechanic, gunner and pilot, and was awarded a Distinguished Service Medal. He then worked for A. V. Roe & Co. in England, bought an Avro Baby from them, and made a record non-stop flight from England to Italy in it in 1920. Unable to continue to Australia as planned, he returned to England. He made a record non-stop flight in the Avro Baby (which had been shipped to Australia) from Sydney to Bundaberg in 1921. After returning to England, Hinkler was chief test pilot at A. V. Roe & Co. until 1926. He made a non-stop flight in his Avro Avian from England to Latvia in 1927. He then made the first solo flight from England to Australia, in the Avro Avian, in 1928, the total time for the trip being fifteen days and two and a quarter hours. Hinkler was unable to find backing to produce the Ibis amphibian aircraft, which he designed and built. He flew solo in his Puss Moth from Canada to New York, and then to London (via several countries), in 1931, creating more records. Hinkler crashed and died in the Italian Alps in 1933, while attempting to fly solo in his Puss Moth from England to Australia.

Hobart (officially Hobart Town until 1881), the capital city of the state of *Tasmania, is situated on the estuary of the Derwent River. It was founded as a convict settlement in 1804 and named after the British Secretary of State for the Colonies. It was proclaimed a city in 1842, and incorporated in 1857. Its population was 128,603 in 1981.

Holman, William Arthur (1871–1934), politician, was born in London. He, his parents (who were both actors) and his brother came to Australia in 1888. A cabinetmaker by trade, Holman became active in the New South Wales labour movement. He became a Member of the New South Wales Legislative Assembly in 1898. He was a vocal opponent of the *Boer War. Holman represented the Labor Party until 1916, when he was expelled from the party because of his support for *conscription, and the Nationalists from then until 1920, when he lost his seat. He was Premier of New South Wales from 1913 until 1920, and held various other portfolios. Holman had been admitted to the Bar in 1903, was appointed King's Counsel in 1920, and became a prominent barrister in the 1920s. He also entered federal politics, and was a Member of the House of Representatives, representing the *United Australia Party, from 1931 until his death.

Holt, Harold Edward (1908–67), politician, was born in Sydney, was educated at Wesley College, Melbourne, and the University of Melbourne, and practised as a solicitor briefly from 1933. He was a Victorian Member of the House of Representatives from 1935 until 1967, representing the *United Australia Party and its successor, the *Liberal Party of Australia. He held various portfolios at different times. During the Second World War, Holt enlisted with the Second AIF, but was recalled to the ministry. He was Deputy Leader of the Liberal Party from 1956 to 1966. When *Menzies retired in 1966, Holt became Prime Minister. It was the time of Australia's growing involvement in the *Vietnam War. While in office, Holt disappeared while swimming near Portsea, Victoria, on 17 December 1967. Although his body was never recovered, he was presumed dead.

Hordern, Anthony (1819–76), merchant, was born in London, and was brought to Sydney by his family in 1826. He was educated by J. D. *Lang, and then lived in Melbourne for several years, before he and his brother Lebbeus (1826–81) established a draper's store on Brickfield Hill, Sydney, in the mid-1840s. Anthony established his own retail business in the Haymarket in 1855, his firm becoming the now-famous Anthony Hordern & Sons after his sons Anthony (1842–86) and Samuel (1849–1909) became partners in 1865 and 1869. After his death, they continued to develop the business. Anthony Hordern & Sons became a private company, with Samuel's son, Sir Samuel (1867–1956) as governing director, in 1912, and a public company in 1926.

Horse-racing, in some form, began in Australia soon after white settlement. Recorded race meetings were first held in New South Wales in 1810, Van Diemen's Land in 1814, Western Australia in 1833, South Australia and the *Port Phillip District in 1838, and the *Moreton Bay District in 1843, and horse-racing has since become a major sport and industry in Australia. The *Melbourne Cup has been the country's best-known horse-race for many years. It was won by the now-legendary *Phar Lap, ridden by James Pike (1892–1969), in 1930. Other notable Australian jockeys have included David Hugh ('Darby') Munro (1913–66), Arthur ('Scobie') Breasley (1914–) and George Moore (1923–   ).

Hotham, Sir Charles (1806–55), *governor, was born in England. His father was an honorary canon. Hotham pursued a naval career, and negotiated a British commercial treaty with Paraguay in 1852.

He administered Victoria from June 1854 until his death in December 1855, first as Lieutenant-Governor, and then as Governor from May 1855. He sent his resignation to England in November 1855. Hotham's administration of the colony, particularly his handling of the *Eureka Rebellion, has been criticized.

Howe, Michael: *Bushrangers

Hughes, William Morris (1862-1952), politician, was born in London, grew up in Wales and England, and became a schoolteacher. He migrated to Australia in 1884, where he held various jobs. Hughes was a Labor Member of the Legislative Assembly of New South Wales from 1894 to 1901, belonged to the Socialist League from 1892 to 1898, was active in union organization of waterside workers, and was a union official from 1899 to 1916. He was admitted to the Bar in 1903. Hughes was a Member of the House of Representatives from 1901 to 1952, representing Labor from 1901 to 1916, National Labor in 1916-17, and then the Nationalists, the *United Australia Party and the *Liberals. (He was expelled from the Labor Party over *conscription, from the Nationalists when he helped to bring down the government in 1929, and from the United Australia Party when he rejoined the Advisory War Council, which the party had left, in 1944.) Hughes was Prime Minister from 1915 to 1923, when *Bruce replaced him as leader of the Nationalists and Prime Minister. During the First World War he tried twice (unsuccessfully both times) to introduce conscription. He attended meetings of the Imperial War Cabinet and Imperial War Conference in 1918, and achieved some success when he sought separate representation for the Dominions at the *Paris Peace Conference, held after the war. At the latter, he argued effectively for war reparations for Britain and Australia, succeeded in gaining a mandate over German New Guinea for Australia, and defended the *White Australia Policy, opposing a Japanese attempt (which ultimately failed) to include a guarantee of the equality of nations in the covenant of the *League of Nations.

Hughes held various other portfolios at different times, and led the United Australia Party from 1941 to 1943. He wrote a number of books.

Hulks were the bodies of dismantled ships, worn out and unfit for sea service, which were used as prisons. Convicts had been transported to the British colonies in America until the American War of Independence. Hulks on the River Thames (and later elsewhere) were then used, supposedly as a temporary expedient until transportation could be resumed, to house convicts. They rapidly became overcrowded. The need for a place to which convicts could be transported was a major factor in the British Government's decision to establish a settlement at *Botany Bay. Hulks continued in use in Britain until the mid-nineteenth century. They were also used in Sydney, in Hobart, and off Williamstown, Victoria.

Hume and Hovell Expedition (1824-5): An important feat of inland exploration. In October 1824 Hamilton Hume (1797-1873) and William Hilton Hovell (1786-1875) left the former's station at Gunning, near present-day Yass, in New South Wales. Their destination was Western Port, in present-day Victoria. During their journey they discovered numerous rivers, including the Hume River (later renamed the Murray), and lands suitable for grazing and agriculture. In December 1824 they arrived at Corio Bay in Port Phillip, which they mistook for Western Port, because of a miscalculation made by Hovell. They followed a similar route back to Gunning, arriving there in January 1825. In 1826 Governor *Brisbane sent a party, including Hovell, to Western Port by sea to establish a settlement. Hovell discovered his mistake, and the settlement at Western Port, which was found to be unsuitable, was abandoned shortly afterwards. Hume and Hovell later disagreed over who deserved credit for leading the expedition, and whether or not Hume had mistaken Port Phillip for Western Port at the time.

Hunter, John (1737-1821), *governor, was born at Leith in Scotland. He considered a clerical career in the Church of Scotland, and briefly attended the University of Aberdeen as an undergraduate, but rejected it in favour of a naval career, during which he had extensive sea-going experience. He sailed to New South Wales with the *First Fleet; he was second captain, under *Phillip, of HMS *Sirius*, and commanded the main convoy after Phillip transferred to the tender *Supply* during the voyage. Hunter held a dormant commission to succeed Phillip in case of death or absence, but was not Lieutenant-Governor. He was involved in survey and legal work in the new colony, and also took the *Sirius* to the Cape of Good Hope for supplies (1788–9). After the *Sirius*, under Hunter's command, was wrecked off *Norfolk Island in 1790, Hunter surveyed that island. He returned to England, arriving in 1792, and his naval career continued. Hunter was appointed Governor of New South Wales in 1794, and assumed office the following year. Like Phillip, he had virtually autocratic power. He faced major problems with the *New South Wales Corps. Hunter was recalled, and handed over office to King in 1800. He then resumed his naval career, later being promoted to vice-admiral (1810). He continued to give advice on New South Wales, and gave evidence to the Select Committee on Transportation (1812). He died in London. Hunter published *An Historical Journal of the Transaction at Port Jackson and Norfolk Island, with the discoveries that have been made in New South Wales and the Southern Ocean since the publication of Phillip's Voyage* (1793) and *Governor Hunter's Remarks on the Causes of the Colonial Expense of the Establishment of New South Wales, Hints for the reduction of such expense and for reforming the prevailing abuses* (1802).

Hydro-Electric Commission of Tasmania: Statutory authority responsible for the generation, distribution and sale of electricity in Tasmania. It was established in 1930, replacing the Hydro-Electric Department, which had been created when the Tasmanian Government acquired the partly completed Great Lake scheme in 1914. Hydro-electric power developments have been constructed in the Great

Lake, Derwent, South Esk, Mersey-Forth, Gordon and Pieman River catchment areas. In the 1980s Tasmania's hydro-electric system was the largest in Australia.

I

Immigration: Australia's first immigrants, the ancestors of the *Aborigines, are believed to have arrived more than 40,000 years ago. *Transportation of convicts, mainly from Britain, provided the next group of immigrants. The first convicts arrived, with the *First Fleet, in 1788; the last arrived in 1868. Free settlers began to arrive in 1793, but did not come in sizeable numbers until the 1830s, when significant assistance schemes were introduced. (Various such schemes have continued intermittently throughout the nineteenth and twentieth centuries.) *Systematic colonization, a theory propounded by *Wakefield and others, had some influence on policies during the 1830s and 1840s. Caroline *Chisholm and others also assisted immigrants. The *gold-rushes of the 1850s attracted many immigrants, including some Chinese people, upon whose entry restrictions were soon placed. Such restrictions foreshadowed the *White Australia Policy, a policy of excluding non-Europeans from Australia, which was pursued for a large part of the twentieth century. *Blackbirding brought some Pacific Islanders to Australia from the 1860s onwards. Immigration virtually ceased during the *Depression of the 1890s, the First World War and the *Great Depression. During the first part of the twentieth century, especially the 1920s, much encouragement was given to British immigrants, through organizations such as the *Big Brother Movement, and government policies such as *'Men, Money and Markets'. Some non-British immigrants arrived during the nineteenth century, and increasing numbers arrived in the period between the two world wars, but the first large-scale non-British immigration did not occur until after the Second World War, initially as a result of *Calwell's introduction of an extensive immigration scheme. Many immigrants worked on projects such as the *Snowy Mountains Hydro-Electric Scheme. Some 4.2 million immigrants, of whom about 60 per cent were assisted, arrived between 1945 and the mid-1980s. About 40 per cent of these came from Britain and Ireland, the remainder from Italy, Greece, Yugoslavia, the Netherlands, Germany, New Zealand, Poland, the United States of America, Vietnam, Turkey, Lebanon and elsewhere.

Industrial Workers of the World (IWW): A syndicalist organization, founded in Chicago in 1905 (syndicalism being a 'movement among industrial workers having as its object the transfer of the means of production from their present owners to unions of workers for the benefit of the workers'). Members of the IWW were also known as 'Wobblies'. The first Australian branch began in Sydney in 1907, and others followed. Australian members, who numbered about two thousand, were very active during the First World War, taking a strong stand against war and *conscription. Tom Barker, the editor of the IWW's journal *Direct Action*, was convicted several times for making statements prejudicial to recruiting, and was jailed. The organization became the focus of controversy when a series of fires occurred in Sydney in 1916. Twelve members were charged with conspiring to commit arson, to secure Barker's release unlawfully, and to excite sedition. All were found guilty on at least one count, and their sentences ranged from five to fifteen years. An appeal in 1917 led to the quashing of two convictions on the second count, and corresponding reductions in sentences. The Street Inquiry of 1918 confirmed the guilt of the accused. The Ewing Royal Commission of 1920 found that six of the twelve had been wrongfully convicted, that four had been rightfully convicted, but had served adequate sentences; that one's sentence should be reduced; and that the other's sentence was confirmed. Ten were released soon after in 1920, one served his full sentence before being released in 1921, and the other was released early in 1921. The organization was banned in 1916, and was virtually dissolved in Australia by the end of 1917.

Irian Jaya

Irian Jaya: A province of Indonesia, comprising the western part of the island of *New Guinea and nearby islands. The Dutch claimed the western part of New Guinea in 1828. It became known in Australia as Dutch New Guinea or West New Guinea. The Dutch transferred authority for it to the United Nations in 1962, and it became part of Indonesia in 1963. For a time it was known as West Irian.

Irrigation is 'the action of supplying land with water by means of channels or streams'. *Deakin was an early supporter of irrigation for Australia. The *Chaffey brothers were largely responsible for establishing Australia's first major irrigation settlements, at Renmark and Mildura, during the late 1880s. Further schemes in various states soon followed. The *Snowy Mountains Hydro-Electric Scheme, begun after the Second World War, provides water for irrigation as well as power. By the 1970s, large areas were under irrigation in Victoria (mainly along the Murray River) and New South Wales (mainly along the Murray and Murrumbidgee Rivers), sizeable areas in Queensland, and smaller areas in South Australia (also mostly along the Murray) and Western Australia (notably on the Ord River, where a scheme was begun in 1960 and completed in 1971); a small area was under irrigation in Tasmania. Irrigation schemes have often proved to be uneconomic, and are considered to have increased salinity in the Murray River.

Isaacs, Sir Isaac Alfred (1855–1948), lawyer, politician and governor-general, was born in Melbourne, was educated at schools in Yackandandah and Beechworth, and was a teacher from 1870 to 1875. He was a clerk in the Crown Law Department from 1875 to 1881, studied law at the University of Melbourne, was admitted as a barrister in 1880, and was appointed Queen's Counsel in 1899. Isaacs was a Member of the Victorian Legislative Assembly (1892–1901), served as Solicitor-General once (1893) and Attorney-General twice (1894–9, 1900–1), and was a member of the *Federal Convention (1897–8). He was a Protectionist Member of the House of Representatives from 1901 to 1906, and was Attorney-General from 1905 to 1906. He was appointed to the *High Court in 1906, becoming Chief Justice in 1930. Isaacs generally favoured the extension of the Commonwealth's powers (in contrast with Sir Samuel *Griffith, the Chief Justice until 1919, who favoured the defence of states' rights). The court's decision in the *Engineers' Case* (1920) reflected a move towards Isaacs's position. He was appointed a Privy Counsellor in 1924. His appointment as the first Australian-born Governor-General of the Commonwealth of Australia early in 1931 was the subject of controversy. He held that position until 1936. Isaacs, who was an anti-Zionist, died in Melbourne.

IWW: *Industrial Workers of the World

J

Jackaroo: An Australian slang term that came into use during the nineteenth century. It was applied to inexperienced colonists, many of whom came from Britain. It often was, and is, used to describe young men gaining experience on station properties in order to become station-managers. It may have originated as a portmanteau of Jack and kangaroo.

Janssen (or Jansz), **Willem** (*c.* 1570–?), Dutch mariner, is the first European known to have discovered Australia. He had sailed from Holland for the Dutch East Indies (present-day Indonesia), in command of the *Duyfken*, in 1603. Janssen charted part of the eastern coast of the Gulf of Carpentaria, which he thought was part of New Guinea, early in 1606. One of his crew was killed in an altercation with Aborigines. Janssen commanded several other vessels in the Dutch East Indies, before returning to Holland for a visit. He became the Governor of Fort Henricus, on Solor, in 1614. He visited Holland again, and while returning to the Dutch East Indies, as supercargo on the *Mauritius*, he landed again in

Australia, near present-day North West Cape, in
1618. Janssen was appointed to the Council of the
Indies in 1619, and fought against the British for
some time. As vice-admiral, later admiral, he served
in a British–Dutch fleet against the Philippines.
From 1623 to 1627 he was the Governor of Banda
(present-day Banda Aceh). After commanding an
expedition to Persia (present-day Iran), he assisted
in the defence of Batavia (present-day Jakarta).
Janssen arrived back in Holland, where he reported
on affairs in the Indies, in 1629.

Jones, David (1793–1873), merchant, was born in
Wales, where he became a grocer's apprentice, and
later worked in a general store. He also worked in
London for some time, before arriving in Sydney in
1835 as the partner of a businessman named Charles
Appleton. After the partnership ended in 1838, Jones
traded from a building on the corner of George Street
and Barrack Lane. He retired in 1856, but returned
to the firm in 1860 when it faced difficulties, and
retired again in 1868. One of his sons followed him
into the business. David Jones was also a Member
of the New South Wales Legislative Council from
1856 to 1860. He died in Sydney.

K

Kalgoorlie (originally Kalgurli) is a mining centre
situated about 600 kilometres east of Perth. After
Patrick ('Paddy') Hannan discovered gold there in
1893, a rush followed, and Kalgoorlie became the
service centre for the nearby Golden Mile, one of the
world's richest gold reefs. Gold production in the area
peaked in about 1902. The population rose to about
200,000 in 1905; it was about 20,000 in the 1980s.
Kalgoorlie was linked by rail with Perth in 1896,
and with Esperance in 1927. The Goldfields Water
Supply, which ensured a permanent water supply
to the area, was opened in 1903. The Western Australian Premier, *Forrest, announced the decision to

construct it in 1895. Charles Yelverton O'Connor, the
engineer responsible for its construction, committed
suicide in 1902, apparently because of criticisms of
the scheme. Although it has declined in latter years,
gold production in the area continues in the 1980s.
Nickel was found near Kalgoorlie during the 1960s,
and it has overtaken gold in importance.

Kalgoorlie Riots: Riots in the Western Australian
mining towns of Kalgoorlie and nearby Boulder in
January 1934. The catalyst for the riots was the death
of Edward Jordan, early on 29 January, following
a brawl with Claudio Mattaboni, a barman from
Gianetti's Home from Home Hotel. Australians destroyed, damaged and stole property belonging to
southern Europeans, predominantly Italians and
Yugoslavs, in Kalgoorlie and Boulder, on 29 January.
On 30 January some Australians decided to strike
unless assured that unnaturalized 'foreigners' would
not be employed in the mines. Also on 30 January
Australians attacked houses and camps, mostly occupied by Yugoslavs, at Dingbat Flat, near the Boulder
railway station. In the fighting, Charlie Stokes, an
Australian, was stabbed to death, and Joseph Katich,
a Montenegrin, was shot and killed. During the two
days, about seventy buildings (including hotels,
clubs, boarding-houses, cafés, shops and houses), and
a similar number of camps, were destroyed or damaged. Extra police arrived from Perth on 31 January
and 2 February, but no further riots occurred after
30 January. A public appeal provided some relief for
the victims. About ninety people were charged with
various offences, mostly relating to looting. Most
were fined; a few received short jail sentences. Mattaboni, who had been charged with manslaughter,
was acquitted, and open findings were recorded
regarding the deaths of Stokes and Katich. Australian resentment towards the southern Europeans was
based partly upon allegations that the latter caused
accidents in the mines (because of lack of knowledge
of English and lack of experience), and that they
paid 'slingbacks' (bribes) in return for jobs. Extreme
heat and excessive drinking of alcohol were also
factors leading to the riots.

Kanakas

Kanakas: *Blackbirding

Kangaroo Island lies about fifteen kilometres off the coast of South Australia. It is about 145 kilometres long, and 55 kilometres wide (at its widest point). *Flinders was perhaps the first white person to discover it, in 1802. *Sealers used the island in following years. South Australia's first permanent white settlers, organized by the *South Australian Company, landed there in 1836.

Kelly, Edward (1855-80), *bushranger, was born in Victoria. His parents were Irish, his father an ex-convict. Ned Kelly had had several altercations with the law before the outbreak of the Kelly gang took place. Fitzpatrick, a police-trooper, claimed that Ned had shot him when he attempted to arrest Ned's brother Dan in 1878. As a result of this incident, Ned's mother and two other people served jail sentences. Rewards of £100 each were offered for Ned and Dan, who hid in the Wombat Ranges, near Mansfield. Joseph (Joe) Byrne and Stephen (Steve) Hart joined them. The four became known as the Kelly gang. The outbreak consisted of four main events, which took place at Stringybark Creek, Euroa, Jerilderie and Glenrowan, between 1878 and 1880. Ned shot and killed three policemen, Michael Kennedy, Thomas Lonigan and Michael Scanlon, who were camped at Stringybark Creek while searching for the gang; a fourth policeman, Thomas McIntyre, escaped. Rewards of £500 for each member of the gang were offered. The gang then took over a station near Euroa. Byrne guarded the captives while the others held up a bank in Euroa, escaping with about £2000. Rewards were increased to £1000 each. Next the gang took over the police station at Jerilderie, New South Wales. Dressed in police uniforms, the gang held up the bank in Jerilderie, escaping with another £2000. They also took over the hotel. Rewards were then £2000 each. Some time after this, Byrne shot and killed Aaron Sherritt, a friend of his who had become a police agent. The gang's final stand was at Glenrowan, where they took over the hotel. Policemen, led by Francis Hare, surrounded the hotel. The members of the gang were dressed in armour made from plough mould-boards. A shoot-out took place. Hare was shot in the arm. Byrne was shot and killed. Kelly was shot several times and eventually was captured. Two bystanders were killed. A policeman set fire to the hotel. Later, the badly burnt bodies of Dan Kelly and Hart were found; they may have committed suicide. Ned Kelly was found guilty of Lonigan's murder, was sentenced to death, and was hanged on 11 November 1880. Before his capture he had written two explanations of his actions; they are known as the 'Cameron Letter' and the 'Jerilderie Letter'. Kelly has become a folk hero. His experiences have inspired stories, ballads, books, paintings, films and other works.

Kidman, Sir Sidney (1857-1953), pastoralist, was born near Adelaide. His father, a farmer, died shortly after his birth. Kidman was educated at private schools at Norwood. He worked variously as a stockman, carter and butcher in New South Wales, established coaching businesses in New South Wales and Western Australia, and bought and sold cattle and horses. He acquired a series of stations, eventually owning or controlling land greater in size than England. Kidman, the 'Cattle King', died in Adelaide.

King, Philip Gidley (1758-1808), *governor, was born in England, and pursued a naval career. He sailed for New South Wales with the *First Fleet. *Phillip chose King to establish a settlement on *Norfolk Island. King did so in 1788 and supervised that settlement until 1796. He briefly visited England to report upon the progress of New South Wales (1790-1), and was appointed Lieutenant-Governor in 1791. King returned to England because of ill health in 1796. After his health improved, he returned to New South Wales and relieved *Hunter in 1800. King promoted farming by small settlers in the colony, encouraged the development of whaling and sealing, and reduced liquor imports (but was unable to put an end to illegal distilling of spirits). Like Hunter, he faced major problems with the *New South Wales Corps. His governorship ended in 1806. He was in very poor health when he sailed for England in 1807, and he died the following year. One of his sons, Phillip Parker King (1791–1856), did a considerable amount of work charting parts of the Australian coastline.

King Island, an island measuring about sixty-five kilometres by twenty-five kilometres, lies in Bass Strait to the north-west of Tasmania, of which it has been a municipality since 1908. William Campbell sighted the island in 1797, John Black named it after Governor *King in 1801, John Murray charted its coast in early 1802, and both *Baudin and Charles Grimes visited it in late 1802. *Sealers and *whalers used the island in the early nineteenth century, and a few settlers followed them, but permanent settlement did not begin until 1888. Tom Farrell discovered scheelite (one of the tungsten ores) at King Island in 1904. Scheelite mining began during the First World War, and has continued intermittently since then; tin and other minerals have also been mined at various times. *Soldier settlement took place after each of the two world wars. The island's pastoral industry has continued throughout the twentieth century. King Island has a notorious reputation for shipwrecks. The population in 1981 was 2701.

Kingsford Smith, Sir Charles Edward (1897–1935), aviator, was born in Brisbane, and educated in Canada and Sydney. During the First World War, he served with the Australian Imperial Force, transferred to the Australian Flying Corps in 1916, and joined the British Royal Flying Corps in 1917. After returning to Australia in 1921, he flew joy-flights and later mail services, and established various businesses involving flying. 'Smithy', as he became called, created numerous records, and broke many others. His flights included a round-Australia flight with Charles Ulm, in record time, in 1927; the first crossing of the Pacific, with Ulm and two Americans, in 1928; the first crossing of the Tasman, with Ulm and two Australians, in 1928; the first east-west crossing of the Atlantic, in 1930; a solo flight from England to Darwin, in record time, in 1930; and the first east-west crossing of the Pacific, with P. G. Taylor, in

1934. Kingsford Smith and J. T. Pethybridge disappeared while on a flight from England to Australia. They are believed to have crashed near Burma on or about 8 November 1935. Kingsford Smith wrote several books.

Kingston, Charles Cameron (1850-1908), politician, was born in Adelaide. His father was an engineer (and later a politician). Kingston was educated at the Adelaide Educational Institution, and practised as a barrister; he was admitted to the Bar in 1873, and was appointed Queen's Counsel in 1888. He was a Member of the House of Assembly from 1881 to 1900, and a Member of the Legislative Council briefly in 1900. Kingston was Premier from 1893 to 1899, and held various other portfolios. His Government introduced women's *suffrage, passed arbitration and conciliation legislation, and established a state bank. Kingston played a prominent role in the *federation movement. In 1901 he entered federal politics, and was a Protectionist Member of the House of Representatives until his death. He was Minister for Trade and Customs from 1901 to 1903.

Kisch Affair: A controversial diplomatic incident in 1934-5. Egon Erwin Kisch, a Czechoslovakian communist writer, was invited to speak at a Melbourne congress, organized by the Australian branch of the Movement Against War and Fascism, in 1934. The *Lyons Government banned Kisch from entering Australia. He was not allowed to leave his ship in Fremantle, jumped ashore at Port Melbourne (breaking his leg in the process), and was taken to Sydney where he failed an immigration test (a dictation test administered in Scottish Gaelic). The case was taken to court, but the *High Court found that Scottish Gaelic was not a 'European language' as required by the *Immigration Act*, and therefore the test was invalid. Kisch spoke at a number of meetings before leaving Australia in 1935. His publications include *Australian Landfall* (1937).

Kokoda Trail: A foot-track that crosses the Owen Stanley Range in Papua New Guinea, beginning near Port Moresby in the south and ending near the small village of Kokoda in the north. It is about 240 kilometres long. During the Second World War Australian and Japanese soldiers fought along the Kokoda Trail for some months in 1942, until the latter were ordered to withdraw. It was the closest that any enemy forces have come to Australia by land.

Korean War (1950-3): Popular name given to the 'police action' that followed the North Korean attack on South Korea on 25 June 1950. The South Koreans were supported by *United Nations Organization forces, made up of representatives from Australia, Belgium, Canada, Colombia, Ethiopia, France, Greece, Luxembourg, the Netherlands, New Zealand, the Philippines, Thailand, Turkey, the Union of South Africa, the United Kingdom and the United States of America (which led the United Nations intervention). The armistice concluded at Panmunjom on 27 July 1953 divided Korea, along the 38th Parallel, into North and South. This was similar to the position before the fighting. Within days of the North Korean attack, Australia offered support to South Korea, and sent members of the *Royal Australian Navy, the *Royal Australian Air Force and the Royal Australian Regiment. There were about 1400 Australian casualties (including 278 deaths), most of them members of the Royal Australian Regiment.

L

Labor Party: *Australian Labor Party

Labour Day: *Eight-Hour Day Movement

Lalor, Peter (1827–89), leader of the *Eureka Rebellion and politician, was born and educated in Ireland. He was a civil engineer before migrating to Australia in 1852. He worked on the construction of the Melbourne–Geelong railway, before going to the goldfields, firstly the Ovens, and then Ballarat, where he became involved in the Ballarat Reform League.

In 1854 Lalor led the *diggers in the Eureka Rebellion, during which he was wounded, losing an arm as a result. He escaped after the Rebellion. A reward of £200 was offered for information leading to his arrest, but was later withdrawn. The public raised money for Lalor, with which he bought land. He entered Victorian politics, and was a Member of the Legislative Council (1855-6), then a Member of the Legislative Assembly (1856-71, 1874-89). He held various offices, including that of Speaker (1880-7). During his political career he was also the director of several mining companies. Lalor died in Melbourne.

Lambert, George Washington Thomas (1873-1930), artist, was born in St Petersburg (present-day Leningrad), Russia. His father, who died before Lambert's birth, was an American railway engineer; his mother was English. The family lived in Germany for some time, and in England (where Lambert was educated), before settling in New South Wales in 1887. Lambert worked variously as a clerk, a station-hand and a grocer's assistant. He studied art under Julian Ashton in Sydney, began to contribute illustrations to the *Bulletin* in 1895, and developed a reputation as a painter in the latter half of the 1890s. After winning the New South Wales Society of Artists' first travelling fellowship, he left Australia in 1900, studied art in Paris for about a year, and then settled in London, where he continued to draw and paint. He became known in particular for his portraits. In 1917, during the First World War, Lambert became an official Australian war artist, a position he held for some years. He settled in Sydney again in 1921. McCulloch says that between 1920 and 1930 Lambert's work 'dominated the Australian scene'.[1] Lambert also executed a number of sculptures during the 1920s. He died at Cobbity, New South Wales. His paintings include *A Bush Idyll* (1896), *Across the Black Soil Plains* (1899), *Portrait of Miss Thea Proctor* (1903), *Anzac, the Landing* (1918-22),

[1] Alan McCulloch, *Encyclopedia of Australian Art* (Hutchinson of Australia, Melbourne, 1968), p. 312.

and *The Charge of the Light Horse at Beersheba* (1920).

Lambing Flat Riots: A number of violent clashes in 1860-1 between Europeans and Chinese *diggers on the Burrangong gold-fields (present-day Young), New South Wales. Lambing Flat was one of the areas where the Chinese were camped. The clashes, also known as the Burrangong Riots, culminated in a confrontation between the European diggers and the authorities on 14 July 1861. Similar riots had occurred elsewhere, notably at Buckland River. At Burrangong, 'roll-ups' of diggers assaulted the Chinese, forced them to leave, and destroyed their property. The main clashes occurred in November and December 1860, and January, February and June 1861. A Miners' Protection (or Protective) League, whose aims included the exclusion of Chinese from the field, was formed at Burrangong early in 1861. It played some part in the riots, until its demise in mid-1861. Military forces were stationed at Burrangong from March to May 1861. The arrest of three diggers on 14 July 1861, on charges relating to the June riot, led to a confrontation with the authorities. About 1000 diggers demanded the release of the prisoners, their demand was refused, and a riot ensued. A digger, William Lupton, was killed; three policemen and about twenty diggers were injured. The commissioners and police withdrew to Yass the following day. Further military and naval forces arrived in Burrangong at the end of July, and some remained there for a year. Several men were arrested on charges relating to the Lambing Flat Riots. Only two were convicted: Claremont Owen and William Spicer were each sentenced to two years' imprisonment. The New South Wales Government paid some financial compensation to the Chinese diggers. Earlier attempts to pass restrictive legislation in New South Wales had failed, but after the Lambing Flat Riots the *Chinese Immigration Restriction and Regulation Act* (1861) was passed. It was repealed in 1867.

Land Rights: A term that, in an Australian context, usually refers to Aboriginal political and property

rights. White settlers established missions and
reserves for *Aborigines, from the early nineteenth
century onwards, but did not consider that Aborigines had legal rights to these or other lands. The
land rights movement began in the 1960s, although
some earlier claims had been made. There has been,
and continues to be, opposition to it. In 1963 Yirrkala
Aborigines from Arnhem Land presented a bark petition to the Commonwealth Parliament, protesting
over a government decision to excise part of their
reserve for mining. A Select Committee inquired into
the protests, but mining went ahead. Some Yirrkala
Aborigines later sought compensation, but Mr Justice Blackburn, in 1971, held that they did not have
legal rights to the land. Aborigines at *Wave Hill
station were among others who played a significant
role in the early stages of the land rights movement.
Aboriginal land trusts, with varying powers, were
established in South Australia in 1966, Victoria in
1970, Western Australia in 1972, and New South
Wales in 1974. In 1972 Aborigines set up a tent
embassy on the lawns of Parliament House in Canberra, for about six months, to publicize the land
rights movement. The Aboriginal Land Rights Commission, under Mr Justice Woodward, was held in
1973 and 1974, and was followed by the passing of
the *Aboriginal Land Rights (Northern Territory) Act*
1976, which led to the granting of some land rights
to Aborigines in the Northern Territory. An Aboriginal Land Fund Commission was established to
administer funds to buy land throughout Australia
for Aborigines, in 1975. (An Aboriginal Development
Commission took over its work in 1980.) In 1981 the
South Australian Government, following extensive
negotiations, granted the Pitjantjatjara people freehold title to some 100,000 square kilometres of land.
Other developments occurred in various parts of Australia during the 1980s.

Lane, William (1861-1917), journalist and trade
unionist, was born in England, was educated at Bristol Grammar School, and worked in various jobs,
including that of journalist, in Canada and the United States of America. He migrated to Brisbane in
1885, where he became prominent in journalism and

the trade union movement. Lane helped to found the *Boomerang* in 1887, the *Worker* in 1890, and the Australian Labour Federation in 1899. He was involved in the *Maritime and *Shearers' Strikes of 1890 and 1891, then led *New Australia, and later Cosme, the two Australian utopian settlements in Paraguay. After leaving Cosme in 1899, Lane briefly edited the *Australian Worker* in Sydney in 1900, before settling in Auckland. He was leader writer of the *New Zealand Herald* from 1900 to 1913, then editor until his death. Lane had become conservative, founding the National Defence League in 1906, and arguing, among other things, for compulsory military training. His publications include *The Working-man's Paradise, An Australian Labour Novel* (1892), published under the pseudonym 'John Miller', and *Selections from the Writings of Tohunga* (1917), a collection of essays reprinted from the *New Zealand Herald*.

Lang, John Dunmore (1799-1878), clergyman, was born in Scotland, and migrated to Australia in 1823. Lang, Sydney's first Presbyterian minister, played a prominent and often controversial role in colonial affairs. He was responsible for the building of Scots Church in Sydney (completed in 1826), broke away from the official Presbyterian Church in 1842 and was not formally reinstated for more than twenty years, and became the Moderator of the General Assembly of the Presbyterian Church in New South Wales in 1872. He promoted education, arranged various emigration schemes from Britain, founded and ran several newspapers, including the *Colonist* (1835-40), the *Colonial Observer* (1841-4) and the *Press* (1851), and wrote many books and pamphlets. Lang, who held radical and republican views, served on the Legislative Council of New South Wales several times during the 1840s and 1850s, and argued for the separation of the *Port Phillip District and the *Moreton Bay District (both of which he represented at different times on the Council) from New South Wales. His publications include *Narrative of the Settlement of the Scots Church, Sydney, New South Wales* (1828), *View of the Origin and Migra-*

tions of the Polynesian Nation (1834), *An Historical and Statistical Account of New South Wales, both as a Penal Settlement and as a British Colony* (1834), which is his best-known book, *Transportation and Colonisation* (1837), *Phillipsland* (1847), *The Coming Event, or the United Provinces of Australia* (1850) and *Freedom and Independence for the Golden Lands of Australia* (1852).

Lang, John Thomas (1876-1975), politician, was born in Sydney, and held various jobs, including that of estate agent, before becoming a Labor Member of the New South Wales Legislative Assembly in 1913. He was Treasurer three times (1920-2, 1925-7, 1932-2), Premier twice (1925-7, 1932-9), led the Opposition three times (1923-5, 1927-30, 1932-9), and also held other offices. His first government restored the 44-hour week, introduced widows' pensions and child endowment, and extended workers' compensation. Lang tried unsuccessfully to abolish the Legislative Council in 1926 and 1930. During the *Great Depression, his so-called Lang Plan, proposed in 1931, was controversial. It has been described as follows:

Lang proposed 'the Lang Plan', that interest payments to British bondholders should be suspended, that interest on Australian government borrowings should be reduced to 3 per cent, and that a new form of currency should be based on 'the goods standard'.[1]

His attempts to deal with the depression led to splits within the Labor Party, and his dismissal from the premiership by Sir Philip Game, the Governor of New South Wales, in May 1932 (followed by his party's electoral defeat a week later). Lang was expelled from the Labor Party in 1943 (but readmitted in 1971), resigned from the New South Wales Parliament in 1946, then served as an Independent Labor Member of the House of Representatives from 1946 to 1949,

---

[1] Bede Nairn, 'John Thomas Lang', in Bede Nairn and Geoffrey Serle (eds), *Australian Dictionary of Biography*, volume 9 (Melbourne University Press, Melbourne, 1983), p. 664.

when he lost his seat. He founded the *Century*, a weekly newspaper, in 1938, and continued to edit it for the rest of his life. His publications include *Why I Fight* (1934), *Communism in Australia, A Complete Exposure* (1944), *I Remember* (1956), *The Great Bust* (1962) and *The Turbulent Years* (1970).

La Pérouse, Jean-François de Galaup, Comte de (1741–88) was a French naval officer. In 1785 he sailed from France in charge of an expedition to explore the Pacific Ocean, his ships being the *Boussole* and the *Astrolabe*. He sailed around Cape Horn to Chile, then to Alaska via the Sandwich Islands (present-day Hawaii), south along the coast to California, across to China and the Philippines, north to Sakhalin and Kamchatka, and then south to Samoa, where islanders killed the *Astrolabe*'s commander and eleven other men. La Pérouse then sailed to *Botany Bay via *Norfolk Island. On 26 January 1788 he entered Botany Bay, and camped on the north shore. He met some members of the recently arrived *First Fleet. His expedition disappeared after leaving there in March, apparently wrecked soon afterwards in the Santa Cruz Islands. Its fate was not known until the 1820s.

Larrikins were the Australian equivalent of hoodlums or hooligans, rowdy males who roamed the streets of Melbourne and Sydney in 'pushes' during the latter part of the nineteenth century. They wore distinctive clothing, and their activities ranged from rowdiness and pranks to rape and murder. The term seems to have originated in Melbourne.

Lasseter's Reef: An apparently mythical gold reef in Central Australia. In 1929 and 1930 Lewis Hubert (Harold Bell) Lasseter claimed, in various conflicting versions of the story, that many years before he had found a huge gold reef. In 1930 a seven-person expedition, led by Fred Blakeley and guided by Lasseter, left Alice Springs to search for the reef. No sign of it was found. Although the rest of the party abandoned the search, Lasseter continued. He died, probably of starvation, in the Petermann Ranges. In 1931 a search party found and buried his body and recovered his diary, in which he claimed to have rediscovered the reef. Ion Idriess's novel *Lasseter's Last Ride* (1931), and Blakeley's account, *Dream Millions* (1972), have helped to keep the myth alive. There have been several other unsuccessful attempts to find Lasseter's Reef.

Latham, Sir John Greig (1877-1964), lawyer, was born in Melbourne, was educated at Scotch College and the University of Melbourne, and taught for some time before studying law. While studying, and shortly after, he tutored and wrote for newspapers. He was admitted to the Bar in 1904. During the First World War, he worked in naval intelligence. He accompanied the Australian delegation to the *Paris Peace Conference. He was appointed King's Counsel in 1922. Latham was a Member of the House of Representatives from 1922 to 1934, first as an Independent, then representing the *Nationalist Party, and finally the *United Australia Party. He held various portfolios at different times, and led the Nationalist Party and the Opposition from 1929 to 1931. He was appointed to the Privy Council in 1933. Latham returned to the Bar in 1934, and was appointed Chief Justice of the *High Court in 1935, a position he held until 1952. He was considered to be a 'centralist' in his interpretation of the Constitution. During the Second World War, he was Australia's first Minister to Japan (1940-1). His publications include *Australia and the British Commonwealth* (1929).

La Trobe, Charles Joseph (1801-75), colonial administrator, was born in London. He taught, travelled, and wrote several books about his travels. In the late 1830s La Trobe wrote three reports on education in the West Indies for the British Government. In 1839 he became Superintendent of the newly settled *Port Phillip District. La Trobe supported separation from New South Wales (although he was not active in the separation movement), but some Port Phillip colonists considered that he was too subservient to Sydney, and an unsuccessful petition requesting his removal was sent to England. In 1851, when the area was separated (and renamed Victoria), he became Lieutenant-Governor. Almost immediately, he was faced with the problem of handling the *gold-rushes. He adopted the New South Wales licence system, which later became a cause of the *Eureka Rebellion. He was responsible for setting aside considerable areas of parkland around Melbourne. La Trobe's term of office ended in 1854, and he left the colony that year. His publications include *The Alpenstock, or Sketches of Swiss Scenery and Manners* (1829), *The Pedestrian, A Summer's Ramble in the Tyrol* (1832), *The Rambler in North America, 1832–1833* (1835), *The Rambler in Mexico, 1834* (1836) and *The Solace of Song* (1837).

Launceston, a city in northern Tasmania, is situated at the junction where the North and South Esk Rivers form the Tamar River, a tidal estuary that runs into Bass Strait at Port Dalrymple some seventy kilometres from Launceston. *Bass and *Flinders discovered Port Dalrymple in 1798, and Hamelin, commanding one of *Baudin's ships, visited it in 1802. The following year, David *Collins sent William Collins from Port Phillip to explore the area. William *Paterson established a settlement, comprising mainly soldiers and convicts, at York Town (near the mouth of the Tamar River on the west side) in 1804, having first camped at the site of George Town (on the east side of the Tamar). He founded a settlement at Launceston (briefly known as Patersonia, but then renamed after *King's birthplace) in 1806, and it soon became the chief settlement in the north of Van Diemen's Land. *Macquarie's attempts to develop George Town in this role, rather than Launceston, failed. Launceston was declared a town in 1826, was made a municipality in 1852, and became a city in 1888. It was connected by rail to Hobart, about 200 kilometres to the south, in 1876. Hydro-electric power has assisted its development. The population of Launceston, Tasmania's second-largest city, was 64,555 in 1981.

Lawson, Henry (1867–1922), poet and short-story writer, was born in New South Wales. His Norwegian

father (Niels Larsen) had been a seaman, was a
*digger at the time of Henry's birth, and later became
a *selector. His mother was Louisa *Lawson. Henry
Lawson was educated at schools at Eurunderee and
Mudgee, and at night-school in Sydney. He was deaf
by the age of fourteen. Lawson held numerous jobs,
including those of farm-worker, apprentice coach-
painter, clerk, house-painter, sawmill worker, telegraph lineman and teacher, in Australia and New
Zealand. He wrote for various newspapers and journals, including the Sydney *Bulletin, the Sydney
Republican, the Brisbane Boomerang and the Sydney Worker. Lawson visited London between 1900
and 1902. Alcoholism was a problem for much of
his life. He died in Sydney. Lawson is one of Australia's best-known poets and short-story writers.
Many of his poems and stories are about the bush
and bush-workers. His poetry includes In the Days
When the World Was Wide and Other Verses (1896),
Verses, Popular and Humorous (1900), When I Was
King and Other Verses (1905), The Skyline Riders
and Other Verses (1910), A Coronation Ode and Ret-
rospect (1911), For Australia and Other Poems (1913),
My Army, O, My Army! and Other Songs (1915), Song
of the Dardanelles and Other Verses (1916), Too Old
to Rat (1917), Joseph's Dreams (1923), From One-
Hundred-and-Three (1924), Winnowed Verse (1924)
and Out Back and Other Poems (1943). His stories
include Short Stories in Prose and Verse (1894), On
the Track (1900), Over the Sliprails (1900), Joe Wilson
and His Mates (1901), The Country I Come From
(1901), Children of the Bush (1902), Send Round the
Hat (1907), The Romance of the Swag (1907), The
Rising of the Court and Other Sketches in Prose and
Verse (1910), Mateship, A Discursive Yarn (1911),
The Stranger's Friend (1911) and Triangles of Life
and Other Stories (1913).

Lawson (née Albury), **Louisa** (1848–1920), feminist,
journalist and social reformer, was born in New
South Wales. Her father was a labourer. She married
Niels Hertzberg (Peter) Larsen (later known as Law-
son) in 1866. She bore several children, including
Henry *Lawson. She worked at various jobs in the

country, including keeping a store and post-office. In the early 1880s Louisa Lawson left her husband and moved to Sydney. She founded the *Republican* (later the *Australian Nationalist*), a short-lived journal, in 1887, and the *Dawn*, which is said to have been Australia's first feminist journal, in 1888. It advocated women's *suffrage and other rights. Louisa Lawson edited and published the *Dawn* until its demise in 1905. She founded the Dawn Club, a women's social reform club, in 1889. She also published books, including Henry Lawson's first, *Short Stories in Prose and Verse* (1894), and some of her own stories and poems. She died in Sydney. Her own publications include *The Lonely Crossing and Other Poems* (1905).

Lawson, William: *Blue Mountains, Crossing of the

League of Nations: An international organization established, under the Treaty of *Versailles, after the First World War. Australia was one of the fifty-eight founding members. The League's main aims were to solve international disputes peacefully, and to foster international co-operation. Its ability to do either was hampered by the fact that the United States of America was never a member, and by the withdrawal of some members. Brazil withdrew in 1926, Japan in 1933, Germany (which had joined in 1926) in 1933, Italy in 1937, and Russia (a member from 1934) in 1940. Its system of sanctions failed. The League's final meeting was held in 1946, shortly after the end of the Second World War. It was superseded by the *United Nations Organization.

Leichhardt, Friedrich Wilhelm Ludwig (1813–48?), naturalist and explorer, was born in Prussia. His father was a farmer. Leichhardt was educated at the Universities of Berlin and Göttingen, but did not take out a degree. After spending some years studying and making field trips in England, France, Italy and Switzerland, he arrived in Sydney in 1842. He led an overland expedition from the *Moreton Bay district to *Port Essington, in the Northern Territory, in 1844–5. He and six members of his party (two others having turned back, and one other having been killed by Aborigines) completed the journey in about fourteen and a half months. Leichhardt was hailed as a hero, was later given awards by geographical societies in London and Paris, and was also later pardoned for being a Prussian military deserter. He planned another expedition, aiming to leave from the Darling Downs and travel across the north to the western coast of the continent, and then to travel south to the Swan River settlement. His first attempt began in 1846, but failed. The party, which consisted of eight including Leichhardt, returned to the Darling Downs in mid-1847. His second attempt began in March 1848. The party, consisting of seven including Leichhardt, was last seen in the Darling Downs in April 1848. At least nine major searches between 1852 and 1938 failed to discover the fate of Leichhardt and his party. Some bones and relics, possibly belonging to them, were found. Leichhardt's publications include *Lectures delivered by Dr. Ludwig Leichhardt, at the Sydney School of Arts, on the 18th and 25th days of August, 1846* (1846), *Journal of an Overland Expedition in Australia, from Moreton Bay to Port Essington, a distance of upwards of 3000 miles, during the years 1844-1845*(1847) and numerous articles.

Lend-Lease: Name given to American aid, such as munitions, materials and services, to neutral and Allied countries during the Second World War. Congress passed the *Lend-Lease Act* (1941) while the United States of America was still neutral. After she became a belligerent, Reciprocal Lend-Lease was introduced. Britain and the United States made a Mutual Aid Agreement in 1942; Australia made similar agreements with the United States in 1942 and Canada in 1944. Lend-Lease was terminated in 1945, after the war ended. In 1946 Australia agreed to pay the United States $US 27 million (of which $US 20 million had already been paid). It was estimated that Australia received Lend-Lease worth approximately £Aust. 466 million, and contributed Reciprocal Lend-Lease worth approximately £Aust. 285 million to the United States.

Lewis, Essington (1881-1961), industrialist, was born in Burra, South Australia. He was educated at

Liberal Party

St Peter's College, Adelaide, and the South Australian School of Mines, and became a mining engineer. Lewis joined the *Broken Hill Proprietary Company Limited (BHP); he was to play a leading role in its development. During the First World War, he managed the Broken Hill Munitions Company Proprietary Limited from 1915 to 1918. He became BHP's assistant general manager in 1918, general manager in 1921, managing director in 1926, and chief general manager in 1938. During the Second World War he held various public offices, including those of director-general of munitions, from 1940 to 1945, and director-general of aircraft production from 1942 to 1945. After the war Lewis continued as chief general manager of BHP until 1950, chaired the company from 1950 until 1952, and then remained on its board until he died. He wrote several publications about the Australian iron and steel industry.

Liberal Party: A political party. By 1913 the *Fusion Party had generally become known as the Liberal Party. *Deakin resigned as the federal parliamentary leader of the Liberal Party, and from Commonwealth Parliament, in 1913. Joseph *Cook replaced him as leader. The Liberals governed federally from June 1913 to September 1914, when they were defeated by Labor. After the Labor Party split over conscription, the Liberals merged with the *National Labor Party to form the *Nationalist Party in 1917. Liberals also governed, sometimes in coalition with other parties, in various states at various times.

Liberal Party of Australia: Australia's major non-Labor political party. It superseded the *United Australia Party in 1945. The Liberal Party governed federally, in coalition with the Country Party (*National Party of Australia), from 1949 to 1972, and again from 1975 to 1983. *Menzies, who was largely responsible for founding the Liberal Party, was its federal parliamentary leader from 1945 to 1966. He was followed by *Holt (1966-7), *Gorton (1968-71), *McMahon (1971-2), Billy Mackie Snedden (1972-5), *Fraser (1975-83), Andrew Sharp Peacock (1983-5) and John Winston Howard (1985-). Liberals have also governed, sometimes in coalition with other parties, in various states at various times.

Light, William (1786–1839), soldier and surveyor, was born in Malaya and educated in England. Before becoming the first Surveyor-General of the new British province of South Australia in 1836, Light's varied experiences included two years' service in the British navy, a military career (during part of which he served in the Peninsular War), and extensive travel. He arrived in South Australia in 1836, chose the site for Adelaide, and began surveys of it. *Hindmarsh later actively opposed the choice of site. Light also began surveys elsewhere in South Australia, but was hampered by insufficient staff and equipment, and his requests to England for more of both were rejected. After being instructed to undertake temporary surveys for the sake of speed, he resigned in 1838. He then became the main partner in a private surveying firm. He died the following year. His publications include *A Brief Journal of the Proceedings of William Light* (1839).

'Light on the hill': *Chifley, Joseph Benedict

Lindsay Family: A well-known Australian artistic and literary family. Its best-known member is **Norman Alfred William Lindsay** (1879–1969), artist and writer. He was born in Victoria. His father was an Irish-born medical practitioner. Norman Lindsay was educated at Creswick Grammar School. He worked as an illustrator in Melbourne for some time. In 1901 he moved to Sydney, where he became an illustrator for the *Bulletin*, a position he held for many years. His prolific artistic output includes cartoons, line drawings, water-colours, oil paintings, etchings, and sculptures. His best-known art works probably are those of his drawings and paintings that are 'dominated by deep-bosomed and heavy-hipped nudes luxuriating in exotic and bacchanalian settings'.[1] His literary output was also prolific. Both

---

[1] Bernard Smith, *Australian Painting, 1788–1970* (Oxford University Press, Melbourne, 1971), p. 197.

his art and writing were considered controversial.
Norman Lindsay, who had travelled in Europe and
America, died at Springwood, in the Blue Mountains,
where he had lived for some fifty years. His novels
include *A Curate in Bohemia* (1913), *Redheap* (1930),
which was banned in Australia for many years, *The
Cautious Amorist* (1932), *Miracles by Arrangement*
(1932), *Saturdee* (1933), *Pan in the Parlour* (1933),
Age of Consent (1938), *The Cousin from Fiji* (1945),
Dust or Polish? (1950) and *Rooms and Houses* (1968).
*The Magic Pudding, Being the Adventures of Bunyip
Bluegum and his Friends, Bill Barnacle and Sam
Sawnoff* (1918), which has become a classic, and *The
Flyaway Highway* (1936) are children's books. *Creative Effort, An Essay in Affirmation* (1920), *Hyper-
borea, Two Fantastic Travel Essays* (1928) and
*Madame Life's Lovers, A Human Narrative Embod-
ying a Philosophy of the Artist in Dialogue Form*
(1929) contain some of his personal philosophies.
Bohemians of the Bulletin (1965), *The Scribblings
of an Idle Mind* (1966) and *My Mask* (1970) are autobiographical. Norman Lindsay also wrote articles for
periodicals such as *Vision*. Other members of the
family include **Sir Daryl Ernest Lindsay** (1890–
1976), one of Norman's brothers, painter and illustrator, who was for many years director of the
National Gallery of Victoria; **Lady Joan à Beckett
Lindsay** (née Weigall) (1896–1964), Daryl's wife,
water-colourist and writer, whose publications
include *Time Without Clocks* (1962) and *Picnic at
Hanging Rock* (1967); **John (Jack) Lindsay** (1900–
), Norman's son, writer and translator; **Sir Lionel
Arthur Lindsay** (1874–1961), another of Norman's
brothers, graphic artist, water-colourist and writer,
whose publications include *The Australian Work of
Arthur Streeton* (1919), *Conrad Martens, the Man
and His Art* (1920), *The Art of Hans Heysen* (1920)
and *Charles Kean, The Artist's Artist* (1934); **Per-
cival (Percy) Charles Lindsay** (1870–1952),
another of Norman's brothers, water-colourist and
illustrator; and **Ruby Lindsay** ('Ruby Lind') (1887–
1919), Norman's sister, illustrator, who married the
cartoonist Will *Dyson.

Logan, Patrick: *Moreton Bay

Longford, Raymond Hollis (né John Walter)
(1878-1959), film director, was born in Melbourne.
He began acting in Australian films about 1909, and
began directing about 1911. Longford, the best-
known Australian silent-film director, directed numerous films (some of which he also acted in) during
the next twenty years, including *The Romantic Story
of Margaret Catchpole* (1911), *The Silence of Dean
Maitland* (1914), *The Mutiny of the Bounty* (1916),
The Sentimental Bloke (1919), often described as an
Australian film classic, *Ginger Mick* (1920), *On Our
Selection* (1920) and *Fisher's Ghost* (1924). Longford
and Lottie Lyell, who starred in many of the films,
formed a partnership to produce some of them; Lyell
also co-directed at least one. Longford continued to
work in the film industry during the 1930s, in various
minor capacities. He spent his last years as a night-
watchman on the wharves in Sydney, where he died.

Lyne, Sir William John (1844-1913), politician,
was born in Apslawn, Tasmania. His father was a
politician. Lyne was educated at Horton College
(Ross, Tasmania) and by a tutor, spent some time
in the Gulf of Carpentaria area, was a council clerk
in Glamorgan, Tasmania, from 1865 to 1875, and
became a pastoralist at Camberoona, near Albury,
in 1875, before entering politics in New South Wales;
he was a Member of the Legislative Assembly from
1880 to 1901. During this time he was Premier from
1899 to 1901 and held various other offices. Hopetoun
invited Lyne, who was a strong opponent of the *federation movement, to become the first Prime Minister
of the Commonwealth of Australia; Lyne was unable
to form a ministry, and *Barton became Prime Minister instead. Lyne was a Member of the House of
Representatives from 1901 until his defeat in 1913,
shortly before his death. He was Minister for Home
Affairs (1901-3), Minister for Trade and Customs
(1903-4, 1905-7) and Treasurer (1907-8). Lyne was
a Protectionist for most of his political career.

Lyons (née Burnell)**, Dame Enid Muriel** (1897-
1981), was born in Tasmania, educated at Stowport
and Burnie State Schools and the Teachers Training
College in Hobart, and taught for a year. She married

Joseph *Lyons in 1915, and had six sons and six daughters. Dame Enid was a Member of the House of Representatives from 1943 to 1951, the first woman to hold that position. She represented the *United Australia Party, and then its successor, the *Liberal Party of Australia. She also became the first woman member of Federal Cabinet; she was the Vice-President of the Executive Council from 1949 to 1951. She was also active in various other organizations. Her publications include *So We Take Comfort* (1965), *The Old Haggis* (1969) and *Among the Carrion Crows* (1972).

Lyons, Joseph Aloysius (1879–1939), politician, was born in Tasmania to Irish parents, was educated at a convent school in Ulverstone, Stanley State School, and the Teachers Training College in Hobart, and became a teacher. He was a Labor Member of the Tasmanian House of Assembly from 1909 to 1929. He was Treasurer (1914-16, 1923-8), Leader of the Opposition (1916-23, 1928-9), Premier (1923-8), and held other portfolios. His government's achievements included improving the state's finances. Lyons was then a Member of the House of Representatives from 1929 until his death, representing Labor (1929-31), and then the *United Australia Party (1931-9). When *Theodore was reinstated as Treasurer in 1931, Lyons and others left the Labor Party, joined with Nationalists, and formed the United Australia Party. Lyons advocated a deflationary policy to deal with the *Great Depression, with reductions in public expenditure, wages and pensions. He led the Opposition from 1931 to 6 January 1932, and then was Prime Minister until his death, leading a United Australia Party Government until 1934, and then one in coalition with the Country Party. He also held other portfolios. Dame Enid *Lyons was his wife.

M

Macarthur, John (1767-1834), pastoralist, was born in England, to Scottish parents. His father was a mercer and draper. Macarthur pursued a military career, arriving in New South Wales in 1790 as a lieutenant in the *New South Wales Corps. He became regimental paymaster at Parramatta in 1792, inspector of public works in 1793, and was promoted captain in 1795. Macarthur's conflicts with authorities eventually earned him his nickname, 'the Perturbator'. He clashed with *Hunter and *King, who sent him to England after he wounded William *Paterson in a duel in 1801. Macarthur resigned from the army before returning to New South Wales, to pursue his mercantile and pastoral interests, in 1805. He played an active role in the *Rum Rebellion of 1808, after which he became Colonial Secretary until July 1808. In 1809 he sailed for England, and remained there for some years, aware that he risked arrest if he returned to New South Wales. When he did return to the colony in 1817, it was on the condition that he did not take part in public affairs. He came into conflict with *Macquarie, and later with *Darling. *Brisbane's attempt, in 1822, to appoint him as a magistrate failed. Macarthur was a Member of the Legislative Council from 1825 to 1832. He played an active role, greatly assisted by his wife Elizabeth, in the development of the Australian fine wool industry; he publicized Australian fine wool during his visits to England; and he is said to have influenced the *Bigge reports. He took control of the *Australian Agricultural Company in 1828. Macarthur died in New South Wales.

McCubbin, Frederick (1855–1917), painter, was born in West Melbourne. His father was a baker. McCubbin studied at the Artisans' School of Design, Carlton, and at the National Gallery School, Melbourne. He taught drawing at the latter from 1886 until his death. He was president of the Australian Art Association once (1912), and of the Victorian Artists' Society several times (1893, 1902–4, 1908–9, 1911–12). He visited Europe in 1907. McCubbin is best known for his landscapes, and was a leading member of the *Heidelberg School. According to Bernard Smith, 'Frederick McCubbin appears to have been the prime mover in promoting the distinctly national quality of the Heidelberg School'.[1] His paintings include *The Lost Child* (1886), *Down on His Luck* (1889), *Bush Burial, Wallaby Track* (1896) and *The Pioneers* (1904).

McEwen, Sir John (1900–80), politician, was born at Chiltern, Victoria, and was educated at state schools, before working in the Crown Solicitor's Office, in Melbourne, from 1916 to 1918. He enlisted in the First Australian Imperial Force, but the First World War ended before he could be sent overseas. He became a soldier-settler, running a dairy farm at Stanhope in the Goulburn Valley. He joined the Victorian Farmer's Union in 1919, and was active in establishing a co-operative dairy factory in his district. McEwen entered federal politics; he was a Victorian Member of the House of Representatives from 1934 to 1971, representing the Country Party. He held several portfolios, and was successful in developing *protection in the period from 1949 to 1967. McEwen was Deputy Leader of the Country Party (1943–58), and then Leader (1958–71). He was Deputy Prime Minister from 1958 to 1971. After *Holt's disappearance, he became Prime Minister as a short-term measure (December 1967–January 1968) until *Gorton was elected. After retiring from politics in 1971, he returned to farming.

MacGregor, Sir William (1846–1919), colonial administrator, was born and educated in Scotland. He became assistant medical officer in the Seychelles in 1873, medical officer in Mauritius in 1874, and chief medical officer in Fiji in 1875. In each of these places he also held administrative positions, including that of acting Governor of Fiji for two periods. MacGregor became the Administrator of British New Guinea in 1888. During his term of office, which lasted until 1898 (his title becoming Lieutenant-Governor in 1895), he established a native police force, organized missionary activity, encouraged European development, and explored extensively. He

---

[1]Bernard Smith, *Australian Painting, 1788–1970* (Oxford University Press, Melbourne, 1971), p. 85.

was Governor of Lagos from 1898 to 1902, Governor of Newfoundland from 1904, and Governor of Queensland from 1909 to 1914. In 1910 MacGregor became the first Chancellor of the University of Queensland, which he had helped to found.

Machine-breakers: *'Swing' Rioters

McIlwraith, Sir Thomas (1835-1900), politician, was born and educated in Scotland. In 1854 he migrated to Victoria, where he worked firstly as a miner, then as an engineer. He began to make investments in Queensland, and eventually moved there permanently. McIlwraith was a Member of the Queensland Legislative Assembly for many years (1870-1, 1873-86, 1888-96). He was Premier three times (1879-83, 1888, 1893), and held various other offices. He unsuccessfully attempted to annex southeastern New Guinea, on Britain's behalf, in 1883. He died in London.

McKay, Hugh Victor (1865-1926), inventor and businessman, was born at Raywood, Victoria. His father was a farmer. McKay's harvesting machine, which stripped, threshed and cleaned grain, was patented in 1885. He established McKay's Harvesting Machine Company at Ballarat in 1891, but moved it to Braybrook (later renamed Sunshine), to the west of Melbourne, in 1906. His application for exemption from excise duties under *New Protection legislation led to the *Harvester Judgement of 1907. McKay's company reputedly was the largest manufacturer of agricultural machinery in the southern hemisphere by the 1920s.

McKell, Sir William John (1891-1985), governor-general, was born in New South Wales, and was educated at Bourke Street Public School, Surry Hills. He became a boilermaker, and was active in the Boilermakers' Union. McKell then entered state politics, and was a Labor Member of the New South Wales Legislative Assembly from 1917 to 1947. He held various portfolios, before becoming Premier and Treasurer (1941-7). He was Governor-General of the Commonwealth of Australia from 1947 to 1953.

McMahon, Sir William (1908-), politician, was born in Sydney, and educated at Sydney Grammar School and the University of Sydney. Before and after the Second World War, he practised as a solicitor. During the war he served with the Militia. He entered federal politics, and was a Liberal Member of the House of Representatives from 1949 to 1982. McMahon held various portfolios, and was Deputy Leader of the Liberal Party from 1966 to 1971, when he became Prime Minister. He was defeated at the 1972 elections. McMahon then resigned as Leader, Billy Mackie Snedden being elected in his place.

Maconochie (né M'Konochie), **Alexander** (1787-1860), penal reformer, was born in Edinburgh, Scotland. He pursued an active career in the navy from 1803 to 1815; during this period, he spent some time as a prisoner-of-war of the French. He helped to found the Royal Geographical Society in London in 1830, and became its first secretary. Maconochie then became the first professor of geography at the University of London in 1833. He went to Van Diemen's Land, where he was secretary to Sir John *Franklin from 1836 to 1839. Maconochie was superintendent of the *penal settlement at *Norfolk Island from 1840 to 1844. During this time he implemented his now well-known Mark System. He did not believe that punishment should be cruel or vindictive. Prisoners should earn their freedom by labour and good behaviour, measured by marks, rather than by time. They should pass through various stages, including one in which they worked as members of a group. After his recall, Maconochie returned to England in 1844. He governed a new prison at Birmingham from 1849 to 1851. His publications include *A Summary View of the Statistics and Existing Commerce of the Principal Shores of the Pacific Ocean, etc.* (1818), *Report on the State of Prison Discipline in Van Diemen's Land...* (1838), *Crime and Punishment, the Mark System, Framed to Mix Persuasion with Punishment, and to Make their Effect Improving, Yet their Operation Severe* (1846) and many pamphlets.

Macquarie, Lachlan (1762-1824), *governor, was born on the island of Ulva in the Inner Hebrides,

Scotland, and pursued a military career, which took him to various parts of the world. He was appointed Governor of New South Wales following the *Rum Rebellion, sailed with the 73rd Regiment in 1809, and took office in 1810. He was the last Governor of New South Wales with virtually autocratic powers. Convict numbers increased dramatically during his term of office, especially after the end of the Napoleonic Wars in 1815. Macquarie used many of the convicts to carry out an extensive program of public works, which included the construction of roads, numerous buildings, many of which were designed by *Greenway, and a number of new towns. His policy towards convicts and *emancipists (such as *Redfern), generally considered to be a supportive one, led to conflict with *exclusives such as *Macarthur, *Marsden and the Bent brothers. He made various attempts to improve public morality, and treated *Aborigines with sympathy. Macquarie (who had been promoted brigadier-general in 1811) resigned in 1821, was relieved by Thomas *Brisbane, and left the colony for England in 1822. The *Bigge reports, the result of an inquiry held in the latter stages of his term of office, distressed Macquarie. He did not hold public office again after leaving New South Wales, and died in London in 1824.

Macquarie Harbour: An inlet, named after *Macquarie, on the western coast of Tasmania. During the *transportation period, a *penal settlement was established there, the first forty-five convicts being sent in late 1821. The main settlement was on Sarah Island; another settlement was located on a nearby smaller island. Convicts sent to Macquarie Harbour, which gained a notorious reputation as a place of punishment, worked at timber-felling, building of vessels, and other pursuits. The settlement was abandoned in late 1833.

Mahogany Ship: The name given to a ship's hull found by sealers in 1836 in the sand dunes near the present-day Victorian city of Warrnambool. Numerous sightings of it were made during the nineteenth century. It was possibly made from mahogany (hence its name) or cedar. The last recorded sighting of it was made in 1880. Numerous searches since then have failed to find it, but have uncovered some relics in the area. It may have been burnt or hidden by sand. Some people believe that the Mahogany Ship may have been a Portuguese vessel of the fifteenth or sixteenth century.

Major's Line: A route from New South Wales to *Australia Felix, named after Major Thomas *Mitchell. The tracks he made on his return from Australia Felix to Sydney in 1836 were visible for some years, and *squatters from New South Wales followed the Major's Line in search of new pastures.

Malayan Emergency: A period of conflict in 1948-60 between Malayan–Chinese communists and British and other forces in Malaya, which at the time was ruled by Britain. Australia, at Britain's request, sent members of the Royal Australian Air Force (1950-8) and the Royal Australian Regiment (1955-62) to Malaya. Eventually, the British defeated their opponents. British tactics of fighting guerrillas during the Malayan Emergency were copied, with far less success, during the *Vietnam War.

Mannix, Daniel Patrick (1864-1963), Roman Catholic archbishop, was born in Ireland. His father was a tenant farmer. Mannix was educated at, taught at, and from 1903 to 1912 was president of, St Patrick's College, Maynooth, in Ireland. He was Coadjutor Archbishop (1913-17) and the Archbishop (1917-63) of Melbourne. Mannix became a controversial public figure. He argued for state aid to Catholic schools, opposed the British response to the Irish Easter Rising of 1916, argued for Irish independence, and spoke out strongly against *conscription during the referendum campaigns of 1916 and 1917. The British refused him entry to Ireland in 1920. Mannix became a strong opponent of communism, and was influential in the establishment of the National Secretariat of Catholic Action (1937) and the Catholic Social Movement, a major force in the creation of the *Democratic Labor Party. During the campaign for the 1958 federal elections he tried to discourage Catholics and others from voting for the Australian Labor Party. Mannix died in Melbourne.

Maori Wars: A series of conflicts in 1860–72 between British troops and Maoris. The basic cause was the struggle for possession of land in the North Island of New Zealand. About 1500 male volunteers sailed from Australia in 1863 to support Britain. They became known as the Waikato Militia (named after the area in which fighting was occurring), which consisted of four regiments. A further 1200 or so male volunteers, and approximately 1000 women and children, followed in 1864. A scheme of military settlement, in which some of the Australians participated, was largely unsuccessful; many of the settlers left their farms.

Maralinga: *Nuclear Tests

Maritime Strike: The name usually given to Australia's first almost-general strike, in 1890. It actually involved a series of strikes between August and November. Maritime workers were the first to strike, hence the popular but somewhat inaccurate name. Transport workers, miners and pastoral workers followed. Some 50,000 men in Victoria, New South Wales, Queensland and South Australia became involved. Workers were fighting for the principles of unionism and the 'closed shop' ('an establishment in which only trade union members are employed', or 'a trade etc. restricted to members of a [particular] trade union'). Employers were fighting for the principle of 'freedom of contract' (the right to employ anyone). Other issues were also involved. The unions were defeated, and some collapsed completely.

Mark System: *Maconochie, Alexander

Married Women's Property Acts: Popular name given to legislation that transferred rights over married women's property from the women's husbands to the women themselves. Such legislation was passed in the Australian colonies from the 1870s onwards.

Marsden

Marsden, Samuel (1764–1838), chaplain, was born at Farsley, Yorkshire, England. He was apprenticed to his father, a blacksmith, and became a lay preacher. The Elland Society (an Anglican organization) sponsored his education at Hull Grammar School and Magdalene College, Cambridge. Marsden's studies were interrupted when he was appointed assistant chaplain of New South Wales. After ordination as a deacon and then as a priest, Marsden arrived in New South Wales in 1794. He visited England (1807–9), and was appointed senior chaplain in 1810. He played a prominent, and sometimes controversial, role in public affairs. His public duties included that of magistrate. He clashed with *Macquarie, especially over the latter's *emancipist policy. Marsden was a noted sheep-breeder. He was active in organizations such as the London Missionary Society, the Church Missionary Society, and the British and Foreign Bible Society; he founded the New South Wales Society for Affording Protection to the Natives of the South Sea Islands and Promoting their Civilization in 1813; he supervised missionaries in the Pacific Islands and New Zealand, and in the course of his missionary work visited New Zealand seven times between 1814 and 1837. Marsden died at Windsor, New South Wales.

Marshall, Alan (1902–84), writer, was born at Noorat, Victoria, where his father was a store-keeper. Marshall was crippled with poliomyelitis in 1908. After attending school in Terang and business college in Melbourne, Marshall worked in various jobs, including those of clerk, bookkeeper and accountant. During the Second World War he wrote as a freelance journalist and then lectured for the Army Education Service. He had begun writing during the 1920s. He travelled widely in Australia and overseas. Best known for his autobiographical *I Can Jump Puddles* (1955), which has been translated into other languages and adapted for film and television, Marshall wrote numerous other stories, histories and travel books, and did much to record Australian folklore.

Martens, Conrad (1807–78), artist, was born in London. His father, a German-born merchant, was for some time Austrian consul in London; his mother was English. He studied landscape painting under the water-colourist Copley Fielding. Martens left England in the *Hyacinth*, bound for India, but joined the *Beagle*, as an artist, at Montevideo, in 1833. While on board the *Beagle*, which was making a scientific survey of Patagonia and Tierra del Fuego, he became friendly with Charles Darwin. Martens left the *Beagle* at Valparaiso in 1834. After visiting Tahiti and New Zealand, he arrived in Sydney in 1835, and lived there for the rest of his life. He undertook various sketching expeditions and gave some art lessons. Martens is best known for his water-colour landscapes and seascapes, many of which are of Sydney Harbour and surrounding areas, although he also produced lithographs and other works. He was a parliamentary librarian from 1863 until his death. His paintings include *View from Neutral Bay* (*c.* 1857-8) and *Sydney from Vaucluse* (1864).

'Marvellous Melbourne': A now-famous term which was, and is, used to describe Melbourne during the boom years of the 1880s, when Melbourne developed rapidly. The term was used because of Melbourne's apparent material, commercial, social and cultural progress. George Augustus Sala, an English journalist touring the colonies, first used the term in newspaper articles published in the London *Daily Telegraph*, the Melbourne *Argus*, the Melbourne *Australasian* and the *Sydney Morning Herald* in 1885. The term's use soon became widespread.

Mawson, Sir Douglas (1882-1958), geologist and Antarctic explorer, was born in England, and came to Australia as a child. He took part in a geological surveying expedition to the New Hebrides (present-day Vanuatu) in 1903. Mawson, who had gained degrees in engineering and science from the University of Sydney, became a lecturer at the University of Adelaide in 1905. From 1907 to 1909 he took part in Ernest Shackleton's British Antarctic Expedition. Mawson and two others became the first people to reach the South Magnetic Pole, in 1909. He led the Australasian Antarctic Expedition (1911-14). The expedition established three bases, mapped a large part of the Antarctic coast, and engaged in scientific research. While on a trip inland, Mawson's two companions died. He returned to base alone. Mawson was knighted in 1914. During the First World War he worked in the British Ministry of Munitions. He became Professor of Geology at the University of Adelaide in 1920. He led the British–Australian–New Zealand Antarctic Expedition (BANZARE) (1929-31), and claimed British possession of part of Antarctica in 1930. He continued to take an active interest in Australia's Antarctic involvement and research until his death. One of the bases in the 'Australian Antarctic Territory was named after him. His publications include *The Home of the Blizzard* (1915).

Mechanics' Institutes: Organizations in Australia that, like their British predecessors, aimed to provide educational facilities for working-class adults (a mechanic being a 'skilled workman, esp. one who makes or uses machinery'). Official attempts to establish such an organization in Sydney in 1826 failed, but one was established by skilled tradesmen in Hobart in 1827, and others were established in Sydney, Adelaide, Melbourne and elsewhere in the 1830s. Such organizations, also known as Schools of Arts and by various other names, eventually were established in many towns and cities. They tended to attract middle-class members. Some were later absorbed by other educational institutions; others later became social rather than educational organizations.

Melba (née Mitchell)**, Dame Nellie** (Helen Porter) (1861-1931), singer, was born in Melbourne. Her father was a building contractor. She was educated at the Presbyterian Ladies' College, Melbourne, and studied singing under Pietro Cecchi, in Melbourne, from 1879. She married Charles Frederick Nesbitt Armstrong, the manager of a Queensland sugar plantation, in 1882, and bore a son the following year. The marriage did not last. She went to Europe in 1886, studied singing under Madame Marchesi in Paris, and made her operatic debut in Brussels, in

Rigoletto, in 1887. Melba, who had adopted her stage name in 1886, went on to sing in London, Paris, New York and elsewhere, becoming the best-known soprano of the time. She toured Australia in 1902 and 1903. From 1909 onwards, she lived alternately in Australia and Europe. In 1911 and 1924 she brought Melba–Williamson Operas to Australia. On occasions she taught at Melbourne's Conservatorium of Music. She was created a Dame of the British Empire in 1918, and a Dame Grand Cross of the Order of the British Empire in 1927. Dame Nellie Melba gave a number of supposedly final performances. Her final Covent Garden performance was in 1926. She sang at the opening of Parliament House, Canberra, in 1927. Her final Australian performance was in 1928. She died in Sydney. Her publications include *Melodies and Memories* (1925).

Melbourne, the capital city of the state of *Victoria, lies on the Yarra River, near its mouth in Port Phillip Bay. Charles Grimes, the Surveyor-General of New South Wales, explored the area in 1803. *Batman, a settler from Van Diemen's Land, followed in 1835, entered into a 'treaty' (later declared invalid) with local Aborigines to buy land, and allegedly noted 'the site for a village'. John Pascoe Fawkner, also from Van Diemen's Land, led a party that settled near Batman's site in 1835. *Bourke, the Governor of New South Wales, visited the settlement in 1837, named it Melbourne after the British Prime Minister, and arranged for its planning and first land sales. Melbourne became a municipality in 1842, and a city in 1847. Melbourne's population was approximately 283,000 in 1881, and 2,578,527 in 1981.

Melbourne Cup: Australia's most famous horse-race. The first Melbourne Cup was run, under the auspices of the Victoria Turf Club, on Thursday, 7 November 1861. It has been run every year since then. The race was taken over by the Victorian Racing Club, which was founded in 1864. Originally it was run over two miles; since 1972 it has been run over 3200 metres. Notable winners have included Archer (1861, 1862), Carbine (1890) and *Phar Lap (1930).

'Men, Money and Markets'

The Melbourne Cup is run at the Flemington race-course on the first Tuesday in November, which is a public holiday in Melbourne.

'Men, Money and Markets': A slogan used to sum up the theory behind many of the policies of the *Bruce-*Page Government (1923-9). 'Men' referred to immigrants, to increase Australia's population; 'Money' referred to capital, mostly to be borrowed from the British Government; 'Markets' referred to Imperial Preference, that is, mutual preference for trade between Great Britain and the Dominions. During the 1920s Australia was more successful in attracting 'Men' and 'Money' than 'Markets'.

Menzies, Sir Robert Gordon (1894-1978), politician, was born in Victoria, and educated at Wesley College and the University of Melbourne. His father was a shopkeeper and politician. Menzies became a barrister in 1918 and was appointed King's Counsel in 1929, was a Member of the Victorian Legislative Council in 1928-9, and a Member of the Victorian Legislative Assembly from 1929 to 1934, representing the Nationalists until 1931, and then their successor, the *United Australia Party. He held various offices. Menzies was then a Member of the House of Representatives from 1934 to 1966, during which time he represented the United Australia Party until 1944, and then the *Liberal Party of Australia, which he had been largely responsible for founding. Menzies held numerous portfolios at different times, and was Prime Minister from 1939 to 1941, when he resigned because of dissatisfaction with his leadership; he led the Opposition from 1943 to 1949, and then was Prime Minister again from 1949 to 1966, when he resigned. He strongly supported close relations with Britain, hosted the first visit to Australia by a reigning monarch (Queen Elizabeth II's visit in 1954), and supported Britain's policy in the Suez Crisis of 1956. During his second term of office, Australian troops were sent to the *Korean War, the *ANZUS Pact and *SEATO treaty were signed, and Australia's involvement in the *Vietnam War began. He supported the Dutch against Indonesia in the conflict over West

New Guinea (*Irian Jaya). Menzies, who was strongly anti-communist, unsuccessfully attempted to outlaw the *Communist Party of Australia, first by legislation, and then by referendum. The *Petrov affair also occurred during Menzies's second term of office. The Commonwealth Government's role in the provision of tertiary education expanded greatly during these years (a particularly notable event being the establishment of the Australian Universities Commission in 1959), as did its role in the field of secondary education. Canberra also developed considerably in this period. Menzies was Chancellor of the University of Melbourne from 1967 to 1972. His publications include *Afternoon Light* (1967) and *The Measure of the Years* (1970), both of which are memoirs.

Mitchell, Helen Porter: *Melba, Dame Nellie

Mitchell, Sir Thomas Livingstone (1792–1855), surveyor-general, was born in Scotland. He pursued a military career, during which he served in the Peninsular War. Mitchell, who had by then attained the rank of major, arrived in Sydney as Assistant Surveyor-General of New South Wales in 1827. He became Surveyor-General in 1828. His work in the colony included leading four major expeditions. On the first, in 1831–2, he travelled north-west from Sydney and explored an area around the Gwydir and Barwon Rivers. On the second, in 1835, he charted the Bogan River, and much of the Darling River. On the third, in 1836, he followed the Lachlan River, then the Murrumbidgee River to the Murray River, followed it to the Darling River, explored part of the latter, and then followed the Murray to the junction of the Loddon River. He then went south-west and discovered an area that he named *Australia Felix, reached the mouth of the Glenelg River, several days later, Portland Bay (where he met *Henty), and then went in a north-easterly direction back to Sydney. *Squatters soon followed the *Major's Line to new pastures. On his fourth expedition, in 1845–6, he attempted to find an inland route to *Port Essington in the north, but failed, reaching an area near the site of present-day Isisford before returning to Sydney. He represented the *Port Phillip District on the Legislative Council of New South Wales in 1844-5. Mitchell, who had visited Britain several times since first coming to the colony, died in Sydney, while still in office. His publications include *Ninety Figures, Showing all the Motions in the Manual and Platoon Exercises* (1825), *Outlines of a System of Surveying for Geographical and Military Purposes* (1827), *Three Expeditions in the Interior of Eastern Australia* (1838), *Journal of an Expedition into the Interior of Tropical Australia* (1848), *Notes on the Cultivation of the Vine and Olive* (1849), *The Australian Geography* (1850), *The Lusiad of Luis de Camoens, closely translated* (1854) and *Report upon the Progress Made in Roads and Public Works in New South Wales* (1856).

Molesworth Committee: A Select Committee of the British House of Commons (1837-8). It was appointed to inquire into *transportation and was chaired by Sir William Molesworth, hence its popular name. Its report criticized transportation in general, and assignment in particular. Shortly afterwards, the British Government abolished assignment in the Australian colonies, and suspended transportation to New South Wales. Many criticisms, some of which are debatable, have been made of the Molesworth Committee, notably that its members were prejudiced, that they were strongly influenced by Wakefieldian ideas, and that their use of evidence was questionable.

Monash, Sir John (1865-1931), engineer and soldier, was born in Melbourne. His father was a German-Jewish merchant. Monash was educated at Scotch College and the University of Melbourne. Before the First World War he practised as an engineer, becoming a pioneer in reinforced concrete construction. He joined the Melbourne University Rifles in 1884, was commissioned in the Garrison Artillery, commanded the Australian Intelligence Corps in Victoria in 1908, and became a colonel of an infantry brigade in 1913. During the First World War he took the 4th Australian Infantry Brigade to Egypt, and commanded it throughout the *Gallipoli campaign. He then took command of the 3rd Division, which he trained in England in 1916, and then took into action in France. His notable characteristics of meticulous planning, and lucid exposition of his plans (particularly to those who had to execute them), were already evident, and were exemplified again in his division's first major engagement, the Battle of Messines, which began on 7 June 1917. In May 1918 he took command of the Australian Corps. He further enhanced his reputation as a commander, particularly in the Battle of Amiens, which began on 8 August 1918. After the war Monash was appointed general manager of the Victorian State Electricity Commission in 1920, and in 1921 chairman of the Commission. He was responsible for the development of brown coal resources in the La Trobe Valley. Monash, who was also active in other public affairs, died in Melbourne. His publications include *The Australian Victories in France in 1918* (1920) and *War Letters* (1933).

Moncrieff, Gladys (1892–1976), singer, was born in Bundaberg, Queensland. She appeared in vaudeville, before being employed by *Williamson. 'Our Glad', as she became known, appeared in many operettas and musical comedies, including *The Maid of the Mountains* (in which she performed more than 3000 times between 1921 and 1952), *The Merry Widow, The Southern Maid, The Chocolate Soldier* and *Rio Rita*. She appeared in London in the mid-1920s, in New Guinea during the Second World War, and in Korea during the *Korean War, but spent most of her life in Australia. Her autobiography, *My Life of Song*, was published in 1971.

Moran, Patrick Francis (1830–1911), Roman Catholic archbishop, was born in Ireland and educated in Rome. He became a priest in 1853, and was Vice-Principal of St Agatha's College, Rome, from 1856 to 1866. Moran then returned to Ireland, where he was private secretary to Bishop Cullen, his uncle, from 1866 to 1872, and was Bishop of Ossory from

1872 to 1884, when he was appointed Archbishop of Sydney. In 1885 he was made a cardinal. Moran was responsible for building many Catholic institutions, including St Patrick's College (a seminary at Manly); supported the labour movement and federation; and advocated Home Rule. He wrote a number of books and pamphlets.

Morant, Harry Harbord ('Breaker'): *Boer War; *Bulletin*

Moreton Bay is a large bay on the Queensland coast near *Brisbane. It is flanked by Bribie, Moreton and Stradbroke Islands. James Cook, who discovered it in 1770, named it after the Earl of Morton. John Oxley explored the area in 1823. A *penal settlement was established on its shores in 1824, but was soon moved to Brisbane, where it remained until 1839. Patrick Logan became the commandant of the settlement in 1826. He was killed by Aborigines in 1830, near present-day Mount Beppo, while on an exploratory expedition. Although free settlers were banned from the Moreton Bay District, some began to arrive in 1840; the ban was lifted in 1842. The Moreton Bay District was separated from New South Wales, and proclaimed the colony of Queensland, in 1859.

Mort, Thomas Sutcliffe (1816–78), businessman, was born in Bolton, Lancashire. His father was a manufacturer. Mort arrived in Sydney as a clerk in 1838, became an auctioneer and broker in 1843, and ran Sydney's first regular wool sales. He became involved in various mining ventures; established a dock and engineering works, where ships and railway locomotives were built, and a system of profit-sharing with employees was implemented for some time, at Balmain; and developed a large dairy estate at Bodalla, New South Wales. Mort contributed much to the development of refrigeration techniques, but died shortly before frozen meat was successfully shipped from Australia.

Mount Isa, one of Australia's major mining centres, lies in the Selwyn Range in north-western Queensland. John Campbell Miles, a prospector, discovered

ore bearing silver and lead at Mount Isa, which he
named, in 1923. Mount Isa Mines Limited was
founded in 1924, soon took over leases, and developed
the field, which has yielded copper, silver, lead and
zinc. The shire became a city in 1968. Mining continues at Mount Isa, sometimes described as the
'Copper City', in the 1980s.

**Mueller, Baron Sir Ferdinand Jakob Heinrich
von** (1825-96), botanist, was born in Rostock,
Schleswig-Holstein. His father was a customs commissioner. Mueller studied pharmacy and botany,
before migrating in 1847 to South Australia, where
he worked as a chemist and then as a farmer. He
moved to Melbourne in 1852, was appointed Government Botanist in 1853 (a position he held until his
death), and undertook several expeditions in Victoria, during which he noted many previously
unknown plant species. He took part in A. C. Gregory's North West Australia Expedition (1855-6).
Mueller was the director of the Melbourne Botanical
Gardens from 1857 to 1873. He also undertook expeditions in Western Australia and Tasmania. Mueller
had extensive interests, belonged to numerous societies, and received many honours. He published
hundreds of papers and books, including *Fragmenta
Phytographiae Australiae* (1858-82), *The Natural
Capabilities of the Colony of Victoria* (1875), *Select
Plants Readily Eligible for Industrial Culture or Nat-
uralization in Victoria* (1876), *Eucalyptographia, A
Descriptive Atlas of the Eucalypts of Australia and
the adjoining Islands* (1879-84) and *Key to the System of Victorian Plants* (1885-8), and assisted with
the preparation of George Bentham's *Flora Austra-
liensis* (1863-78)).

Munro-Ferguson, Sir Ronald Craufurd: *Novar,
Ronald Craufurd Munro-Ferguson, Viscount

Murdoch, Sir Walter Logie Forbes (1874-1970),
essayist, was born in Scotland, the son of a Presbyterian minister. He came to Victoria with his family
in 1884, was educated at Scotch College and the
University of Melbourne, became a schoolteacher,
and also began writing for newspapers. Murdoch

lectured in English at the University of Melbourne from 1903 to 1911, was Professor of English at the University of Western Australia from 1912 to 1939, and was Chancellor of the latter from 1943 to 1947. Western Australia's second university was named after him. His best-known works are his essays, which he contributed to newspapers for many years. Many of these were later published in collections such as *Speaking Personally* (1930), *Saturday Mornings* (1931) and *Moreover* (1932). He also edited a number of anthologies, including *The Oxford Book of Australian Verse* (1918). His other publications include *Alfred Deakin, A Sketch* (1923).

Murray, Sir John Hubert Plunkett (1861-1940), administrator, was born in Manly, New South Wales, and educated in Australia and England, where he was called to the Bar from the Inner Temple in 1886. After returning to Australia, he practised as a barrister. During the Boer War, he commanded the New South Wales Irish Rifles. He was appointed chief judicial officer of British New Guinea in 1904, became acting Administrator of the area in 1907, and served as the first Lieutenant-Governor of Papua under Australian rule from 1908 to 1940. He attempted to encourage European enterprises in Papua, did much to bring Papua under government control, and introduced welfare measures in fields such as education and health. Difficulties facing him included problems relating to the First World War, antagonism displayed by some white settlers (especially in the period around 1920), the effects of the *Great Depression, and a general lack of finance. Sir Hubert Murray died while in office.

Music Conservatoriums have been founded in various places in Australia. One in Melbourne, attached to the University of Melbourne, was founded in 1894. Some of its functions have since been transferred to the Victorian College of Arts, which first took music students in 1974. The Conservatorium became known as the University's Faculty of Music. The Elder Conservatorium of Music, attached to the University of Adelaide, was founded in 1898. The New

South Wales State Conservatorium of Music (the first director of which was Henri Verbrugghen) was founded in 1916, and the Newcastle Conservatorium of Music in 1952. The Queensland Conservatorium of Music was established in 1957, and the Tasmanian Conservatorium of Music in 1962. The latter institution became part of the University of Tasmania in 1981, and that University's Faculty of Music in 1984. A number of other schools of music and university departments of music have also been established.

Myall Creek (near present-day Inverell), New South Wales, was the scene of the killing of at least twenty-eight Aboriginal men, women and children, by white station-hands in June 1838. As a result, eleven whites were tried for murder, but were acquitted. However, seven of them were retried, found guilty and hanged. There was much public protest. Prosecution of whites for such an occurrence was unusual.

Myer, Sidney (né Simcha) **Baevski** (1878–1934), businessman and philanthropist, was born in Russia. He came to Victoria in the late 1890s, and initially sold clothing and drapery. He and his brother bought a business in Bendigo in 1908, and then one in Bourke Street, Melbourne, in 1911. A public company was established, and other businesses, including woollen mills in Ballarat, were acquired. Myer donated money for various philanthropic causes, including the building of the Yarra Boulevard during the Great Depression, and left money for the establishment of a Sidney Myer Trust. Other family members continued in the business after his death. In 1985 the Myer organization merged with the company founded by *Coles.

N

Namatjira, Albert (1902–59), artist, was born at the Lutheran Hermannsburg Mission, near Alice Springs, in the Northern Territory. He was an Aborigine of the Aranda people. He was educated at the mission school. In the mid-1930s Rex Battarbee tutored him in the use of water-colours. Namatjira became famous for his water-colour landscapes of central Australia. He was granted Australian citizenship in 1957. He became the subject of controversy in 1958, when he was charged with supplying liquor to members of his people (who were not Australian citizens). He was found guilty and sentenced to six months' imprisonment (later commuted to three months'). He was allowed to serve his sentence in the open. He died in Alice Springs.

National Council of Women of Australia (NCWA): An independent, non-sectarian, non-political women's organization. The International Council of Women, to which the NCWA belongs, was founded in the United States of America in 1888. The *National Council of Women of New South Wales was formed in 1896. National Councils of Women were later formed in the other Australian states and territories. The national organization was formed in 1931. Members of the National Councils of Women have worked for causes such as *equal pay, the introduction of policewomen, and uniform divorce laws. Notable members have included Rose *Scott, Vida *Goldstein and Alice *Henry.

National Country Party: *National Party

Nationalist Party: A political party formed during the First World War. The *National Labor Party and the *Liberal Party merged to form it early in 1917, following the split in the *Australian Labor Party. Its full title was the Australian National Federation; at times it was also called the National Party. The Nationalist Party, stressing a 'Win-the-War' policy, defeated Labor in the federal elections of 1917. It continued in government until 1929, governing in coalition with the Country Party from 1923 onwards. *Hughes led the party until 1923, when he was forced to resign as leader before the Country Party would join the Nationalists in a coalition. *Bruce succeeded him. The Bruce–*Page Government, many of whose policies were summed up in the slogan *'Men, Money and Markets', was defeated by Labor in the elections of 1929. Bruce lost his own seat. *Latham succeeded Bruce as leader. The Nationalist Party was absorbed into the newly formed *United Australia Party in 1931. Nationalists also governed in each of the states, either alone or in coalition with other parties, at various times.

National Labor Party: A political party. During the First World War the *Australian Labor Party split, basically over the issue of *conscription. After the first conscription referendum, *Hughes, the Prime Minister, either left or was removed from (a debatable point) the Labor Party on 14 November 1916. He took with him thirteen Labor Members of the House of Representatives and eleven Labor Senators. Hughes and his followers called themselves the National Labor Party. This rump party governed federally with the support of the *Liberal Party. National Labor and the Liberals merged to form the *Nationalist Party on 9 January 1917.

National Party (1917-31): *Nationalist Party

National Party of Australia: A political party that largely represents rural interests. Farmers' representatives were elected to colonial (later state) parliaments from the 1890s onwards. The First World War acted as a catalyst in the formation of Australian country parties. By the early 1920s they existed (under various names) in all states. A number of farmers' candidates were elected to Commonwealth Parliament in the elections of 1919, and in 1920 they formed the Australian Country Party. It has governed federally in coalition with the *Nationalist Party (1923-9), the *United Australia Party (1934-9, 1940-1) and the *Liberal Party of Australia (1949-72, 1975-83). Its federal parliamentary leaders have included William James McWilliams (1920-1), *Page (1921-39), Archie Galbraith Cameron (1939-40), *Fadden (1941-58), *McEwen (1958-71), John Douglas Anthony (1971-83) and Ian McCahon Sinclair (1983-). Three have become Prime Ministers, albeit for very brief periods—Page (1939), Fadden (1941) and

McEwen (1967–8). The party has also governed (under various names), mostly in coalition with other parties, for periods in New South Wales, Victoria, Queensland, South Australia, Western Australia and the Northern Territory. The party's national name was changed to National Country Party in the mid-1970s, and to the National Party of Australia in 1982. Several of the state branches share the latter name.

National Security Act: An Act passed in 1939, and later amended a number of times, that gave the Commonwealth Government very wide powers, both general and specific, relating to public safety and defence. It operated during, and for some time after, the Second World War. Its equivalent during the First World War was the *War Precautions Act.*

National Service Scheme: *Conscription

Native Police (also known as Black Police): Forces of Aboriginal police, which were used in some parts of Australia during the nineteenth century. The forces consisted of black troopers led by white officers. During the period of the *Port Phillip Protectorate, native police were introduced in the Port Phillip District in 1842, and operated there until 1852. They were re-formed briefly to hunt *Kelly and his gang during the 1870s. Native police were introduced in New South Wales in 1848, and used mainly in the northern districts (part of present-day Queensland). When Queensland became a separate colony in 1859, it inherited the system. Native police continued to operate in Queensland until the late 1890s. The force there usually consisted of between 100 and 200 men. Most were used to patrol the frontiers of white settlement. The native police were engaged in many conflicts with the Aborigines, and killed many of them.

Navy: *Royal Australian Navy

NCWA: *National Council of Women of Australia

New Australia was the name given to the first of two utopian settlements founded by Australian socialists in Paraguay. After the failure of the *Maritime and *Shearers' Strikes of 1890 and 1891, a New Australia Co-operative Settlement Association was formed. About 200 settlers, led by *Lane, left Australia on the *Royal Tar* on 16 July 1893. They established New Australia on land provided by the Paraguayan Government at Puesto De Las Ovejas, 175 kilometres south of Asunción, on 28 September 1893. Another group of settlers arrived on 31 December 1893. Lane, and sixty-three others, left the settlement in May 1894 and founded another, called Cosme, in July. An imbalance of men and women, together with economic, physical and leadership difficulties, contributed to New Australia's demise. A new agreement with the Paraguayan Government was reached, and the settlement's assets were divided in 1897. Cosme faced similar problems, and its assets were divided in 1929. Descendants of the settlers still lived in Paraguay in the 1980s.

New Australians: A term used in Australia during the late 1940s and 1950s to describe migrants, especially those from European countries. *Calwell, Minister for Information and Immigration in the *Chifley Labor Government, introduced the term during the period of mass *immigration following the Second World War. Its public use was encouraged. Its purpose was to assist migrants to assimilate. It was designed to replace derogatory terms such as 'Balt', 'Dago', 'Pommy' and 'Reffo'.

Newcastle, a city and port in New South Wales, is situated at the mouth of the Hunter River. John Shortland found the site in 1791 while searching for escaped convicts, named the river, and discovered coal, some of which was exported in 1799. In 1801 small numbers of soldiers and convicts settled at Coal Harbour (as it was then called) to mine coal, but were withdrawn the following year. A *penal settlement existed at the site, renamed Newcastle, from 1804 to 1824, convicts being employed in timber-getting, coal-mining and lime-burning. The *Australian Agricultural Company became involved in coal-mining at Newcastle in the 1820s, developing a monopoly that lasted until 1850. Newcastle became a municipality in 1859, and a city in 1885, and was connected by rail to Sydney (a distance of 168 kilometres) in 1889. The *Broken Hill Proprietary Company Limited opened iron and steel works at Newcastle in 1915. These and coal-mining were still important in the 1980s. The city's population in 1981 was 135,194.

New England New State Movement: The most significant of a number of movements towards the formation of new Australian states that have occurred since Federation in 1901. The area concerned is that of New England in New South Wales. *Page led the first attempt at Grafton in 1915. The Cohen Royal Commission, appointed by the New South Wales Government, recommended against the formation of any new states in 1925. The New England movement revived during the *Great Depression; it adopted a draft state constitution at Maitland in 1931, and unsuccessfully asked the Commonwealth Government to hold a referendum on the subject. In 1935 the Nicholas Royal Commission, also appointed by the New South Wales Government, reported that New South Wales could be divided into three areas, each of which could vote on the matter at a referendum. The New South Wales Government did not act on this report. The New England movement revived again at Armidale in 1948; Nicholas's suggested boundaries were accepted, and a draft state constitution was adopted in 1949. A constituent assembly of New England was established in 1954, holding its first meeting the following year. A referendum was finally held in the area on 29 April 1967. The proposal was defeated: 198,812 people voted against it, 168,103 in favour of it.

New Guard: A quasi-fascist organization formed during the *Great Depression. A small group, led by Eric Campbell, left the Movement,[1] or Old Guard (as it became known), and formed the New Guard at

---

[1]This organization is not to be confused with the Catholic Social Movement, also known as the Movement.

a meeting held at the Imperial Service Club in Sydney in 1931. Several weeks later Campbell was elected leader. At its peak in 1932 the New Guard probably had more than 50,000 members, many of whom were ex-servicemen. It published two journals, the *New Guard* (1931-2) and *Liberty* (1932-4). Campbell heavily criticized J. T. *Lang, the New South Wales Premier, at a Lane Cove rally in 1932; he was fined £2 for using insulting language, but successfully appealed. In 1932 the New Guard petitioned Philip Woolcott Game, the New South Wales Governor, for the dismissal of the Lang Government. Francis de Groot, a New Guard member, slashed the ribbon at the opening of the *Sydney Harbour Bridge in 1932; he was fined £5, with £4 costs, for offensive behaviour. Eight New Guard members attacked 'Jock' Garden, one of the founders of the *Communist Party of Australia, in 1932; each was convicted of assault and was sentenced to three months' jail. Police were said to be preparing charges of seditious conspiracy against New Guard leaders shortly before the dismissal of the Lang Government; charges were not pressed. A Royal Commission and a commission of inquiry were proposed, but neither eventuated. The Centre Party, a political wing of the New Guard, fielded several candidates, including Campbell, at the New South Wales elections of 1935. All were unsuccessful. The New Guard was virtually dissolved by the end of 1935.

New Guinea is a large island in the Pacific Ocean, to the north of Australia. It is divided from Australia by Torres Strait, which was discovered by Luis Vaez de Torres, a Spanish navigator, in 1606. Portuguese navigators were the first Europeans to visit it, during the sixteenth century. It was already inhabited. Spanish, Dutch, British and French navigators later followed the Portuguese. Permanent white settlement did not begin in New Guinea until the 1870s. New Guinea is now divided, at longitude 141°E, into *Irian Jaya (in the west) and *Papua New Guinea (in the east).

New Holland: The early name by which the Australian continent was known. Seventeenth-century

New Italy

Dutch navigators named the western part of the continent *'Nova Hollandia'*, and the name came to be used to describe the entire continent. It was used until about the 1820s, by which time the name 'Australia' was in wide use.

New Italy: Popular name given to an Italian settlement near Woodburn on the Richmond River, New South Wales. A group of about 200 Italian people arrived in Sydney in 1881, after unsuccessfully attempting to settle in New Ireland. Some time later they founded the settlement that became known as New Italy. In 1885 it consisted of fifty-three farms. The settlement lasted into the twentieth century, although some of its members had begun to leave about ten years after its foundation.

New Norcia: A Benedictine mission settlement in Western Australia, on the Moore River, about 130 kilometres north of Perth. Two Spanish Benedictine monks, Dom Salvado and Dom Serra, founded a mission, first known as Central, in the area in 1846. In 1847 they chose the present site and name (after St Benedict's birthplace, Norcia, in Italy). Their main aim was to teach *Aborigines to become Christians. A church, a monastery, schools and a farm were established. Aborigines were taught farming and other skills there. The mission was separated from the Diocese of Perth in 1859, and the monastery was made an abbey in 1867. New Norcia continues to exist in the 1980s.

New Protection: The name given to a socio-economic policy. In 1907 *Deakin, one of its chief exponents, described New Protection in the following way:

The 'Old' Protection contented itself with making good wages possible. The 'New' Protection seeks to make them actual. It aims at according the manufacturer that degree of exemption from unfair outside competition which will enable him to pay fair and reasonable wages without impairing the maintenance and extension of his industry, or its capacity to supply the local market. It does not stop here. Having put the manufacturer in a position to pay good wages, it goes on to assure the public that he does pay them.[1]

Such ideas had been discussed in Australia since the 1890s. Deakin's Protectionist Government, supported by the Labor Party, attempted to implement them between 1905 and 1908. It introduced legislation such as the *Excise Tariff (Agricultural Machinery) Act 1906* and the *Australian Industries Preservation Act 1906*. Such legislation was designed to introduce New Protection by means of bounties, rebates, regulations and restrictions. The *Harvester Judgement was an outcome of New Protection. The Labor Party incorporated New Protection into its party policy in 1908. The *High Court found much of the New Protection legislation to be constitutionally invalid, for example, in *Barger's Case* (1908).

New South Wales: A state of the *Commonwealth of Australia since the latter's creation in 1901. In 1770 James *Cook took possession for Britain of the eastern part of present-day Australia. In 1786 Britain decided to establish a penal colony, Australia's first white settlement, at *Botany Bay. In 1788 the *First Fleet arrived at Port Jackson. *Transportation to New South Wales ended in 1840. Partial representative government was granted in 1842; *responsible government was proclaimed in 1855. Originally New South Wales comprised much of Australia. *Van Diemen's Land (present-day Tasmania) was separated from New South Wales in 1825, the *Port Phillip District (present-day Victoria) in 1851, the *Moreton Bay District (present-day Queensland) in 1859; the Northern Territory was annexed to South Australia in 1863, and land for the Australian Capital Territory was transferred to the Commonwealth in 1911. *New Zealand was administered from New South Wales in 1840 and 1841.

New South Wales Corps: A unit of the British Army, raised in England in 1789 by *Grose, specifically to police the colony of *New South Wales. It

---

[1]Cited in W. Murdoch, *Alfred Deakin, A Sketch* (Constable, London, 1923), p. 236.

replaced the marines who had sailed with the *First
Fleet. The first detachment, consisting of 100 men
commanded by Nicholas Nepean, arrived in New
South Wales in 1790, having sailed with the *Second
Fleet. *Macarthur was one of the officers. The second
detachment, commanded by Grose, arrived in 1792.
Some remaining marines formed a company, commanded by George Johnston, of the Corps. The
Corps, which has since been dubbed the 'Rum Corps'
because of its involvement in the rum trade, greatly
increased its power and influence during the interregnum (1792-5). It quelled the *Castle Hill Uprising
of 1804. Johnston, and the Corps, played a major
role in the *Rum Rebellion of 1808. As a result, the
Corps was replaced by the 73rd Regiment, which
some of the men joined; most of the officers, and
some of the men, returned to England in 1810. The
Corps became the 102nd Regiment when it was
recalled to England. Johnston was cashiered in 1811.

New Unionism is the term used to describe the
expansion of the trade union movement in Australia,
and changes in its nature, from the late 1870s and
1880s onwards. Before then most trade unions had
been small craft unions, restricted to skilled and semi-
skilled workers. They charged high membership fees,
were local in organization, and were concerned with
issues such as hours, pay and benefits (for example,
for sickness). The so-called 'new' unions aimed at
mass membership of unskilled and semi-skilled
workers in large industries such as shearing and
mining. They charged low fees, were inter-colonial
in organization, and were more prepared to resort
to strikes and political action to gain their demands
that the earlier unions had been. The Amalgamated
Miners' Association (AMA) and the Amalgamated
Shearers' Union (ASU) are examples of 'new' unions
formed during the 1880s.

New Zealand, a country situated in the southern
Pacific Ocean, comprises the North Island, the South
Island and a number of smaller islands. Its first
inhabitants were Polynesians. The first Europeans

known to have visited present-day New Zealand were *Tasman (1642), James *Cook (1769–70, 1773, 1777), and the French explorers Jean de Surville (1769) and Marion du Fresne (1772). Europeans seeking seals, whales, timber and flax went there from the 1790s. Missionaries, notably *Marsden, began to go there from 1814. There were probably about 2000 European settlers in New Zealand by the late 1830s. A British Resident, James Busby, arrived in 1833. The New Zealand Company (originally Association), which was formed in Britain by *Wakefield and others in 1839, established settlements in New Zealand from the 1840s. New Zealand was briefly a dependency of *New South Wales in 1840 and 1841. William Hobson, the first Lieutenant-Governor of New Zealand, arrived in January 1840, signed the Treaty of Waitangi with Maoris in the North Island in February 1840, and formally annexed New Zealand for Britain in May 1840. New Zealand was proclaimed a separate British colony in 1841, with Hobson becoming its first Governor. A form of self-government was granted in 1852, responsible government in 1856, and dominion status in 1907. New Zealand showed some interest in federation with the Australian colonies, but finally did not join. New Zealand ratified the *Statute of *Westminster* (1931) in 1947, and is a member of both the *Commonwealth of Nations and the *United Nations Organization. Some Australians took part in the *Maori Wars during the nineteenth century. Australians and New Zealanders, known as *Anzacs, have fought together at Gallipoli and elsewhere this century. Australia, New Zealand and the United States of America signed the *ANZUS Pact in 1951.

Nineteen Counties: The official area of white settlement in *New South Wales during the 1830s. The counties, which were proclaimed in the *Sydney Gazette* on 17 October 1829, were Argyle, Bathurst, Bligh, Brisbane, Camden, Cook, Cumberland, Durham, Georgiana, Gloucester, Hunter, King, Murray, Northumberland, Phillip, Roxburgh, St Vincent, Wellington and Westmoreland. *Squatters (some with authorization, others without) settled beyond the Nineteen Counties.

Nolan, Sir Sidney Robert (1917-), artist, was born in Melbourne. His father was a tram-driver. Nolan was educated at state and technical schools in Melbourne, and worked in various jobs before taking up painting in the 1930s. During the Second World War he served in the *army from 1942 to 1945. He was stationed in the Victorian Wimmera, which inspired some of his paintings. Nolan has travelled, lived, worked and exhibited his work in numerous countries. McCulloch has said of him: 'By 1962 Nolan had achieved a more extensive international reputation than any other Australian painter of his own or preceding generation.'[1] He is perhaps best known for his paintings based on the theme of Ned *Kelly. Many of his other paintings are of Australian historical and outback subjects. Nolan has been awarded numerous prizes and fellowships, including the Dunlop Australian Art Contest (1950), an Italian Government Scholarship (1956), a Commonwealth Fund Fellowship to the United States of America (1958) and the Britannica Australian Award (1969).

Norfolk Island, a small Pacific Island, has been an Australian external territory since 1914. James *Cook was the first white person to discover the island, in 1774. It was uninhabited at the time. *Phillip established a convict settlement there, as a branch of New South Wales, in 1788. Attempts to develop a flax industry were unsuccessful, and the first settlement was abandoned in 1814. A second, mainly for convicts undergoing secondary punishment, was established in 1825. *Maconochie experimented in penal reform there from 1840 to 1844. The second settlement was finally abandoned in 1856, the year in which Pitcairn Islanders (descendants of *Bounty* mutineers and Tahitian women) settled on the island. Many of their descendants still live there.

---

[1] Alan McCulloch, *Encyclopedia of Australian Art* (Hutchinson of Australia, Melbourne, 1968), p. 415.

North Australia (also known as the Gladstone Colony) was a short-lived British colony on the central coast of present-day Queensland. The British Secretary of State for the Colonies, William Ewart Gladstone, established it in 1846. The colony was to comprise all of New South Wales (as it then was) north of latitude 26°S. Its population was to consist of expirees (convicts whose terms of transportation had expired) and conditionally pardoned convicts from Van Diemen's Land, and *exiles from Britain. There was vigorous opposition in New South Wales to the proposal. The new colony's Superintendent, George Barney, chose Port Curtis as the site for the capital in November 1846. He and the other first settlers, who included officials, soldiers and civilians, arrived there from Port Jackson in January 1847. More soldiers and civilians arrived soon after. The settlers at Port Curtis faced a number of problems, mostly relating to the climate. Meanwhile, Earl Grey, who had succeeded Gladstone as Secretary of State for the Colonies, wrote to Governor FitzRoy in November 1846, telling him of the British Government's decision to abandon the new settlement. This news reached Port Curtis in April 1847, and the settlement was abandoned shortly after. The town (later city) of Gladstone was later established on the site.

Northern Territory: A self-governing territory of Australia. The Dutch ship *Arnhem*, the first known European contact, visited the coast in 1623. *Tasman (1644), *Baudin (1801, 1803), *Flinders (1803) and Phillip Parker King (1818) followed. Several attempts were made to establish a permanent British commercial and strategic settlement in the north of Australia, partly because of fears that the French or others might settle in the area. The first party from New South Wales arrived at *Port Essington in 1824, took formal possession of the area, and founded Fort Dundas on Melville Island. Fort Dundas was abandoned in 1829. Fort Wellington, at Raffles Bay, lasted from 1838 to 1849. *Stuart crossed Australia from Adelaide to the northern coast in 1862, and the Northern Territory was annexed to South Australia in 1863.

Palmerston, at Escape Cliffs, was founded in 1864, but this site was abandoned in 1867. A new site was chosen for Palmerston in 1869. This settlement, later renamed *Darwin, proved to be permanent. The Commonwealth took over the administration of the Northern Territory in 1911. The Northern Territory was divided into North Australia and Central Australia, each separately administered, between 1926 and 1931. A Legislative Assembly was created in 1974, and the Northern Territory was granted self-government in 1978.

Novar, Ronald Craufurd Munro-Ferguson, Viscount (1860–1934), governor-general, was born in Scotland, and privately educated. He served in the Grenadier Guards from 1879 to 1884, was a Member of Parliament for many years (1884–5, 1886–1914), and was made a Privy Counsellor in 1910. As Sir Ronald Craufurd Munro-Ferguson, he was the Governor-General of Australia from 1914 to 1920. He was created a viscount in 1920, and was the Secretary for Scotland from 1922 to 1924.

Nuclear Tests were conducted in Australia by the British Government, with the agreement of the Australian Government, during the 1950s. Three bombs were exploded in the Monte Bello Islands in 1952 and 1953, two at Emu in 1953, and seven at Maralinga in 1956 and 1957. (The latter two sites both lie within the Woomera rocket range area.) Growing concern about the effects on the population led to the appointment in 1984 of a Royal Commission, headed by Mr Justice James McClelland, to inquire into the nuclear tests.

O

Olympic Games: The first of the modern Olympic Games, international sporting contests usually conducted every four years, was held in Athens in 1896. Australians have participated in each of the modern Olympic Games. Melbourne hosted the 1956 Olympic

Games, in which Australia was placed third, having won thirteen gold, eight silver and fourteen bronze medals, behind Russia and the United States of America.

'Our last man and our last shilling': A famous phrase originally used during the First World War. *Fisher promised that Australia would defend Britain to 'our last man and our last shilling' in several speeches given during the federal election campaign that coincided with the outbreak of war. As newly elected Prime Minister, he promised: 'We shall pledge our last man and our last shilling to see this war brought to a successful issue.'[1]

Overlanders: Popular name given to Australian stockmen, especially during the nineteenth century, who drove cattle and sheep over very long distances. The journeys of the early overlanders, into previously unoccupied areas of Australia, usually took months, sometimes years. Overlanding from New South Wales to the *Port Phillip District began in 1836; from New South Wales and the Port Phillip District to South Australia in the late 1830s; from New South Wales to the *Moreton Bay area in 1840; and across northern Australia in the 1880s. The main routes used in the late nineteenth century were the Murranji Track, from the Northern Territory to Queensland; the Birdsville Track, from Queensland to South Australia; and a track from Queensland to Victoria. Droving along these and other routes continues, but has declined since the development of rail and road transport, and refrigeration.

Overland Telegraph Line: Australia's first transcontinental telegraph system. It was completed in 1872. Charles (later Sir Charles) Todd, the South Australian Postmaster-General and Superintendent

---

[1]*Parliamentary Debates, LXXV,* cited in Ernest Scott, *Australia During the War* (Angus and Robertson, Sydney, second edition, 1937), p. 23. This is the eleventh volume of C. E. W. Bean (ed.), *The Official History of Australia in the War of 1914–1918* (Angus and Robertson, Sydney, 1921–37). This particular speech was given on 14 October 1914, but the phrase had been used earlier.

of Telegraphs, was largely responsible for the construction of the line, running from Port Augusta in South Australia to Port Darwin in the Northern Territory, a distance of about 2900 kilometres. The South Australian Government paid for the line, which enabled Australia, for the first time, to be linked (via Java) with the telegraph systems of Asia and Europe. The Overland Telegraph Line played an important role in Australia's overseas communication system for about ninety years.

P

Pacific Islanders: *Blackbirding

Page, Sir Earle Christmas Grafton (1880–1961), politician, was born at Grafton, New South Wales, was educated at Grafton State School, Sydney High School and the University of Sydney, and then practised as a surgeon. During the First World War he served in the Australian Army Medical Corps, in Egypt and France, from 1916 to 1918. Early in the war Page had been active in the *New England New State movement; after the war he entered federal politics. He was a Member of the House of Representatives from 1919 to 1961, representing the Country Party from 1920 onwards. He led that party from 1921 onwards. Page was Deputy Prime Minister in coalition Governments from 1923 to 1929, and from 1934 to 1939, and briefly Prime Minister following the death of *Lyons in 1939. He was Treasurer from 1923 to 1929, and was responsible for the establishment of the Loan Council, which he chaired from 1924 to 1929, and for the introduction of the *Financial Agreement. He was Chancellor of the University of New England from 1955 to 1960. Page was defeated at the 1961 elections. He died during the election count.

Palmer, Edward Vivian (Vance) (1885–1959), writer and critic, was born in Queensland. His father was a schoolteacher. Palmer was educated at Ipswich

Grammar School. He then worked in various jobs, including those of clerk, journalist, tutor and book-keeper, in Australia and overseas. During the First World War he enlisted with the Australian Imperial Force, but did not see action. He spent most of his life in Australia. Like his wife, Janet (Nettie) *Palmer, he did much to foster Australian literature. He wrote poetry, prose and drama; he helped to found a dramatic group, the Pioneer Players, which existed from 1922 to 1926; he was active on the Advisory Board of the Commonwealth Literary Fund, which he chaired from 1947 to 1953; and he encouraged other writers. His poetry includes *The Forerunners* (1915) and *The Camp* (1920). His collections of short stories include *The World of Men* (1915), *Separate Lives* (1931), *Sea and Spinifex* (1934) and *Let the Birds Fly* (1955). His novels include *The Man Hamilton* (1928), *Men Are Human* (1930), *The Passage* (1930), *Daybreak* (1932), *Legend for Sanderson* (1937), *Cyclone* (1947), *Golconda* (1948), *Seedtime* (1957) and *The Big Fellow* (1959); the last three form a trilogy. His plays include *The Black Horse and Other Plays* (1924) and *Hail Tomorrow, A Play in Four Acts* (1947). His critical works include *National Portraits* (1940), *A. G. Stephens, His Life and Work* (1941), *Frank Wilmot* (1942) and *The Legend of the Nineties* (1954).

Palmer (née Higgins), **Janet (Nettie) Gertrude** (1885-1964), writer and critic, was born in Victoria. She was educated at the Presbyterian Ladies' College, Melbourne, and at the University of Melbourne. She married Edward Vivian (Vance) *Palmer in 1914. She spent most of her life in Australia. Nettie Palmer did much to foster Australian literature. She wrote in various genres, lectured for organizations such as the Commonwealth Literary Fund and the Melbourne University Extension Board, and encouraged other writers. She died in Melbourne. Her poetry includes *The South Wind* (1914) and *Shadowy Paths* (1915). Her critical works include *Modern Australian Literature, 1900-23* (1924), *Henry Bournes Higgins, A Memoir* (1931), *Talking It Over* (1932) and *Henry Handel Richardson, A Study* (1950). Her *Fourteen*

Years, Extracts from a Private Journal, 1925-1939
(1948) is autobiographical. She also edited *Australian
Storybook, A Selection from the Best Australian
Short Stories Written in the 20th Century* (1928).

Palmerston: *Darwin

Papua New Guinea: An independent member of
the *Commonwealth of Nations. It comprises the
eastern part of the island of *New Guinea and nearby
islands. Britain rejected Queensland's annexation in
1883 of south-eastern New Guinea, proclaimed a protectorate over this area in 1884, and finally annexed
it in 1888, after Queensland, New South Wales and
Victoria had agreed to contribute financially to its
administration (which was to be handled by Britain
and Queensland). British New Guinea was transferred to the newly created Commonwealth of Australia in 1902. The latter formally took control in
1906; British New Guinea became Papua. Germany
had administered north-eastern New Guinea from
1884 onwards. Australia captured German New Guinea in 1914, at the beginning of the First World War;
she administered the Territory of New Guinea, as
it became known, under a *League of Nations mandate from 1921 and under United Nations trusteeship
from 1946. Japan occupied much of New Guinea during the Second World War. Australia administered
Papua and the Territory of New Guinea together from
1946 onwards. The two territories were formally
united as Papua New Guinea in 1949. Papua New
Guinea gained self-government in 1973 and independence in 1975.

Paris Peace Conference: A meeting of the Allied
and Associated Powers, held in Paris in 1919-20,
shortly after the conclusion of the First World War.
Its purpose was to determine the peace settlement.
The provisions of the Treaties of *Versailles, St Ger-
main, Neuilly, Trianon and Sèvres were determined.
In a significant move for Australia, the Dominions
were represented at the Conference. *Hughes, as one
of Australia's two representatives, played an active
and controversial role in the proceedings.

Parkes, Sir Henry (1815-96), politician, was born in England. His father was a tenant farmer, later a gardener. Parkes's formal education was limited. He held labouring jobs before serving an apprenticeship as a bone and ivory turner. He then founded a business, which, like several of his later businesses, failed. Parkes and his wife sailed to Sydney as bounty immigrants in 1839. He worked as a labourer, then in an ironmongery and brass-foundry, and then in the Customs Department from 1840 to 1844. Parkes contributed to a number of newspapers, including the *Atlas*, the *Australasian Chronicle*, the *Launceston Examiner* and the *Sydney Morning Herald*, during the 1840s. He established, edited and owned the *Empire* newspaper, which was published from 1850 to 1858. Parkes's political career was extensive. He was active in a number of political campaigns (notably opposing *transportation, supporting Robert Lowe, and supporting J. D. *Lang), before serving as a Member of the Legislative Council of New South Wales (1854-6). He was then a Member of the colony's Legislative Assembly (1856, 1858, 1859-61, 1864-70, 1872-84, 1885-95). He was Colonial Secretary (1866-8, 1872-5, 1877, 1878-83, 1887-89, 1889-91), Premier (1872-5, 1877, 1878-83, 1887-89, 1889-91) and Secretary for Lands (1883). Parkes lectured on *immigration in England between 1861 and 1863. His role in the *federation movement earned him the title 'Father of Federation', but there has been some speculation about his motives. He eschewed the Federal Council, but later declared his support for federation, notably in his *Tenterfield Oration. The Australasian Federation Conference discussed his proposals in 1890. He chaired the *Federal Convention in Sydney in 1891. Parkes died in New South Wales. He wrote poetry and prose, including *Stolen Moments* (1842), *Murmurs of the Stream* (1857), *Australian Views of England* (1869), *Studies in Rhyme* (1870), *Speeches on Various Occasions* (1876), *The Beauteous Terrorist and Other Poems* (1885), *Fragmentary Thoughts* (1889), *The Federal Government of Australasia* (1890), *Fifty Years in the Making of Australian History* (1892) and *Sonnets and Other Verses* (1895).

Parliaments: The term commonly used to describe the legislatures of each of the states (formerly colonies) and the *Commonwealth of Australia. Legislative Councils with nominated members first met in New South Wales in 1823, Van Diemen's Land in 1825, Western Australia in 1832 and South Australia in 1842. Councils with nominated and elected members first met in New South Wales in 1843, Victoria, South Australia and Van Diemen's Land in 1851, and Western Australia in 1870. Bicameral parliaments (those with two legislative chambers), based partly on the British system, first met in Victoria, New South Wales, South Australia and Tasmania (former Van Diemen's Land) in 1856, Queensland in 1859, and Western Australia in 1890. Members of the lower houses (called the Legislative Assembly in New South Wales, Victoria, Queensland and Western Australia, and the House of Assembly in South Australia and Tasmania) were, and are, elected. Manhood *suffrage for these houses was introduced in South Australia in 1856, Victoria in 1857, New South Wales in 1858, Queensland in 1859, Western Australia in 1893, and Tasmania in 1900. Female suffrage was introduced in South Australia in 1894, Western Australia in 1899, New South Wales in 1901, Tasmania in 1903, Queensland in 1905 and Victoria in 1908. Members of the Western Australian Legislative Council were nominated between 1890 and 1893, and then elected. Members of the New South Wales Legislative Council were nominated until 1934, then indirectly elected until 1978, then directly elected. Members of the Queensland Legislative Council, which was abolished in 1922, were nominated. Members of the Legislative Councils in Victoria, South Australia, Western Australia (from 1893) and Tasmania, were elected, but a special franchise system (based on qualifications such as property, profession, education or age) operated in them for many years, eventually being abolished in all four states between 1950 and 1973. According to the Constitution, the federal parliament consists of 'the Queen, a Senate, and a House of Representatives'. The Senate and the House of Representatives first met in 1901. Members of these two houses have always been elected. Those people eligible to vote for the lower house in each state were eligible to vote for both houses of the federal parliament at the first federal election, full adult suffrage for both houses being introduced in 1902. Methods of dealing with deadlocks between the two houses vary in some of the parliaments.

Parramatta, now a city that forms part of the Sydney metropolitan area, is situated about twenty-four kilometres west of Sydney Cove. Governor *Phillip, who explored the area in April 1788, established a farming settlement there, the second white settlement in Australia, in November 1788. The settlement was originally known as Rose Hill; its name was changed to Parramatta (an Aboriginal name that probably means 'head of the river' or 'head of the waters') in 1791.

Paterson, Andrew Barton (1864-1941), poet, was born near Orange, New South Wales. His father was a grazier. Paterson was educated at Sydney Grammar School and the University of Sydney, practised as a solicitor for some time, and then became a journalist. He was a war correspondent for the *Sydney Morning Herald* during the *Boer War and the *Boxer Rising. After his return to Sydney, Paterson continued in journalism; he edited the Sydney *Evening News* from 1904 to 1906, and the Sydney *Town and Country Journal* from 1907 to 1908. He was then a pastoralist for about six years. During the First World War he served as an ambulance officer in France and as a remount officer in Egypt. After the war he again returned to journalism and other writing, sometimes using the pseudonym 'The Banjo', and he is still usually referred to as 'Banjo' Paterson. He is best known for his bush ballads, which attained wide popularity. His poetry (much of which was first published in the *Bulletin*) includes *The Man from Snowy River, and Other Verses* (1895), *Rio Grande's Last Race, and Other Verses* (1902), *Saltbush Bill, J.P., and Other Verses* (1917), *The Collected Verse of A. B. Paterson* (1921) and *The Animals Noah Forgot* (1933). Paterson wrote the words of the famous

Australian song, *'Waltzing Matilda', in 1895, and edited *The Old Bush Songs, Composed and Sung in the Bushranging, Digging and Overlanding Days* (1905). Paterson's other publications include *An Outback Marriage* (1906), *Three Elephant Power and Other Stories* (1917), *The Shearer's Colt* (1936) and *Happy Dispatches* (1934), which is autobiographical.

Paterson, William (1755–1810), colonial administrator, was born in Scotland, pursued a military career, helped to raise the *New South Wales Corps, and arrived in New South Wales in 1791. Shortly afterwards he went to *Norfolk Island, where he commanded a detachment of the Corps until 1793. Paterson took control of the colony, following *Grose, from December 1794 to September 1795. Ill health forced Paterson to leave New South Wales in 1796, but he returned in 1799, when *King appointed him Lieutenant-Governor. Paterson administered the new settlement of Port Dalrymple, in *Van Diemen's Land, from 1804 to 1809. He returned to Sydney in the aftermath of the *Rum Rebellion, took over from *Foveaux, and remained in control from early in 1809 until *Macquarie took office early in 1810. Paterson sailed for England with the New South Wales Corps in 1810, but died while still at sea. He had also been an active botanist.

Patriotic Six: The popular name given to six non-official members of the *Van Diemen's Land Legislative Council who were involved in political controversy in 1845. They were Richard Dry, Michael Fenton, Thomas Gregson, William Kermode, John Kerr and Charles Swanston. Van Diemen's Land was still experiencing the *depression of the 1840s. The Six clashed with *Eardley-Wilmot, the Lieutenant-Governor, over annual estimates of expenditure for 1846. They opposed the use of local revenue for the payment of police and jails, believing that Britain should bear the cost, because it was caused by British *transportation. The Six walked out of the Council on 31 October, leaving it without a quorum, and resigned shortly afterwards. Eardley-Wilmot replaced them with other people, but was himself recalled in 1846, allegedly for neglecting the convict system. The Six were later reinstated, but the British Government's policy remained unchanged.

Payment of Members: The principle of payment of members of the lower houses of parliament was introduced in Victoria (on a temporary basis for some years) in 1870, Queensland in 1886, South Australia in 1887, New South Wales in 1889, Tasmania in 1890 and Western Australia in 1900. The payment of members of the upper houses followed later. It has always existed for the Commonwealth House of Representatives and Senate.

Penal Settlements: Settlements to which convicts who had committed further crimes within the Australian colonies were sent. *Newcastle, in New South Wales, was used as a penal settlement from 1804 to 1824. The first convicts sent there were some of those involved in the *Castle Hill Uprising. Port Macquarie (1821–30) and *Moreton Bay (1824–39) were also used as penal settlements. *Norfolk Island was resettled as a penal settlement in 1825; the last convicts left there in 1856. A penal settlement was established at *Macquarie Harbour, in Van Diemen's Land, in 1822. Building of *Port Arthur began in 1830, and the last convicts from Macquarie Harbour were transferred there several years later. Port Arthur, perhaps the best-known penal settlement, was closed in 1877.

Perth, the capital city of *Western Australia, lies on the banks of the Swan River, some sixteen kilometres from the mouth of the river. British free settlers, led by *Stirling, founded Perth in 1829. Perth was proclaimed a city in 1856. Its population was 36,274 in 1901, 348,647 in 1954, and 809,035 in 1981.

Petrov Affair: A controversial diplomatic incident that occurred in Australia in 1954–5, during the Cold War. Vladimir Petrov, of the Soviet Embassy in Canberra, defected on 3 April 1954. He gave documents and information relating to alleged Soviet espionage in Australia to the *Australian Security Intelligence Organization. Shortly after, *Menzies announced news of the defection and that a Royal Commission into Espionage would be held. Petrov's wife, Evdokia, also of the Embassy, defected on 20 April. Diplomatic relations between Australia and Russia ceased, and were not resumed until 1959. The Petrov affair became an issue in the campaign for the federal elections of May 1954, which saw the return of the Menzies Government. The Royal Commission's report was tabled in 1955. It found that the Petrov papers were authentic, and that there had been leaks from the Department of External Affairs between 1945 and 1948, but none after 1948. No prosecutions were launched. *Evatt, who represented two of his staff members before the Royal Commission until his leave to appear was withdrawn, claimed that Menzies had used the defections for electoral purposes, which Menzies denied. The Petrov affair has been seen as a catalyst in the split of the *Australian Labor Party in the mid-1950s.

Phar Lap (1926–32), Australia's most famous racehorse, was foaled in New Zealand, but raced mostly in Australia. He won many races, including the *Melbourne Cup of 1930. His death in California, shortly after he had won the Agua Caliente in Mexico, was probably due to colic. It aroused much suspicion in Australia. At the time of his death, Phar Lap was said to be third highest stake winner in the world, his winnings totalling £66,738. Phar Lap has become part of Australia's folklore.

Phillip, Arthur (1738–1814), *governor, was born in London. His father was a language teacher. Phillip pursued a naval career; after completing an apprenticeship, he saw active service in the Seven Years' War. During his naval career he served with both the Portuguese and British navies. Phillip was involved in survey work when he was appointed the first Governor of New South Wales in 1786. He sailed with the *First Fleet in 1787. He decided that the landing would be made at Port Jackson, rather than at *Botany Bay as intended, in 1788. Phillip's commissions and instructions gave him virtually autocratic power. He took control of all of the continent east of the 135th meridian and the adjacent islands (including *Norfolk Island). His major difficulties in establishing the new settlement included the personalities of some of the settlers (both officers and convicts), the settlers' inadequate farming knowledge and experience, and a lack of equipment and supplies. Phillip sailed for England in 1792 to seek medical treatment, and resigned on medical advice in 1793. He resumed his naval career in 1796. He retired in 1805 and spent the rest of his life at Bath. Phillip was promoted to admiral shortly before his death.

Pinjarra, Battle of: A violent conflict on 28 October 1834 between twenty-five whites (police, soldiers and settlers, led by Governor *Stirling) and about seventy or eighty Aborigines in the Murray River district (near present-day Pinjarra) of Western Australia. The whites attacked the blacks in retaliation for several killings and attacks on property. One white was killed, and another injured; estimates of black deaths range from about fifteen to fifty.

Playford, Sir Thomas (1896-1981), politician, was born at Norton's Summit, South Australia. His grandfather, Thomas Playford (1837-1915), had been the Premier of South Australia twice (1887-9, 1890-2). Playford was a Member of the South Australian House of Assembly from 1933 to 1967, when he retired. He was the Premier of South Australia, leading Liberal and Country League Ministries, from 1938 to 1965, a record continuous term for a parliamentary leader in the *Commonwealth of Nations. (An electoral system favouring rural electorates helped him to stay in office for such a long period.) Playford also held various other portfolios. He encouraged the growth of secondary industry, opened the Leigh Creek coalfield, and nationalized electricity supplies. South Australia's population increased markedly during his term of office. After the Labor Party defeated his Government at the elections of 1965, Playford led the Opposition until 1966.

Plural Voting: A system in which some electors can vote more than once. Plural voting at elections

for the lower houses of parliament was abolished in
New South Wales in 1893, Victoria in 1899, Tasmania
in 1901, Queensland in 1905 and Western Australia
in 1907. It had not existed for the lower house in
South Australia. It has never existed at elections for
the Commonwealth House of Representatives or
Senate.

Point Puer: *Port Arthur

Police Strike: A group of policemen in Melbourne
refused to go on beat duty on 31 October 1923. By
2 November more than 600 metropolitan policemen
were on strike. The total Victorian police force numbered about 1800 at the time. The introduction of
a system of special supervisors, nicknamed 'spooks'
by the policemen, was the immediate cause of the
strike, but there was a background of other grievances. Melbourne did not have a proper police force
for a week, during which time there was rioting,
looting and illegal gambling in the streets. A *Public
Safety Preservation Act* was passed, giving the State
Government wide emergency powers, and special
policemen were recruited. Victorian Government
requests to the Commonwealth Government for
troops were not granted, except to guard Commonwealth property. Six hundred and thirty-four policemen were discharged, and two dismissed; none were
reinstated, but special supervisors were not used
again. The Police Strike led to a Royal Commission,
chaired by *Monash, and investigation into the
police force.

Port Arthur is an inlet, about 100 kilometres by
road from Hobart, on Tasman's Peninsula in south-
eastern Tasmania. A *penal settlement for male convicts undergoing secondary punishment (that is,
those convicts who had committed further crimes
within the colonies) was founded there in 1830. One
of the site's main advantages was that it was only
a short distance by sea from Hobart. Port Arthur
continued as a prison after *transportation ended,
finally being abandoned in 1877. A boys' prison,
established at nearby Point Puer in 1834, continued

until 1849. At its peak it held about 730 boys. Some of the buildings at Port Arthur have been restored, and the area has become a major tourist attraction.

Port Dalrymple: *Launceston

Port Essington, an inlet on the Cobourg Peninsula, was the site of a short-lived British settlement, the third white settlement in the area that now forms the *Northern Territory. Like its predecessors, Fort Dundas (1824-9) on Melville Island and Fort Wellington (1827-9) at Raffles Bay, this settlement, which became known as Victoria, was established mainly for commercial and strategic reasons. Captain James John Gordon Bremer had landed at Port Essington in 1824, but had then decided to establish the first settlement on Melville Island instead, because of a lack of fresh water at Port Essington. However, he returned to Port Essington, and established a settlement there, in 1838. The tropical climate led to many problems for the settlers, and the settlement was abandoned in 1849. A fourth white settlement, at Escape Cliffs (1864-7), near the mouth of the Adelaide River, also failed.

Port Jackson: *Botany Bay

Port Phillip Association: An organization formed by fifteen people, including John Batman, in *Van Diemen's Land in 1835. It was originally known as the Geelong and Dutigalla Association, but soon became known as the Port Phillip Association. Batman entered into a so-called treaty with local Aborigines in 1835, exchanging various items, including tomahawks, shirts and blankets, for some 243,000 hectares of land. Batman and other members of the Association settled in the area, which became known as the *Port Phillip District. The British Government did not accept the validity of the treaty, but did allow the association a remission of £7000 on land purchase price, as recognition of its initial expenses in settling the area. The Port Phillip Association was superseded by the Derwent Association, which lasted until 1842.

Port Phillip District

Port Phillip District: The name given to present-day *Victoria in its early years of white settlement. *Bass, *Flinders, James Grant and John Murray explored its coast in the years between 1797 and 1802. *Collins, sent from England, unsuccessfully attempted to establish a convict settlement on the eastern coast of Port Phillip (near present-day *Sorrento) in 1803, but soon moved to *Van Diemen's Land. The *Hume and Hovell expedition explored parts of the area in 1824. Another convict settlement, on the eastern coast of Western Port, lasted from 1826 to 1828. Three attempts at settlement from Van Diemen's Land proved to be more permanent. *Henty settled at Portland Bay in 1834. John Batman and John Pascoe Fawkner established separate settlements on the site of present-day *Melbourne in 1835. *Squatters settled *Australia Felix soon after its discovery by Thomas *Mitchell in 1836. *La Trobe became Superintendent of the Port Phillip District in 1839. A small number of convicts went to the Port Phillip District from New South Wales and Van Diemen's Land. Some of them were employed on public works, others accompanied settlers as assigned servants. A few *exiles, most of whom were employed by squatters, were sent there in the late 1840s. The Port Phillip District was part of New South Wales until 1851, when it became a separate colony, named after Queen Victoria.

Port Phillip Protectorate: An organization designed to control and protect Aborigines in the *Port Phillip District. It was the most elaborate of a number of protectorates (others operated in South Australia and Western Australia). The British Government established the Port Phillip Protectorate in 1838, colonial land revenue being used to fund it. A Chief Protector, *Robinson, and four other protectors were appointed. Each was to cover a different area. They were to travel with the Aborigines, learn their language, protect them and their property, and persuade them to settle on reserves where they would live like Europeans. The protectors established the reserves, which had farms and schools, and dispensed rations and religious instruction. *Squatters opposed the Protectorate, Aborigines generally did not wish to settle on reserves, and lack of finance was a problem. The Legislative Council of New South Wales abolished the Port Phillip Protectorate in 1849.

Premier's Plan: *Great Depression

Prichard, Katharine Susannah (1883–1969), writer, was born at Levuka, Fiji, where her father was the editor of the *Fiji Times*. (He returned to Australia in 1886 to edit the Melbourne *Sun*, later the Launceston *Daily Telegraph*, and then the *Australian Mining Standard*.) Prichard was educated at the South Melbourne College, before becoming a governess, and then a journalist, writing for Australian and English newspapers. She travelled widely throughout her lifetime. Her first novel appeared in 1915, and she married Hugo Vivian Hope Throssell in 1919. Katharine Susannah Prichard helped to found the *Communist Party of Australia, was a lifelong member, and wrote several political works, including *Why I am a Communist* (1957). She died at her home near Perth. Her works of fiction include *The Pioneers* (1915), *Windlestraws* (1916), *Black Opal* (1921), *Working Bullocks* (1926), *The Wild Oats of Han* (1928), *Coonardoo, The Well in the Shadow* (1929), *Haxby's Circus, The Lightest Brightest Little Show on Earth* (1930), *Kiss on the Lips and Other Stories* (1932), *Intimate Strangers* (1937), *Moon Desire* (1941), *Potch and Colour* (1944), *The Roaring Nineties, A Story of the Goldfields of Western Australia* (1946), *Golden Miles* (1948) and *Winged Seeds* (1950). Many have distinctively Australian settings; many are concerned with social injustice; and many have been translated into other languages. Her other publications include *Clovelly Verses* (1913), *The Earth Lover and Other Verses* (1932) and *Child of the Hurricane* (1963), an autobiography.

Prime Minister: The term used to describe the chief minister of the Federal Cabinet. The Prime Ministers (up to the mid-1980s) have been Edmund *Barton (1901–3), Alfred *Deakin (1903–4, 1905–8, 1909–10), John Christian *Watson (1904), George Houston

Probation

*Reid (1904-5), Andrew *Fisher (1908-9, 1910-13, 1914-15), Joseph *Cook (1913-14), William Morris *Hughes (1915-23), Stanley Melbourne *Bruce (1923-9), James Henry *Scullin (1929-32), Joseph Aloysius *Lyons (1932-9), Earle Christmas Grafton *Page (1939), Robert Gordon *Menzies (1939-41, 1949-66), Arthur William *Fadden (1941), John *Curtin (1941-5), Francis Michael *Forde (1945), Joseph Benedict *Chifley (1945-9), Harold Edward *Holt (1966-7), John *McEwen (1967-8), John Grey *Gorton (1968-71), William *McMahon (1971-2), Edward Gough *Whitlam (1972-5), John Malcolm *Fraser (1975-83) and Robert James Lee *Hawke (1983-   ). The chief minister of each state is known as the Premier.

Probation: *Transportation

Protection: The 'theory or system of protecting home industries against foreign competition by imposing duties or the like on foreign productions'. Victoria pursued protectionist policies from the 1860s onwards, while New South Wales pursued *free trade policies. The other colonies adopted various policies. The Commonwealth Government introduced a compromise tariff in 1902, and a national policy of tariff protection in 1908. Since then, Australia in general has pursued protectionist policies.

Protectionist Party: The Protectionist Party was one of the two main non-Labor political parties, the other being the *Free Trade Party, in the early Commonwealth Parliament. Members of the Protectionist Party held a wide range of views regarding the extent to which *protection should be practised. The Protectionist Party governed federally from 1901 to 1904, and from 1905 to 1908. Some Protectionists, led by McLean, governed in coalition with the Free Traders in the *Reid-McLean Government (1904-5). Some joined with moderate Free Traders, and became known as the Tariff Reformers, in 1906. The Protectionist Party was led by *Barton (1901-3) and *Deakin (1903-9). The Protectionist merged with the Free Traders and the Tariff Reformers, to form the *Fusion Party, in 1909. There were also some colonial (from 1901, state) protectionist parties in the late nineteenth and early twentieth centuries.

Q

Qantas is Australia's international airline. Fergus McMaster, P. J. McGinness, W. Hudson Fysh and others founded Queensland and Northern Territory Aerial Services Limited in 1920. Its headquarters were at Winton, Queensland, and it operated a passenger, mail and cargo service in western Queensland and the Northern Territory. In 1934 Qantas and Imperial Airways Limited founded its successor, Qantas Empire Airways Limited, which flew the southern leg of the route to Britain. This was Australia's first international air service. The headquarters were transferred to Sydney in 1938, and Qantas expanded its international services. The Commonwealth Government nationalized Qantas in 1947. Its name was charged to Qantas Airways Limited in 1967.

Queensland, a state of the Commonwealth of Australia, was known as the *Moreton Bay District in its early years of white settlement, when it formed part of New South Wales. It was separated from New South Wales, renamed Queensland and granted *responsible government in 1859. It became a state of the newly created Commonwealth of Australia in 1901. Cattle production, the sugar industry (which for many years relied heavily upon the labour of Pacific Islanders brought to Australia during the *blackbirding period) and mining (especially since the 1950s and 1960s) have been particularly significant in Queensland's history.

Queensland and Northern Territory Aerial Services: *Qantas

Queenstown, a town in western Tasmania, owes its existence to copper mining at nearby Mount Lyell, six kilometres to the north-east. Gold discoveries at Mount Lyell in the early 1880s were followed by

discoveries of copper and silver. Queenstown, named
after Queen Victoria, was Tasmania's third largest
town in 1901, with a population of over 5000. It
became a municipality in 1907. Logging, smelter
fumes and erosion have largely denuded the hills
around Queenstown. The population in 1981 was
3714.

R

RAAF: *Royal Australian Air Force

Radio Australia: *Australian Broadcasting Commission

Raffles Bay: *Northern Territory; *Port Essington

Railway-building began in Australia during the
1850s. The first public steam railways to open in each
of the colonies were those between Melbourne and
present-day Port Melbourne, in Victoria, in 1854;
Redfern and Granville, in New South Wales, in 1855;
Adelaide and Port Adelaide, in South Australia, in
1856; Ipswich and present-day Grandchester, in
Queensland, in 1863; *Launceston and Deloraine, in
Tasmania, in 1871; and Geraldton and Northampton,
in Western Australia, in 1879. The Northern Territory's first railway, between Darwin and Pine Creek,
opened in 1889. Some lines were built by private
companies, but colonial governments soon took
responsibility for most railways (and the Commonwealth Government also became involved from 1911).
The length of railway lines increased from 243 miles
in 1861 to more than 10,000 miles in 1890,[1] and further
lines were built during the twentieth century. (The
opening in 1917 of the transcontinental railway from
Port Augusta, in South Australia, to *Kalgoorlie in
Western Australia, built as a condition of Western
Australia joining the Commonwealth, was a particu-

---

[1]These figures are from A. G. L. Shaw, *The Economic Development
of Australia* (Longman, Melbourne, fifth edition, 1966), p. 84.

larly notable event.) The use of gauges of three different widths (3 feet 6 inches, 4 feet 8½ inches—standard gauge—and 5 feet 3 inches) in various parts of the country caused numerous problems. Some lines have since been converted to standard gauge, and additional standard gauge lines have been built. Diesel and electric power replaced steam during the 1950s and 1960s.

RAN: *Royal Australian Navy

Rats of Tobruk: Popular name given to the Allied servicemen who defended Tobruk, Libya, while it was under siege by the Axis Powers in 1941, during the Second World War. 'Lord Haw-Haw' (William Joyce) coined the term; during a German radio broadcast he described the men as 'the Rats of Tobruk, those self-supporting prisoners of war'. He meant the term to be derogatory. Instead, the men adopted it as their name. Many Australians were involved during the siege; more than 800 Australians were killed, more than 2200 wounded, and about 700 captured.

Redfern, William (1774?–1833), surgeon, was probably born in Canada, but grew up in England. He was commissioned surgeon's mate in HMS *Standard*, whose crew was involved in the mutiny of the fleet at the Nore in 1797. Refern was court-martialled and sentenced to death. He was reprieved, spent four years in jail, and was then transported to New South Wales. He was assistant surgeon at *Norfolk Island from 1802 to 1808. *King granted him a free pardon in 1803. Redfern was assistant surgeon in New South Wales from 1808 to 1819, when he resigned because he was not appointed as principal surgeon. His report on mortality rates on three convict ships, written in 1814, led to significant reforms. As well as his hospital work, he had the colony's largest private medical practice. Redfern was also active in public affairs. *Macquarie appointed him a magistrate in 1819, but Bathurst, the British Secretary of State for the Colonies, vetoed the appointment in 1820. In 1821 Redfern sailed to England, where he and Edward Eager successfully petitioned for the lifting of certain

restrictions imposed upon *emancipists. In 1824 he
returned to New South Wales, where he concentrated
more on farming and less on his practice, which he
gave up in 1826. Redfern went to Edinburgh in 1828,
and died there.

Reibey (née Haydock), **Mary** (1777-1855), business-
woman, was born in England. She was convicted
of horse-stealing and sentenced to seven years'
*transportation in 1790. After her arrival in Sydney
in 1792, she was assigned to *Grose. She married
(Sydney) Thomas Reibey, an Irish free settler, in
1794. (The surname has also been spelt Reiby, Raby
and Rabey.) Mary Reibey bore seven children and
assisted her husband with his business interests.
After his death in 1811 she maintained and expanded
those interests. She and two of her daughters visited
England (1820-1). Mary Reibey was also active in
colonial public affairs, notably those relating to religion, education and charity. She died at Newtown,
Sydney.

Reid, Sir George Houston (1845-1918), politician,
was born in Scotland, the son of a Presbyterian minister. Reid's family migrated to Melbourne in 1852,
and moved to Sydney in 1858. Reid left school at
the age of 13 and worked as a clerk. After studying
law, he was admitted to the Bar in 1879. He was
a Free Trade Member of the Legislative Assembly
in New South Wales from 1880 to 1884, and again
from 1885 to 1901, and was Premier and Treasurer
from 1894 to 1899. He implemented economies in
government spending, introduced land tax, and
established a 'non-political' public service board.
Reid, who had earlier been dubbed 'Yes-No' Reid
because of his attitude towards federation, was a
Member of the House of Representatives from 1901
to 1909. He led the Free Traders in the first Commonwealth Parliament, then became Prime Minister
and Minister for External Affairs, leading a coalition
of Free Traders and Protectionists in 1904-5. After
the defeat of his Government (sometimes known as
the Reid-McLean Government) he continued to lead
the Opposition until his retirement as Free Trade
Leader in 1908. Reid became the first Australian

High Commissioner in London in 1910, holding this position until 1916, in which year he was elected to the British House of Commons. He died in London.

Remittance Men were immigrants in Australian and other colonies during the nineteenth century who survived on remittances from home (usually Britain or Europe), rather than wages. In some cases, their families paid them to stay abroad. They were often looked upon with scorn.

Reserve Bank of Australia: Australia's central bank. In 1959 the Commonwealth Bank of Australia was divided into the *Commonwealth Banking Corporation and the Reserve Bank of Australia. The latter's functions include regulating the Australian monetary and banking system; acting as banker for the government, trading and savings banks, and other financial institutions; printing and distributing Australian currency notes and distributing Australian coinage; holding Australian gold and foreign currency reserves; and administering exchange control. It is responsible to the Commonwealth Treasurer.

Responsible Government: A form of self-government. Responsible government was proclaimed in New South Wales, Victoria and Tasmania in 1855, in South Australia in 1856, in Queensland in 1859 and in Western Australia in 1890. The colonial constitutions established bicameral *parliaments, and these continue in the states, except Queensland, which abolished its Legislative Council in 1922.

Returned Services League of Australia (RSL): A pressure group representing the interests of ex-servicemen and ex-servicewomen. It is the largest of a number of similar Australian organizations, formed in 1916 as the Returned Sailors' and Soldiers' Imperial League of Australia, during the First World War. Its name was changed in 1940 to the Returned Sailors', Soldiers' and Airmen's Imperial League of Australia, during the Second World War. It was changed again, to its present name, in 1965. The organization has worked mainly in areas such as repatriation and welfare, has spoken out on topics such as defence and foreign policy, and claims to be non-political. Before 1982 members needed to have served in a theatre of war; since then, anyone who served in the regular defence forces for six months or more has been eligible. There were about 270,000 members in 1983.

RFDS: *Royal Flying Doctor Service of Australia

Richardson, Ethel Florence Lindesay: *Robertson, Ethel Florence Lindesay

'Richardson, Henry Handel': *Robertson, Ethel Florence Lindesay

Ridley's Stripper, a mechanical wheat harvester, has been described as 'one of the most important technical inventions in the history of Australian farming'.[1] The first such machine was apparently made by John Ridley (hence its popular name), and was first used in South Australia in 1843. J. W. Bull, also of South Australia, had earlier suggested a similar idea.

Ripon Regulations: Land regulations for the Australian colonies, introduced in 1831 by the British Secretary of State for the Colonies, Viscount Goderich (created Earl of Ripon, 1833). They replaced the existing system of disposal of Crown land, a combination of sales and grants, with a system of sales (except in cases where grants had already been promised). Henceforth, Crown land was to be sold at auction at a minimum price of five shillings an acre. The proceeds of the land sales were to be used to assist the *immigration of free settlers.

Roberts, Thomas William (1856-1931), painter, was born in England, and came to Melbourne with his widowed mother in 1869. He worked as a photographer's assistant, and later drew for newspapers and journals. He studied at night, first at the Col-

---

[1] Frank Crowley, *A Documentary History of Australia*, volume 2, *Colonial Australia, 1841-1874* (Nelson, Melbourne, 1980), p. 55.

lingwood Artisans' School of Design, and then at the National Gallery School. In 1881 he went to England, where he continued to draw for newspapers, and studied at the Royal Academy School. He and several friends went on a walking tour of Spain in 1883. He returned to Australia in 1885. Tom Roberts was largely responsible for founding the *Heidelberg School. He and the group's other members established artists' camps in Box Hill and Heidelberg in the 1880s. Roberts and *Streeton then established a camp at Mosman, Sydney, in 1891. Roberts also taught, and painted portraits, in Melbourne and later in Sydney. He became the foundation president of the New South Wales Society of Artists in 1895. Bernard Smith says of Roberts's achievements between 1885 and 1900:

he had been responsible to a greater extent than any other artist for bringing an independent Australian school of painting into existence. In his own work he had achieved distinction in painting both rural and urban landscapes; he had made a reputation second to none in the country in portraiture; and he had painted the most memorable history paintings of Australian rural life. His personal influence upon his fellow artists had been profound ... He had played a leading and creative role in the politics of the art societies.[1]

Roberts lived abroad, mainly in England, from 1903, and continued to paint. During the First World War he worked as a hospital orderly in England. He returned permanently to Australia in 1923. His paintings include *Bourke Street* (1885-6), *The Artists' Camp* (1886), *A Summer Morning's Tiff* (1886), *Coming South* (1886), *Reconciliation* (1887), *Holiday Sketch at Coogee* (1888), *Shearing the Rams* (1889-90), *The Breakaway* (1891), *Mountain Muster* (1898) and *Opening of the First Commonwealth Parliament* (1901-3).

Robertson (née Richardson), **Ethel Florence Lindesay** (1870-1946), novelist, more commonly known

---

[1] Bernard Smith, *Australian Painting, 1788-1970* (Oxford University Press, Melbourne, 1971), p. 122.

by her pseudonym 'Henry Handel Richardson', was born in East Melbourne. Her Irish-born father was a medical doctor; her mother later became a postmistress. She was educated at the Presbyterian Ladies' College, Melbourne, and the Leipzig Conservatorium. After leaving Australia for Leipzig in 1887, she spent most of her life in England, returning only once to Australia, in 1912, while researching *The Fortunes of Richard Mahony*. She is best known for this trilogy, which was first published separately as *The Fortunes of Richard Mahony* (usually known as *Australia Felix*, part of its half-title) (1917), *The Way Home, Second Part of the Chronicle of the Fortunes of Richard Mahony* (1925) and *Ultima Thule, Third Part of the Chronicle of the Fortunes of Richard Mahony* (1930). The trilogy, set largely in colonial Australia, traces the decline of Richard Mahony, a character modelled upon the author's own father. Her other novels and stories include *Maurice Guest* (1908), *The Getting of Wisdom* (1910) and *The End of a Childhood and Other Stories* (1934). *Myself When Young* (1948) is an unfinished autobiography.

Robertson, Sir John (1816–91), politician, was born in England, and came to New South Wales with his family in 1822. He became a *squatter in the 1830s. Robertson entered New South Wales politics, and was a Member of the Legislative Assembly for most of the period from 1856 to 1886 (and a Member of the Legislative Council twice during that time). He was the Premier of New South Wales five times (1860–1, 1868–70, 1875–7, 1877, 1885–6) and held various other portfolios. Robertson was largely responsible for the introduction of land reforms in New South Wales in 1861.

Robinson, George Augustus (1788–1866), protector of *Aborigines, was born in England. His father was a builder. Robinson received little formal education, and worked for the Engineers' Department at Chatham before migrating to Australia in 1824. He worked as a builder in Hobart. In 1829 he was appointed to work with Aborigines. For the next few years, Robinson travelled around *Van Diemen's

Land, making contact with Aborigines and persuading them to live in captivity. Those persuaded were taken to a series of settlements on Bass Strait islands. From 1835 to 1839 Robinson himself took charge of the final such settlement, on Flinders Island. In 1838 he was appointed Chief Protector of the newly formed *Port Phillip Protectorate, and held that position until the abolition of the Protectorate in 1849. In 1852 he returned to England, living there and in Europe for the rest of his life. He died at Bath, England. Some of his writings were later published in *Friendly Mission, The Tasmanian Journals and Papers of George Augustus Robinson 1829-1834* (1966), edited by N. J. B. Plomley.

Rocks, The: An area on the western side of Sydney Cove, which takes its name from the large sandstone rocks found there. Makeshift buildings were erected there as early as 1788; most of the early buildings were for maritime, defence and commercial purposes. During the nineteenth century the Rocks gained a notorious reputation for harbouring groups of criminals, prostitutes and *larrikins. Many of the nineteenth-century buildings at the Rocks have been preserved and restored, and the area has become a tourist attraction.

Rose Hill: *Parramatta

Royal Australian Air Force (RAAF): The most recently established of the Australian armed services, the others being the *Royal Australian Navy and the *army. The Australian Flying Corps (AFC) was formed in 1915, during the First World War. Its members served in the Middle East and on the Western Front. Some formed part of the *Australian Imperial Force, others part of the British Royal Flying Corps. The AFC was disbanded after the war. Its successor, the RAAF, was established in 1921. Its early development was slow, but it expanded greatly during the Second World War. Australia participated in the Empire Air Training Scheme, the purpose of which was to share the Dominions' resources to train airmen, which began in 1939. RAAF members served in Europe, the Middle East, Asia and the Pacific during the war (some of them as part of the British Royal Air Force). Women were first accepted in the air force as nurses in 1940, and in some other positions in 1941. The women's auxiliary, but not the nursing service, was disbanded in 1947. Women were again accepted in the air force from 1950. Since the Second World War, RAAF members have served overseas in the *Korean War, the *Malayan Emergency and the *Vietnam War, and in several peace-keeping operations.

Royal Australian Navy (RAN): One of Australia's three armed services, the others being the *army and the *Royal Australian Air Force. The Royal Australian Navy was formally established in 1911. Previously, the Australian colonies had depended largely upon Britain for naval defence, paying subsidies for this purpose from 1887. Small colonial naval forces had also been raised during the second half of the nineteenth century. A naval contingent took part in the *Boxer Rebellion. The Commonwealth Government took responsibility for the various local forces following Federation in 1901. Australian ships, placed under British Admiralty command, were largely engaged in convoy work during the First World War. Naval forces were involved in the capture of German New Guinea, and the *Sydney* destroyed the German raider *Emden* at the Cocos Islands in November 1914. Two Australian submarines were destroyed during the war; the *AE1* was lost near New Guinea in 1914, and the *AE2* was sunk in the Sea of Marmara in 1915. During the Second World War, Australian ships served in many parts of the world, and were engaged in much action. The sinking of the Italian cruiser *Bartolomeo Colleoni* by the *Sydney* off Crete in July 1940 was particularly notable. More than thirty Australian vessels were lost during the war, including the *Sydney*, which was sunk off Western Australia in November 1941. The Royal Australian Navy was also involved in the *Korean War and the *Vietnam War, and has taken part in a number of peace-keeping operations. Women were first accepted in the navy in 1941.

Royal Flying Doctor Service of Australia (RFDS): An organization that provides a medical service, using radio and aeroplanes, for outback areas. The Reverend John Flynn was largely responsible for the foundation of the Aerial Medical Service in 1928. Based at Cloncurry in Queensland, it was founded under the auspices of the Presbyterian Church's Australian Inland Mission, of which Flynn was founder and superintendent. Responsibility for the organization was transferred from the Australian Inland Mission to the states in 1933, and it became known as the National Aerial Medical Service. In 1942 its name was changed to the Flying Doctor Service of Australia, the word 'Royal' being added to its title in 1954. The organization receives public and private funding, and now has bases in many parts of Australia. Its radio network has also been used for the Schools of the Air (an educational service), and for sending telegrams.

RSL: *Returned Services League of Australia

'Rudd, Steele': *Davis, Arthur Hoey

Rum Corps: *New South Wales Corps

Rum Jungle, in the Northern Territory, was the site of Australia's first large uranium project. Uranium was found there in 1949, and production began in the early 1950s. It had ceased by 1971.

Rum Rebellion: Popular name given to the overthrow in 1808 of the Governor of New South Wales, *Bligh, by leading colonists and officers of the *New South Wales Corps. The Corps has become known as the Rum Corps because of its members' involvement in the rum trade. Background causes of the Rum Rebellion included the personalities of some of those involved, especially Bligh and *Macarthur, and Bligh's successful attempts to limit the powers of the rum traders. Immediate causes included the last of a series of legal cases involving Macarthur. George Johnston led the Corps to arrest Bligh on 26 January. He dubbed himself 'Lieutenant-Governor' and controlled the colony until July, when *Foveaux took

control. William *Paterson later took over from
Foveaux and remained in control until the next Governor, *Macquarie, took office in 1810. Macarthur
was Colonial Secretary during the period when Johnston controlled the colony. Bligh was confined in
Sydney for some time, then sailed to Van Diemen's
Land in 1809, returned to Sydney in 1810, and finally
sailed for England that year. Johnston returned to
England, where he faced a court martial; he was
found guilty and cashiered in 1811. Bligh was virtually exonerated at Johnston's court martial. Macarthur returned to England, where he remained until
1817, aware that he risked arrest if he returned to
the colony. The New South Wales Corps was recalled.

Ryan, Thomas Joseph (1876–1921), politician, was
born at Port Fairy, Victoria, and was educated at
Port Fairy State School, Xavier College, Melbourne,
and the University of Melbourne. Ryan, whose father
was a grazier, taught at schools in several states,
and practised as a lawyer in Queensland, before serving as a Labor Member of the Queensland Legislative
Assembly from 1909 to 1919 (becoming parliamentary Leader of his party in 1912). He was Premier,
Chief Secretary and Attorney-General from 1915 to
1919. His Government was responsible for much
industrial legislation, including Acts dealing with
arbitration and workers' compensation, established
a number of state enterprises, among which were
butchers' shops, station properties, an insurance
office and a hotel, and unsuccessfully attempted to
abolish the Legislative Council. Ryan's strong stand
against *conscription brought him into conflict with
the Prime Minister, *Hughes. Ryan was a Labor
Member of the House of Representatives, representing West Sydney, from 1919 until he died. He was
Deputy Leader of the federal parliamentary Labor
Party from 1920.

S

Savery, Henry (1791–1842), writer, was born in England, and became a sugar broker in Bristol. He went

bankrupt, was convicted of forgery, and was transported for life, arriving in 1825 in Hobart, where he worked in government offices. While imprisoned for debt, Savery wrote a series of sketches about life in Hobart, which were published in the *Colonial Times* during 1829 under the pseudonym of 'Simon Stukeley'. The sketches were published anonymously in book form as *The Hermit in Van Diemen's Land* (1829), said to be the first volume of Australian essays, and became the subject of a libel action in 1830. Savery also wrote the first Australian novel, the partly autobiographical *Quintus Servinton* (1830-1), which was published anonymously in three volumes. He became a farmer, was granted a *ticket-of-leave in 1832 (withdrawn for some time in 1833), and received a conditional pardon in 1838. Savery become insolvent again in 1839, was convicted of forgery a second time in 1840, and was sent to *Port Arthur, where he died.

Schools of Arts: *Mechanics' Institutes

Scott, Rose (1847-1925), feminist and social reformer, was born in New South Wales. She is perhaps best known for her work in the movement for women's *suffrage. She and others founded the Womanhood Suffrage League in Sydney in 1891, and she remained secretary of the League until it was dissolved in 1902, after women in New South Wales had gained the vote. Rose Scott then founded, and was president of, the Women's Political Educational League, which existed until 1910. She was also involved in other organizations, advocating peace and women's rights, and she campaigned for legislative reforms in areas relating to women and children. She died in Sydney.

Scottish Martyrs: Political prisoners transported to New South Wales after celebrated Scottish sedition trials in 1793 and 1794. They were Thomas Muir, Thomas Fyshe Palmer, William Skirving, Maurice Margarot and Joseph Gerrald. All had been active in organizations, influenced by the French Revolution, advocating political reform. Palmer was sentenced to seven years' *transportation, the others to fourteen years'. All but Gerrald arrived in New South Wales in 1794; he arrived the following year, and died of tuberculosis in 1796. As political prisoners, they were excused from compulsory labour. Muir farmed until his escape on the *Otter*, an American ship, in 1796. After facing extreme difficulties, including injury and imprisonment, he reached Paris in 1797. He died at Chantilly, near Paris, in 1799. Palmer farmed and traded until he sailed for England in 1801. He reached Guam, where he died in 1802. Skirving farmed until his death in 1796. Margarot continued his political activities; he is said to have helped to plan the *Castle Hill Uprising of 1804. He was sent to *Norfolk Island, *Van Diemen's Land and *Newcastle. In 1810 he returned to England, where he died in 1815.

Scullin, James Henry (1876–1953), politician, was born in Victoria, was educated at Mt Rowan State School (later attending night classes), and worked variously as a gold-miner, shopkeeper and organizer for the *Australian Workers' Union. He was a Labor Member of the House of Representatives from 1910 to 1913, and again from 1922 to 1949. After losing his seat in 1913, Scullin worked as a journalist and edited the *Ballarat Evening Echo*. He led the Opposition in 1928-9, and then was Prime Minister and Minister for External Affairs from 1929 to January 1932. As Prime Minister, he was confronted with deteriorating economic conditions and deepening divisions within his own party. His Government greatly increased tariffs in an unsuccessful attempt to reduce unemployment. In 1931 he appointed the first Australian Governor-General, *Isaacs, despite opposition from King George V. After the defeat of the Labor Government, Scullin led the Opposition from 1932 to 1935. In 1935 he resigned as federal parliamentary leader of the Labor Party, but did not retire from the Commonwealth Parliament until 1949.

Sealers from Australia, Britain, America and elsewhere operated around Australia from the 1790s until about the 1830s. Seals were hunted for their skins and oil. The Bass Strait islands and *Kangaroo

Island were important sealing grounds during the early years. Sealers then moved to places such as New Zealand and Macquarie Island. Whale and seal products were Australia's main exports until the 1830s. Fur seals were almost extinct by the late 1850s.

SEATO: *South-East Asia Treaty Organization

Secession Movement: A significant secession attempt by *Western Australia during the *Great Depression. Western Australia wished to secede from the *Commonwealth of Australia, becoming instead a self-governing member of the *Commonwealth of Nations. A Dominion League of Western Australia, advocating secession, was formed in 1930. Western Australians voted two-to-one in favour of secession at a referendum, at which voting was compulsory, held in 1933, and a deputation petitioned the British Parliament in 1934. The petition was rejected the following year. The main reasons for the movement were emotional and financial (especially increasing dissatisfaction with the Commonwealth Government's *protection policy).

Second Fleet: Popular name for the second group of ships bringing convicts and supplies from England to New South Wales, in 1790. (The *Lady Juliana*, carrying about 220 female convicts, sailed from England in July 1789, between the *First Fleet and the Second Fleet, and arrived in early June 1790.) The *Surprize*, the *Neptune* and the *Scarborough*, carrying about 1000 convicts, left England together on 19 January 1790, and arrived in late June of that year. The *Justinian*, a store ship, went with them. Conditions on board were grim, and about a quarter of the convicts died during the voyage. Officers and men of the *New South Wales Corps sailed with the Second Fleet.

Second World War (1939-45): A major war, in which many countries were involved, fought between the Allied Powers and the Axis Powers. The Allied Powers included Britain (1939-45), the United States of America (1941-5), France (1939-40), China (1941-

Second World War

5) and Australia (1939–45). The Axis Powers included Germany (1939–45), Italy (1940–3, but a 'co-belligerent' with the Allies from 1943 onwards) and Japan (1941–5). Dozens of other countries were also involved. The long-term causes, which were complex and numerous, included the inadequacy of the peace settlement reached after the *First World War, the rise of Nazism in Germany, and the rise of Fascism in Italy and elsewhere. The short-term cause was the German invasion of Poland on 1 September 1939. Britain declared war on Germany two days later, and other countries soon became involved. The main theatres of war were in Europe, North Africa and the Pacific. Germany surrendered on 7 May 1945. Japan, following the dropping of atomic bombs on Hiroshima on 6 August 1945, and on Nagasaki on 9 August 1945, agreed to accept Allied terms on 14 August, and formally surrendered on 2 September. Australia, as a member of the British *Commonwealth of Nations, on 3 September 1939 automatically followed Britain to war, as she had at the beginning of the First World War. Australia declared war on Italy in 1940, Japan, Finland, Hungary, Rumania and Bulgaria in 1941, and Thailand in 1942. The *Royal Australian Navy, the Australian *army and the *Royal Australian Air Force all participated in the war. The gross enlistments during the war were 45,800 men and 3100 women in the Royal Australian Navy; 691,400 men and 35,800 women in the army; and 189,700 men and 27,200 women in the Royal Australian Air Force. Australia's main expeditionary force was the Second *Australian Imperial Force, whose members were all volunteers. From 1940 onwards, members of the Second AIF served in the Middle East, where some became the now-famous *Rats of Tobruk. Some also fought in Greece and Crete. Other members of the Second AIF went to Malaya in 1941; many of those were taken prisoner by the Japanese following the fall of Singapore on 15 February 1942. Some others remained in Australia. The Australian troops in the Middle East returned to the Pacific in 1942 and 1943, following Japan's entry into the war on 7 December 1941. Second AIF troops served in the Pacific region (which

includes Australia) for the remainder of the war. Militia forces, whose members were conscripts, served in Australia, New Guinea and some other islands. The RAAF and RAN served in many parts of the world. Australian battle casualties (including those of prisoners-of-war) included 1900 deaths in the RAN, 6460 in the RAAF, and 18,713 in the army. More than 30,000 Australians were taken prisoners-of-war, mainly by the Japanese. The *Menzies United Australia Party Government reintroduced military *conscription for home service in 1939. The *Curtin Labor Government introduced a limited form of military conscription for overseas service in 1943. A form of industrial conscription, for men and women, was also introduced. Women eventually were accepted in the armed services, albeit in restricted roles, during the war, and an Australian Women's Land Army was formed. Various volunteer home defence forces were raised. The Commonwealth Government, whose powers were increased during the war, notably through the introduction of *uniform taxation, had introduced wartime legislation such as the *National Security Act. However, the *'Fourteen Powers' Referendum failed. The *Communist Party of Australia was banned for some time. The *Australia First Movement was suppressed. More than 25,000 German, Italian and Japanese prisoners-of-war were held in Australia during the war. A large number of Japanese prisoners attempted to escape in the *Cowra outbreak. Rationing of petrol, clothing, food and other goods and services was introduced. The Japanese launched air raids on *Darwin on 19 February 1942. In the following months there were further air raids on Darwin, Wyndham, Broome, Derby and elsewhere. There were some hundreds of casualties and some property damage. Three Japanese midget submarines attacked Sydney Harbour on 31 May 1942, also causing some casualties and property damage. Submarines shelled Sydney and Newcastle on 7 June 1942, but with little effect. The *Kokoda Trail was the closest the Japanese forces came to Australia by land. There was controversy over the alleged existence of the *Brisbane Line, beyond which Australia would not be defended. Following Japan's entry into the war, Australia turned increasingly towards the United States of America for support. The latter had already been providing *Lend-Lease aid to Australia. Americans began to arrive in Australia from late 1941. General Douglas MacArthur, who went on to command the Allied operations in the south-west Pacific, arrived in Australia in March 1942. The Battle of *Brisbane has become part of Australia's folklore. Australia's increased reliance upon the United States of America was later reflected in the signing of the *ANZUS Pact after the war.

Secret Ballot: A method whereby electors cast their votes in secret. It is known also as the Australian ballot. Australia led the world in introducing the secret ballot for political elections. Victoria and South Australia first introduced provision for it (for both houses) in 1856, Tasmania (for both houses) in 1858, New South Wales (for the lower house) in 1858, Queensland (for the lower house) in 1859, and Western Australia (for the upper house) in 1877. The secret ballot has always been used for elections for the Commonwealth House of Representatives and Senate.

Selectors: Popular name given to a large number of small farmers in Australia during the second half of the nineteenth century. By the 1850s *squatters had acquired most of the land suitable for agricultural and pastoral purposes. Increasing demands were made, especially by those who had come to the colonies during the gold-rushes, for land to be made available at low cost for small farms. All of the colonies introduced systems providing for farms of limited size and the sale of land on credit. Selectors generally were not very successful in New South Wales, but fared better in Victoria and South Australia. There were few selectors in Tasmania, and Queensland and Western Australia remained largely pastoral colonies. Factors leading to the failure of many selectors included the unsuitability of much Australian land for agriculture, the use of devious and obstructive tactics by some squatters, and many selectors' ignorance of farming and lack of capital.

Shearers' Strikes: Major strikes in Queensland and New South Wales in 1891 and 1894. Shearers were fighting for the principles of unionism and the 'closed shop' ('an establishment in which only trade-union members are employed', or 'a trade restricted to members of a [particular] trade union'). Pastoralists were fighting for 'freedom of contract' (the right to employ anyone). The strikes were marked by violence and bitterness on both sides. Non-union labour was used. Union leaders, including some from the now-famous *Barcaldine shearers' camp of 1891, were arrested on charges such as conspiracy, seditious language and riot. Some were jailed. The unions were defeated.

Sheffield Shield: *Cricket

***Shenandoah*:** A ship whose visit to Melbourne during the American Civil War led to a diplomatic incident. The *Shenandoah*, an American Confederate ship, visited Melbourne from 25 January to 18 February 1865, against the wishes of the United States Consul. Her captain, James Waddell, with permission from the Victoria Governor, Sir Charles Darling, had repairs made and bought supplies; without permission, he also recruited sailors. After the American Civil War ended, the American Government made the British Government pay compensation for damage done to Union ships by the *Shenandoah* after she left Melbourne.

Smallpox: A highly contagious and usually fatal disease. Apparently there were smallpox epidemics among *Aborigines, in at least the eastern part of Australia, in 1789 and between about 1829 and 1831. There is debate about the way the disease spread. There was also an outbreak of smallpox among white settlers in Australia in the 1880s.

Smith, Sir Keith Macpherson (1890–1955) and **Sir Ross Macpherson** (1892–1922), aviators, were brothers, born in Adelaide and educated there and in Scotland. During the First World War Ross served with the *Australian Imperial Force and the Australian

231

Snowy Mountains Hydro-Electric Scheme

Flying Corps, and Keith with the Royal Flying Corps. After the war they made the first flight from England to Australia. In 1919 the Commonwealth Government offered a prize of £10,000 for the first Australians to make such a flight in thirty days or less. Ross (pilot), Keith (co-pilot and navigator) and two mechanics, J. M. Bennett and W. H. Shiers, left Hounslow, on 12 November 1919. They arrived in Darwin twenty-seven days and twenty hours later. The Smith brothers won the prize and were knighted. Sir Ross Smith and Bennett were killed on 13 April 1922, while testing an amphibian aircraft in preparation for another long-distance flight. Sir Keith Smith, who later chaired the Australian branch of Vickers Limited, died in Sydney.

Snowy Mountains Hydro-Electric Scheme: A major engineering feat. The Scheme generates electricity for the Australian Capital Territory, New South Wales and Victoria, and also provides water for the Murray and Murrumbidgee irrigation areas. It involves the diversion of water from the Snowy River through tunnels in the Snowy Mountains, in south-eastern New South Wales. Its construction, almost entirely funded by the Commonwealth Government, began in 1949 and ended in 1972.

Social Credit: A theory of economic reform propounded by a Scottish engineer named Clifford H. Douglas, and so known also as Douglas Credit. Although Douglas's ideas circulated in Australia during the 1920s, they were not influential until the *Great Depression. Social Credit organizations were formed from 1930 onwards; Social Credit newspapers, such as the *New Era, Freedom* (later *New Economics*), *New Times* and *New World* were published; Douglas himself visited Australia in 1934; Social Credit political parties, such as the Douglas Credit Party, were formed. No official Social Credit candidates were ever elected to parliament. The Social Credit movement had virtually dissolved in Australia by 1940, except in Queensland, where it continued until the 1960s. Its supporters have mainly been absorbed into other organizations.

'Socialist tiger': During the federal election campaign of 1906, *Reid, leader of the Free Traders, referred to the *Australian Labor Party as a 'socialist tiger'. The slogan formed part of a broader 'anti-socialist' campaign that Reid had begun in 1904.

Socialization Objective: A term that usually refers to an objective included in the *Australian Labor Party platform at the party's federal conference in Brisbane in 1921. The Objective was 'The socialization of industry, production, distribution and exchange', and it was followed by Methods. It was passed by twenty-two votes to ten. The Blackburn Declaration qualified it, and the Objective has been reviewed a number of times. It remained unaltered, but the Methods were revised, at the federal conference of 1927. It was reaffirmed at the federal conference of 1948; the Blackburn Declaration still stood. An Interpretation was added at the federal conference of 1951. The Objective, as determined at the federal conference of 1981, said: 'The Australian Labor Party is a democratic socialist party and has the objective of the democratic socialization of industry, production and exchange to the extent necessary to eliminate exploitation and other anti-social features in these fields.' It was accompanied by an Interpretation.

Soldier Settlement: A land policy implemented after each of the two world wars. It was a form of *closer settlement designed to establish returned soldiers on small farms, often in previously unsettled regions. Governments gave soldier settlers credit and other assistance. There were about 37,000 soldier settlers after the First World War, along the Murray and Murrumbidgee Rivers, in the wheat-growing regions of South Australia and Western Australia, in the Mallee in Victoria, and elsewhere. They frequently faced problems such as lack of experience and capital, farms that were too small, and unproductive land. Many left their farms during the 1920s and 1930s, and the Commonwealth Government had to cover many of their debts. Soldier settlement was implemented on a smaller scale after the Second World War.

Sorell, William (1775-1848), soldier and colonial administrator, was probably born in the West Indies, where he later served during his military career. He served in other places, including the Cape of Good Hope, where he demonstrated his administrative ability, before resigning from the army in 1813. He replaced Thomas Davey as the Lieutenant-Governor of *Van Diemen's Land in 1817. Sorell reduced bushranging in the colony; introduced numerous administrative reforms; established a *penal settlement at *Macquarie Harbour and built convict barracks in Hobart; encouraged the development of the wool and wheat industries; and helped to found the Bank of Van Diemen's Land. After *Arthur succeeded him in 1824, Sorell returned to England. He did not hold administrative office again.

Sorrento is a small town on the eastern shore of Port Phillip. The British, motivated partly by fears that the French might settle in the area, established a convict settlement, the first white settlement in present-day Victoria, near the site of Sorrento in 1803. About 500 settlers (convicts, troops and free settlers), under the command of *Collins, arrived from England in October of that year. The settlement soon faced problems, including reluctance on the part of settlers, lack of fresh water, and heat. The leaders were also worried about the difficulties of access by sea. Collins withdrew the party, and established a new settlement in *Van Diemen's Land, early in 1804. The last of the party left the area in May 1804, except *Buckley, an escaped convict.

South African War: *Boer War

South Australia: A state of the *Commonwealth of Australia since the latter's creation in 1901. Dutch sailors are the first Europeans known to have sighted its coast, in 1627. Other Europeans, including *Flinders and *Baudin, later explored the coast. *Sealers began to use *Kangaroo Island in the early 1800s. *Sturt, and later Collet Barker, explored some areas inland. Settlement of the British province of South Australia, based partly upon *Wakefield's theory of *systematic colonization, began in 1836. The British Government and a Colonization Commission initially shared responsibility for the province. The first immigrants settled on Kangaroo Island, and on the mainland near present-day Glenelg and Adelaide. The first two Governors of South Australia were *Hindmarsh and *Gawler. The province went bankrupt. Its debt having been paid by Britain, it became a conventional colony in 1842, and was granted *responsible government in 1856. Alone among the Australian colonies, South Australia never received convicts. It was Australia's most important wheat-growing state for much of the second half of the nineteenth century. South Australia annexed the *Northern Territory in 1863, and administered it from then to 1911.

South Australian Company: A company founded by George Fife Angas and others in England (1835-6) with the purpose of encouraging investment and development in the new British province of *South Australia. The Company bought 13,770 acres (at twelve shillings per acre) and the pastoral rights to a further 220,000 acres (at ten shillings per square mile). It ran a whaling base at Kingscote on *Kangaroo Island from 1836 to 1841. As it grew, its activities came to include land speculation, trading, banking and shipping. Its activities in South Australia ended in 1949.

South-East Asia Treaty Organization (SEATO): An organization established under the South-East Asia Collective Defence Treaty (the Treaty also becoming known as SEATO), which was signed at Manila in 1954. The signatories were Australia, Britain, France, New Zealand, Pakistan, the Philippines, Thailand and the United States of America. The Treaty, which covered South-East Asia and part of the South-West Pacific, included the following statements:

Each Party recognizes that aggression by means of armed attack in the Treaty Area or against any State or territory which the Parties by unanimous agreement may hereafter designate would endanger its own peace and safety, and agrees that it will in that event act to meet the common danger in accordance with its constitutional processes.

If in the opinion of any of the Parties, the inviolability or the integrity of the territory or the sovereignty or political independence of any Party in the Treaty Area or of any State... is threatened in any way other than by armed attack... the Parties shall consult immediately in order to agree on the measures which should be taken for the common defence.

Pakistan withdrew from the Organization in 1973, and France in 1974. The Organization itself was dissolved in 1977, although the Treaty remained in existence.

Southern Cross Flag: *Eureka Flag

'Spanish' Influenza Pandemic (1918-19): A pandemic (a disease 'prevalent over the whole of a country or of the world') that swept the world towards the end of the *First World War and in the immediate post-war period, causing an estimated twenty to thirty million deaths. Returning Australian soldiers, who were among the first victims, brought the disease into Australia. Protective measures were taken, such as quarantine between some of the states, closure of public places, the wearing of face masks, and inoculation. However, about 12,000 Australians had died from the disease by the end of 1919.

Spence, Catherine Helen (1825-1910), writer, feminist and social reformer, was born in Scotland. Her family migrated to South Australia in 1839. She was a governess for some time. Catherine Spence wrote novels, works of non-fiction, and articles for newspapers and journals; she campaigned for various causes, including children's welfare, electoral reform, girls' education, female *suffrage, and political education of women; she became Australia's first female political candidate when she ran, unsuccessfully, for the *Federal Convention in 1897; and she preached in churches in Australia and the United States of

America (having joined the Unitarian Church about 1856). Her publications, some of which were published anonymously, include *Clara Morison, A Tale of Australia During the Gold Fever* (1854), which is said to be the first novel about Australia written by a woman, *Tender and True, A Colonial Tale* (1856), *A Plea for Democracy, Mr. Hare's Reform Bill applied to South Australia* (1861), *Mr. Hogarth's Will* (1865), *The Author's Daughter* (1868), *The Laws We Live Under* (1880), which is a textbook, *An Agnostic's Progress from the Known to the Unknown* (1884), *A Week in the Future* (1889), *State Children in Australia, A History of Boarding-Out and its Development* (1907) and *An Autobiography* (1910), which was completed by Jeanne Young.

Spence, William Guthrie (1846–1926), trade unionist and politician, was born in the Orkney Islands, Scotland. His father was a stonemason. In 1852 the family migrated to Australia. Spence was not formally educated. He held various jobs, including those of shepherd, butcher boy and miner, in Victoria, and then became involved in trade union organization. He was secretary of the Creswick Miners' Union, which he helped to found in 1878; he was secretary of the Amalgamated Miners' Association from 1882 to 1891; he helped to found, and from 1886 until 1893 was the first president of the Amalgamated Shearers' Union of Australasia; he was actively involved in the *Maritime Strike (1890) and the *Shearers' Strike (1891); in 1894 he helped to found the *Australian Workers' Union, of which he was secretary from 1894 to 1898, and president from 1898 to 1917. He was a Member of the Legislative Assembly of New South Wales from 1898 to 1901. He then entered federal politics, and was a New South Wales Member of the House of Representatives from 1901 to 1917 (representing Labor, then National Labor), and then a Tasmanian Member from 1917 to 1919 (representing the Nationalists). Spence was Postmaster-General (1914–15) and Vice-President of the Executive Council (1916–17). He died at Terang, Victoria. Spence's publications include *Australia's*

Squatters

Awakening, Thirty Years in the Life of an Australian Agitator (1909), *History of the A.W.U.* (1911) and various pamphlets and articles.

Squatters: A term with several meanings. In the early nineteenth century it was a derogatory term in New South Wales; the first squatters, many of whom were ex-convicts, occupied land without authority and often stole stock. By the 1830s the meaning had begun to change, and the many pastoralists who settled beyond the *Nineteen Counties were called squatters. Most were involved in the wool industry. They were granted grazing rights, for an annual licence fee, in 1836. They demanded security of tenure and pre-emptive rights, which they gained in 1847. There were also some squatters in South Australia and Western Australia, although in much smaller numbers than in New South Wales and Victoria. Squatters gained a monopoly over much of Australia's land that was suitable for agricultural and pastoral purposes. They became a very powerful group, socially, economically and politically. Squatters and *selectors struggled bitterly over land during the second half of the nineteenth century. Squatters continued to be known by that name even after they acquired their land freehold, and the term was eventually applied to all large pastoralists in Australia.

State Socialism: A term open to various interpretations. It can involve simply the public ownership of essential services such as gas, water and electricity. More strongly, it can involve the communal ownership of the means of production, distribution and exchange. In Australia the term has most commonly been used to describe the Labor Party's advocacy of the nationalization of monopolies, and the establishment of public corporations, such as the Commonwealth Bank, to compete with private enterprise.

Statute of Westminster: *Westminster, Statute of

Stead, Christina Ellen (1902–83), writer, was born in New South Wales. Her father was a naturalist.

She was educated at various schools, including Sydney Girls' High School, business college, night schools, and Sydney Teachers' College. She taught in Sydney for some time, before leaving Australia in 1928. Christina Stead spent most of her life in Britain, Europe and the United States of America. She worked in various jobs, including those of Hollywood scriptwriter and instructor at New York University. She was married to William James Blake (né Blech). She visited Australia in 1969, returned to live in Australia in 1974, and died in Sydney. She is best known for her novels, which include *Seven Poor Men of Sydney* (1934), *The Beauties and the Furies* (1936), *House of All Nations* (1938), *The Man Who Loved Children* (1940), which is perhaps her most famous work, *For England Alone* (1944), *Letty Fox, Her Luck* (1946), *A Little Tea, A Little Chat* (1948), *The People with the Dogs* (1952), *Dark Places of the Heart* (1966), *The Little Hotel* (1973) and *Miss Herbert (The Suburban Wife)* (1976). She also wrote *The Salzburg Tales* (1934) and *The Puzzleheaded Girl* (1967), both of which are collections of stories.

Stirling, Sir James (1791-1865), *governor, was born in Scotland, and pursued a naval career. He sailed to Sydney with currency in 1826, explored the south-western coast of Australia in 1827, and then transferred the garrison in northern Australia from Melville Island to Raffles Bay. Stirling recommended the Swan River area as a site for British settlement, and administered the new colony of *Western Australia from its foundation in 1829 until 1832, when he visited England, and again from 1834 to 1839. (He became Governor of Western Australia in 1832, having originally been appointed Lieutenant-Governor.) He was involved in the Battle of *Pinjarra in 1834. After leaving Western Australia in early 1839, Stirling continued his naval career, eventually becoming an admiral in 1862. He died in England.

Streeton, Sir Arthur Ernest (1867-1943), artist, was born in Victoria. His father was a schoolteacher. Streeton was apprenticed to a lithographer, and studied at the National Gallery School in Melbourne. He became one of the leading members of the *Heidelberg School. According to Patrick McCaughey, 'Streeton was the most various, the most unpredictable and, arguably, the most naturally gifted member of the Heidelberg School.'[1] He contributed forty works to the controversial Exhibition of 9 × 5 Impressions, and later held a number of successful Australian exhibitions of his own. Streeton's early landscapes are now considered to be his best works. From 1898 he lived in England, returning to Australia for several exhibitions in 1907. During the First World War he served in the Royal Army Medical Corps and as an official war artist. Streeton lived in Australia again from 1919 to 1921. He also lived in the United States of America for some time, before settling permanently in Australia in 1924. Streeton's paintings include *Still Glides the Stream and Shall Forever Glide* (1889), *'Fire's On', Lapstone Tunnel* (1891) and *Purple Noon's Transparent Might* (1896).

Strutt, William (1825–1915), artist, was born in England. He studied art in Paris, and completed many illustrations for books, before arriving in 1850 in Melbourne, where John Pascoe Fawkner became his patron. Strutt remained in Australia until 1862, except for a period in 1855–6 when he lived in New Zealand. He produced many engravings and lithographs, some of which he was employed to do for the *Illustrated Australian Magazine*; sketched and painted numerous significant events; and painted a number of portraits, including those of Fawkner, Frederick Sargood, *Coppin and John O'Hara Burke. Strutt returned to England in 1862, and became well known for his paintings of animals. His best-known works about Australia are his history paintings, such as *Black Thursday* (1862–4) and *Bushrangers on the St. Kilda Road* (c. 1887). The Library Committee of the Parliament of Victoria published Strutt's *Victoria the Golden, Scenes, Sketches and Jottings from Nature, 1850–1862*, in 1980. The Parliament's Library has held the original album since 1907.

[1] Patrick McCaughey and Jack Manton, *Australian Painters of the Heidelberg School, The Jack Manton Collection* (Oxford University Press, Melbourne, 1979), p. 82.

Stuart, John McDouall (1815–66), explorer, was
born in Scotland. His father was an army captain.
Stuart was educated at the Scottish Naval and Military Academy. In 1839 he arrived in South Australia,
where he worked as a surveyor. Stuart was a
draughtsman with Charles *Sturt's expedition to central Australia (1844–6). In 1858 he explored an area
near Lakes Torrens and Gairdner. In 1859 he led
an expedition to search for a permanent route to the
north, travelling to an area beyond Lake Eyre. He
surveyed that area in another expedition later that
year. In 1860 he made his first attempt to cross the
continent from south to north; he reached the centre
of Australia, and discovered nearby Central Mount
Sturt (later Stuart). His second attempt, funded by
the South Australian Government and in competition with the *Burke and Wills expedition, took place
in the first half of 1861. It also failed. His third
attempt, made in 1861 and 1862, was successful.
Burke and Wills had beaten him, but died on their
return trip. The *Overland Telegraph Line was built
along Stuart's successful route. Stuart, almost blind
from the hardships he had experienced, left Australia
for Scotland in 1864, and died in London in 1866.

Stump-jump Plough: An agricultural implement,
which behaves as its name suggests. It was significant in the development of the Mallee areas of New
South Wales, South Australia and Victoria. A farmer
named Mullins apparently devised the theory behind
it, and R. B. and C. H. Smith put the theory into
practice. The stump-jump plough was registered in
1877 and patented in 1881, and is still used in the
1980s.

Sturt, Charles (1795–1869), explorer, was born in
India, the son of a judge in Bengal. He was educated
in England, entered the army, and served in Europe
and Canada before arriving in Sydney as a captain
in 1827. Sturt was largely responsible for solving the
'riddle of the rivers' in eastern Australia. On his first
expedition, in 1828–9, he explored the Macquarie
River, discovered the Darling River and explored part
of the Castlereagh River. On his second expedition,
in 1829–30, he explored much of the Murrumbidgee

River, entered the Murray River (which he named, unaware that it was the same river that Hume and Hovell had discovered further upstream, and had named the Hume) and followed it to its mouth on the southern coast (exploring part of the Darling River at its junction with the Murray along the way), then returned along the rivers. Sturt went temporarily blind as a result of hardships experienced during this expedition. He served on *Norfolk Island for some time, before returning on sick leave to England, where he retired from the army. In 1835 he returned to New South Wales. In 1838, while overlanding cattle to Adelaide, he explored the rest of the Murray River. In 1839 he returned to Adelaide, where he expected to become Surveyor-General, but due to some confusion became assistant Commissioner of Lands. He was later demoted to Registrar-General. On his final expedition, from 1844 to 1846, he explored part of central Australia. He became Colonial Treasurer as well as Registrar-General. He left for England in 1847, on leave, and returned to Adelaide in 1849. He soon became Colonial Secretary, resigned in 1851, and returned permanently to England in 1853. Sturt's publications include *Two Expeditions into the Interior of Southern Australia 1828–31* (1833) and *Narrative of an Expedition into Central Australia* (1849).

'Such is life': A famous phrase, reputedly *Kelly's final words before being hanged at the Melbourne Gaol on 11 November 1880. There is some disagreement as to whether he actually said this, or 'Ah well, I suppose it has come to this.' The phrase is also the title of *Furphy's well-known book.

Sudan Contingent: A contingent sent from New South Wales to support the British in the Sudan. After news of General Gordon's death at Khartoum reached Australia, the New South Wales Government offered, in February 1885, to send troops. The offer was accepted. Further offers from Victoria, South Australia and Queensland were declined. The contingent, consisting of about 750 male volunteers, accompanied by 200 horses, sailed from Sydney in the *Australasian* and *Iberia* on 3 March 1885, and arrived at Suakin on the Red Sea on 29 March 1885. The men saw some fighting at Tamai; three were slightly wounded. They mostly worked on railway fatigues. Fifty formed part of a camel corps. The contingent sailed again, in the *Arab*, on 17 May 1885, arrived in Sydney on 23 June, and disbanded shortly afterwards. Nine of the Australians involved died from disease.

Sudds and Thompson Affair: A controversial affair in New South Wales in 1826. Joseph Sudds and Patrick Thompson, who were privates in the 57th Regiment, were convicted of theft and each sentenced to seven years' *transportation. *Darling, wishing to stamp out the practice of soldiers obtaining discharges from the *army by committing minor civil crimes, commuted their sentences to seven years' hard labour. Sudds and Thompson were paraded in iron collars, chains and leg-irons, and drummed out of their regiment. Sudds died five days later. It has been argued by some that Darling's actions were illegal. Later he was ordered to release Thompson. Darling's opponents used the affair to attack him, and *Wentworth threatened to impeach him. Parts of the press pursued the issue for political reasons. Darling responded by attempting to legislate against the press, and the *Newspaper Regulating Act* (1827) was passed. Thompson was released in mid-1827, and returned to his regiment. After Darling's return to England, a Select Committee inquiring into his conduct in New South Wales exonerated him in 1835.

Suffrage: The 'right of voting in political elections'. Manhood suffrage for the lower houses was introduced in South Australia in 1856, Victoria in 1857, New South Wales in 1858, Queensland in 1859, Western Australia in 1893, and Tasmania in 1900. Adult suffrage (that is, for women as well as men) for the lower houses was introduced in South Australia in 1894, Western Australia in 1899, New South Wales in 1902, Tasmania in 1903, Queensland in 1905, and Victoria in 1908. Adult suffrage for the Commonwealth House of Representatives and Senate was introduced in 1902 (those people eligible to vote for the lower house in each state had been eligible to vote at the first federal election).

Sunshine Harvester: *McKay, Hugh Victor

Sutherland, Dame Joan (1926-   ), soprano, was born and educated in Sydney, where she made her operatic début in Goossen's *Judith.* She went to London in 1951, studied with Clive Carey at the Royal College of Music, and made her Covent Garden début as the First Lady in *The Magic Flute* in 1952. Her performance in the title role of *Lucia di Lammermoor,* at Covent Garden in 1959, and La Scala, Milan, in 1961, confirmed her reputation as a great soprano. She also made highly successful débuts in Italy, France, Austria and the United States of America in 1960, and has often returned to Australia to sing. Her husband, Richard Bonynge, has conducted most of her performances for many years.

Sutherland, Margaret (1897-1984), composer, was born in Adelaide, but spent most of her life in Melbourne. Her father was a journalist. She studied at the Albert Street Conservatorium of Music, Melbourne (later the Melba Memorial Conservatorium). She went to Europe in 1923, spending time in London (where she studied composition under Arnold Bax) and Vienna, before returning to Australia in 1925. Margaret Sutherland composed some twenty orchestral works, an opera entitled *The Young Kabbarli* (1965), based upon the life of Daisy *Bates, more than twenty chamber works, two ballets, and a number of piano, choral, vocal and incidental works. She also organized midday chamber music concerts for the Red Cross during the Second World War; played a leading role in the Combined Arts Centre Movement, the object of which was to have an arts centre established on land in St Kilda Road (the site of the present Victorian Arts Centre), during the 1940s and 1950s; was a founding member of the Council of Education, Music and the Arts in the 1940s; was a council member of the National Gallery of Victoria during the 1950s and 1960s; was a member of the Australian

Unesco Music Committee during the 1960s; and was a member of the Advisory Board of the Australian Music Fund, also during the 1960s.

Swagmen were itinerant labourers. Their name came from the swags, or bundles of personal belongings, they carried. They tramped around country areas, seeking employment on stations in return for supplies. Many travelled alone. They were most common at the turn of this century and during the *Great Depression of the 1930s. Swagmen have become part of Australian folklore.

Swan River: *Western Australia

Swimming has been one of Australia's most popular sports for many years. The first swimming championship to be held in the Australian colonies reputedly took place in Sydney in 1846, and the Amateur Swimming Union of Australia was founded in 1909. Australian swimmers have competed in international competitions since the 1890s, with considerable success, particularly in the *Olympic Games held in Melbourne in 1956 (at which Australia won eight gold medals for swimming). Notable Australian swimmers have included members of the Cavill family, one of whom was Richard Cavill (1884-1938), said to have been the first person to use the stroke that became known as the Australian crawl in a competition (in 1899), Frederick Lane (1880-1969), Sir Frank Beaurepaire (1891-1956), Annette Kellermann (1886-1975), Sarah (Fanny) Durack (1889-1956), Andrew ('Boy') Charlton (1907-75), Lorraine Crapp (1939-), Dawn Fraser (1937-), Murray Rose (1939-), John Konrads (1942-), Ilsa Konrads (1944-) and Shane Gould (1957-). Non-competitive swimming also has been, and continues to be, very popular in Australia. Surfing, competitive and non-competitive, has become increasingly popular among Australians too, especially since the 1960s.

'Swing' Rioters: English agricultural labourers who took part in the 'Swing' Riots of 1830, agrarian riots in wheat-growing areas such as Hampshire,

Wiltshire and Berkshire. Their conditions were poor,
they saw the introduction of new threshing machines
as a threat, and they smashed machines, burnt ricks,
rioted over wages, and sent threatening letters to
farmers. They took their name from that of their
mythical leader, 'Captain Swing', whose signature
often appeared on the threatening letters. They are
known also as the machine-breakers. After the riots,
1976 people appeared before ninety courts. Nineteen
were hanged. Four hundred and seventy-six, two of
whom were women, were transported to Australia;
of these 332 were sent to Van Diemen's Land, the
remaining 144 to New South Wales. Almost all
arrived in the colonies in 1831 and were assigned.
Most received free pardons between 1836 and 1838.
Very few appear to have returned to England. The
'Swing' Rioters formed the largest single group of
protesters to be transported to Australia.

Sydney, the capital city of *New South Wales, is
Australia's oldest city. *Phillip, having rejected
*Botany Bay as the site for Britain's new penal col-
ony, explored to the north and chose a site on Port
Jackson. He named it Sydney Cove, after the British
Secretary of State for the Colonies. Settlers from the
*First Fleet landed there on 26 January 1788. Sydney
was proclaimed a city in 1842. Sydney's population
was slightly more than 1000 in 1788, 224,939 in 1881,
and 2,874,415 in 1981.

Sydney Harbour Bridge: A toll bridge, which
crosses Sydney Harbour from Dawes Point to Mil-
son's Point. John Job Crew Bradfield was largely
responsible for its design. Its construction began in
1923. J. T. *Lang, the New South Wales Premier,
officially opened it on 19 March 1932, although Francis Edward de Groot, a member of the *New Guard,
slashed the ribbon before him (and consequently was
arrested).

Sydney Morning Herald: *Fairfax, John

Sydney Opera House: A striking white building,
in appearance like a series of wind-filled sails, situ-

ated at Bennelong Point, on the edge of Sydney Harbour. Joern Utzon, a Danish architect, was largely responsible for its design. In 1957 he won a competition run by the New South Wales Government, but resigned amid controversy in 1966. Construction, mostly funded by lotteries, began in 1959 and ended in 1973. The building houses a concert hall, drama and opera theatres, restaurants, and other facilities.

Syme, David (1827–1908), newspaper proprietor, was born in Scotland and educated by his father, who was a schoolmaster. He also travelled and studied in Germany. Syme went to the Californian goldfields in 1851, then was a *digger on the Victorian gold-fields from 1852 to 1855, before becoming a road contractor. His brother, Ebenezer Syme (1826–60), bought the Melbourne *Age* in June 1856. David Syme, who became Ebenezer's partner in September 1856, published and edited the *Age* from 1859 until his death. His policies included the opening of land for *selectors, the *protection of local industries, the introduction of democratic reforms, support for *free, compulsory and secular education, and reforms in working conditions. He wielded considerable political influence, especially during the 1890s. The newspaper's circulation increased from about 2000 in 1860 to about 120,000 in 1899. After his death, his sons continued the newspaper as a trust, which was superseded by a public company in 1948. Syme's publications include *Outlines of an Industrial Science* (1876), *Representative Government in England* (1881), *On the Modification of Organisms* (1890), *The Soul, A Study and an Argument* (1903) and various journal articles relating to political economy.

Systematic Colonization: A socio-economic theory expounded by *Wakefield and others, which influenced British colonial policies, particularly during the 1830s and 1840s. The theory proposed a balance between land, labour and capital. Colonial lands should be sold at a so-called 'sufficient price', which would delay, but not stop, labourers from becoming land-owners. Capital raised could be used to finance emigration from the mother country. Colonies eventually would become self-governing. Theoretically, the system would be self-regulating, and of mutual benefit to mother country and colonies. Some principles of this theory were applied to the white settlement of Australia, in particular to that of *South Australia. Wakefield was critical of the way in which South Australia was settled, and dissociated himself from it.

T

TAA: *Trans Australia Airlines

Tailoresses' Strike: A strike in 1882-3 said to have been the first organized women's strike in Australian history. Tailoresses employed in Melbourne factories went on strike over alleged sweating. The main periods of the strike were in December 1882 and February 1883. The Trades Hall Council, the *Age* and many members of the public supported the strikers. Estimates of the numbers of striking tailoresses range from about 400 to 2000. Most of the employers involved agreed to the demands of the Tailoresses' Union in February 1883. Some writers claim that the Tailoresses' Union was formed shortly after the strike began, others that it was already in existence.

Tasman, Abel Janszoon (1603?-59), Dutch mariner, was born near Groningen, in the Netherlands. He joined the Dutch East India Company in 1632, and participated in various military, trading and exploratory voyages before being appointed to command a voyage to explore the southern and eastern seas in 1642. On this voyage, he discovered *Van Diemen's Land, which he claimed for the Dutch and named after the Governor-General of the Dutch East Indies (part of present-day Indonesia); he also discovered *New Zealand, the Tonga Islands, and some of the Fiji Islands; he returned to Batavia (present-day Jakarta) along the northern coast of *New Guinea. In 1644 Tasman led another voyage to the area. He confirmed that New Guinea and *New Holland (present-day Australia) were not joined, but that Carpentaria (part of present-day Queensland) and De Witt's Land (part of present-day Western Australia) each belonged to the same land mass. He charted the northern and north-western coast from the Gulf of Carpentaria to present-day North-West Cape. After returning to Batavia, he was confirmed as commandeur and was appointed to the Council of Justice. He led a diplomatic mission to Siam (present-day Thailand) in 1647. He then led a fleet of eight vessels against the Spanish in 1648, but the following year was removed from office for maltreating a sailor on that voyage. He was reinstated in 1651, but retired soon afterwards, and became a merchant in Batavia. He died there in 1659. Van Diemen's Land was renamed *Tasmania, after him, in 1855.

Tasmania, a state of the *Commonwealth of Australia since the latter's creation in 1901, consists of a large island, separated from mainland Australia by Bass Strait, and a number of smaller nearby islands. In its early years of white settlement, which began in 1803, it was known as *Van Diemen's Land. The colony was renamed Tasmania, after *Tasman, in 1855. *Responsible government was also granted that year. The first responsible ministry took office the following year. The development of Tasmania from the 1930s was greatly assisted by the *Commonwealth Grants Commission.

'Temper, democratic; bias, offensively Australian': A now-famous phrase, first used by *Furphy to describe his novel, *Such is Life, Being Certain Extracts from the Life of Tom Collins* (1903). The complete sentence read: 'I have just finished writing a full-sized novel: title, *Such is Life*; scene, Riverina and northern Vic; temper, democratic; bias, offensively Australian.'[1] Furphy wrote this in a letter that accompanied his manuscript when he sent the latter to the Sydney *Bulletin* for advice in 1897.

---

[1]Cited in Stephen Murray-Smith (ed.), *The Dictionary of Australian Quotations* (Heinemann Publishers Australia, Melbourne, 1984), p. 87.

Tench, Watkin (1758?–1883), soldier and writer, was born in England. He entered the marine corps in 1776, and served in the American War of Independence, during which he was a prisoner-of-war for some months. He sailed to New South Wales with the *First Fleet, as one of the two captain-lieutenants of the detachment of marines. He remained in the colony until 1792, when he sailed to England with the marines. Tench was again a prisoner-of-war for some time during the war with France. He retired, with the rank of lieutenant-general, in 1821. He died in England. Tench is best known in Australia for two books, both based upon his journal: *A Narrative of the Expedition to Botany Bay, with an Account of New South Wales, its Productions, Inhabitants &c* (1789) and *A Complete Account of the Settlement at Port Jackson, in New South Wales, including an Accurate Description of the Situation of the Colony, and of its Natural Productions, taken on the Spot* (1793). He also published *Letters Written in France, to a Friend in London, between the Month of November 1794 and the Month of May 1795* (1796).

Tennis has been for many years one of Australia's most popular sports, for both spectators and participants, with access to tennis courts being widely available. It was first introduced to the Australian colonies during the 1870s. The Lawn Tennis Association of Australia (originally Australasia) was founded in 1904. The Australian championships, first played in 1905, form part of the 'grand slam', the four main international tennis championships for players competing as individuals (the others being held at Wimbledon, in France and in the United States of America). Many Australians have been successful in these championships over the years, particularly during the 1950s and 1960s. Australia (in partnership with New Zealand until 1923) first competed in the Davis Cup (the International Lawn Tennis Challenge Trophy) competition, the main men's international tennis team competition, in 1905, and won twenty-four times (six of those with New Zealand) up to and including 1977. Australia also won the Federation Cup, the sport's main women's international team competition, seven times between 1963 (when that competition began) and 1978. Australia's many notable tennis players have included Sir Norman Brookes (1877-1968), Ken Rosewall (1934-), Lew Hoad (1934-), Roy Emerson (1936-), Rod Laver (1938-), Margaret Court (née Smith) (1942-), John Newcombe (1944-) and Evonne Cawley (née Goolagong) (1951-).

Tent Embassy: *Land Rights

Tenterfield Oration: A now-famous speech given by Sir Henry *Parkes, the Premier of New South Wales, at Tenterfield, New South Wales, on 24 October 1889. He argued for the federation of the Australian colonies, largely for defence reasons.

***Terra Nullius*:** A Latin term meaning land belonging to no-one, or unoccupied land. At the time of white discovery and settlement of *New South Wales, the British apparently considered that the area was *terra nullius*, because the *Aborigines did not occupy the land in a European sense. The British believed that if the land was *terra nullius* (according to their definition), then the first Europeans to discover it, and to occupy it, were entitled to it.

Theodore, Edward Granville (1884-1950), politician and businessman, was born at Port Adelaide, South Australia. His father was a tugboat operator. Theodore left school at twelve and worked in various local jobs, then in mining and other jobs in several states. His union involvement included founding the Amalgamated Workers' Association in Queensland in 1907, and being president of the *Australian Workers' Union, also in Queensland, in 1913. Theodore was a Labor Member of the Queensland Legislative Assembly from 1909 to 1925. He held various portfolios, and was Premier from 1919 to 1925, when he resigned in order to enter federal politics. Theodore, who had become known as 'Red Ted', was a Labor Member of the House of Representatives from 1927 until he was defeated in the elections held in December 1931. He was Deputy Leader of the Labor

Party, and of the Opposition in 1929, and Treasurer in the *Scullin Government. He resigned from the ministry in July 1930, following allegations by a Queensland Royal Commission that his conduct relating to the sale of the Mungana mines, while Premier of Queensland, had been fraudulent and dishonest. His reinstatement in January 1931 was an immediate factor in a major split in the *Australian Labor Party. Later in 1931 a court exonerated him over his actions in the Mungana affair. As Treasurer, Theodore advocated a mildly inflationary approach to deal with the *Great Depression. Following his electoral defeat he pursued business interests. During the Second World War, he was Director-General of Allied Works from 1942 to 1944. He died in Sydney.

Third Fleet: Eleven ships, carrying convicts and supplies, that sailed from England and Ireland to New South Wales in 1791, after the *First Fleet and *Second Fleet. The ships of the Third Fleet were the *Active, Admiral Barrington, Albemarle, Atlantic, Britannia, Gorgon* (a supply ship), *Mary Ann, Matilda, Salamander* and *William and Ann*. About 185 convicts died during the voyage; about 1865 other convicts, some in very poor health, arrived in the colony.

'Thirty-six faceless men': A derogatory phrase that was used to describe the thirty-six member *Australian Labor Party federal conference, and its supposed relationship with the Party's federal parliamentary leadership. There is some debate as to who first used the phrase; it has usually been attributed to Alan Reid, a journalist. A special federal conference met in 1963 to decide party policy on a proposed United States naval communications base at North West Cape. At that time the parliamentary leader (*Calwell) and the deputy leader (*Whitlam) did not have the right to attend such conferences. Press photographs showed Calwell and Whitlam having to wait outside while the conference decided party policy. *Menzies used the phrase during the federal election campaign later that year, claiming that the Australian Labor Party was subject to anonymous external control. The incident led to the Party's parliamentary leader and deputy leader gaining the right to attend and to speak, although not to vote, at federal conferences.

'Three Elevens': A now-famous phrase used by *Deakin in a speech given in Melbourne on 1 February 1904. He likened the situation in the Commonwealth Parliament to a cricket game with 'three elevens' competing instead of two. After the general election held on 16 December 1903, the seats were distributed almost equally among the three parties. In the House of Representatives, the Protectionists held twenty-five seats, the Free Traders twenty-four and Labor twenty-five, and there was one Independent; in the Senate, Labor held fourteen, the Free Traders thirteen and the Protectionists nine. Deakin's full sentence ran as follows: 'What kind of a game of cricket, compared with the present game, could they play if they had three elevens instead of two, with one playing sometimes with one side, sometimes with the other, and sometimes for itself?'[1]

Tichborne Case: A sensational English legal case. Roger Tichborne, the heir to a baronetcy and fortune, disappeared in a shipwreck off the South American coast in 1854. His mother later advertised in search of him. One Thomas Castro, a butcher's assistant from Wagga Wagga in New South Wales, responded to the advertisement in 1855, claiming to be Tichborne. The Tichborne Claimant, as he was called, went to England in 1866. He convinced Tichborne's mother, but not the rest of the family, that he was Tichborne. A civil action to establish his claims failed in 1872. He was then charged with perjury, found guilty and sentenced to fourteen years' imprisonment. It appears that he was a butcher's son named Arthur Orton, who was born in Wapping, London, in 1834. He went to South America in 1849, returned to England in 1851, and then sailed for Australia in 1852. He had various jobs in Australia, before

---

[1] Cited in Stephen Murray-Smith, *The Dictionary of Australian Quotations* (Heinemann Publishers Australia, Melbourne, 1984), p. 63.

becoming a butcher's assistant (under the name of Castro) in Wagga Wagga in 1864. After his release from jail in 1884, he became a music-hall actor. In 1895 he 'confessed' to being an impostor, but later withdrew his 'confession'. He died in London in 1898. The Tichborne case attracted much press and public interest, in both England and Australia.

Ticket-of-leave: A certificate that could be granted to a convict during the *transportation period. It allowed the convict to be excused from compulsory labour, to choose his or her own employer, and to work for wages. There were some restrictions, and the ticket-of-leave could be withdrawn. It was usually granted for good conduct, but sometimes for other reasons, such as economy.

Tolpuddle Martyrs (also known as the Dorchester Labourers): The popular name given to six agricultural labourers from the village of Tolpuddle, in England, who were transported to Australia in 1834. They were James Brine, James Hammett, James Loveless, George Loveless (the group's leader), John Standfield and Thomas Standfield. Their ostensible crime was 'administering unlawful oaths'; their actual 'crime' was organizing a trade union (the Friendly Society of Agricultural Labourers), although it was not illegal to do so. The six were tried at the Dorchester Assizes, were found guilty, and each was sentenced to seven years' transportation. All were transported to New South Wales, except for George Loveless, who was transported to Van Diemen's Land. All were assigned to settlers. After much protest in England, they were granted free pardons and free passages in 1836, and all returned to England between 1837 and 1839. Hammett alone returned to Tolpuddle; the others farmed in Essex for about two years, before migrating to Canada. George Loveless described the experiences of the Tolpuddle Martyrs in *The Victims of Whiggery* (1837).

Torrens System: A system for registration of ownership of land. It takes its name from Robert Richard Torrens, a politician and former Collector of Customs and Registrar-General of Deeds, who introduced a bill, which incorporated it, in the South Australian Parliament in 1857. The bill was passed in 1858. Douglas J. Whalan has described the main principles of the system thus:

land titles no longer passed by the execution of deeds but by the registration of dealings on a public register; once registered the title of a purchaser became indefeasible unless he was guilty of fraud; and innocent dealers with interests in registered land were guaranteed either their interest in the land or monetary compensation therefor.[1]

The system was adopted in Queensland, New South Wales, Victoria and Tasmania during the 1860s, and in Western Australia during the 1870s. It was also adopted in other countries.

Towns, Robert (1794-1873), merchant, was born in England, and went to sea when young. From 1827 he visited Australia many times in charge of vessels, sometimes his own. He settled in Sydney in 1843, where he already held investments and property, and became a successful merchant and ship-owner, trading in the Pacific and elsewhere. He also acquired much land, particularly in Queensland in the 1860s. Towns introduced *blackbirding to Australia in 1863, when he began importing Pacific Islanders to work on his cotton plantations near Brisbane; the practice was to play a significant role in the development of the Australian sugar industry. In 1864 J. M. Black, an agent acting for Towns, established a settlement at Cleveland Bay, which formed the basis of the town (later city) and port of *Townsville. Towns was a director of the *Bank of New South Wales (1850-5, 1861-7); was involved in its reorganization in 1851; and was its president twice (1853-5, 1866-7). He was a Member of the New South Wales Legislative Council (1856-61, 1863-73), and was president of the Sydney Chamber of Commerce several times. He wrote *South Sea Island Immigration for Cotton Culture* (1863).

---

[1]Douglas J. Whalan, 'Sir Robert Richard Torrens', in Geoffrey Serle and Russel Ward (eds), *Australian Dictionary of Biography*, volume 6 (Melbourne University Press, Melbourne, 1976), p. 293.

Townsville

Townsville is a city and port in northern Queensland, located on Cleveland Bay. J. M. Black, acting for Robert *Towns, established a settlement (which he originally called Castletown) on the site in 1864. Townsville was gazetted a town and port in 1865, was declared a municipality in 1866, and became a city in 1903. Queensland gold discoveries in the 1870s, particularly at Charters Towers, greatly assisted Townsville's development. An artificial harbour was built before the end of the nineteenth century. Australian and American troops were stationed there during the Second World War. Townsville is connected by rail with Brisbane (1340 kilometres to the south-east), Cairns, Charters Towers, *Mount Isa and Cloncurry, and the port serves mining, pastoral, sugar and other industries. The James Cook University of North Queensland and the Australian Institute of Marine Science are situated in Townsville. Townsville's population in 1981 was 86,112.

Trade Diversion Policy: A controversial trading policy introduced by the *Lyons *United Australia Party–Country Party Government in 1936. In theory, trade was to be diverted away from bad customers (that is, those that sold much more to Australia than they bought) towards those that were good customers. Australian industry also was to be protected, using bounties, duties and import licences. In practice, the main targets were Japan (a good customer) and the United States of America (a bad customer); trade in textiles was to be diverted from Japan towards Britain, and trade in motor vehicle bodies was to be diverted from the United States of America towards locally based, British-owned, manufacturers. Britain (a good customer) was the main beneficiary. This policy was dropped within about two years. Japanese and American exports to Australia quickly returned to pre-1936 levels, while their imports from Australia remained at much lower levels.

Trans Australia Airlines (TAA): One of Australia's two main domestic airlines, the other being *Ansett Airlines of Australia. The *Chifley Labor Government attempted to nationalize civil aviation, through the establishment of the Australian National Airlines Commission, in 1945. The attempt failed when the *High Court found it to be unconstitutional. However, Trans Australia Airlines, run by the Australian National Airlines Commission, was founded in 1946, with a daily return service between Melbourne and Sydney. The extent of the services was soon increased and TAA became very successful. The *Menzies Liberal–Country Party Government introduced a new policy regarding Australia's domestic airlines, which later became known as the 'two-airline policy', in 1952. The two airlines were TAA and its chief competitor, the privately owned, and ailing, Australian National Airways (ANA). The main stated principles behind the policy were:

(1) Each operator to be given a proper and substantial share of air mail.

(2) Government business to be freely available to both airlines.

(3) Each operator to be assisted financially to acquire new heavy flying equipment…

(4) The level of air-routes charges paid by operators should be substantially reduced.

(5) Routes, time-tables, freights and fares should be rationalized to avoid overlapping, to give the most effective service, and to bring earnings into a proper relation to overall costs.

(6) The operators should confer on the subject of rationalization with a view to agreement and that, failing agreement, an independent chairman should settle any difficulties in relation to rationalization of services.[1]

When Ansett Transport Industries took over ANA in 1957, the 'two-airline policy' was applied to Ansett–ANA (later known as Ansett Airlines of Australia) and TAA. In 1986 it was announced that TAA's name would be changed to Australian Airlines.

---

[1] *Commonwealth Parliamentary Debates*, House of Representatives, 24 October 1952, vol. 220, pp. 3739–40, 3743, cited in Frank Crowley, *A Documentary History of Australia*, volume 5, *Modern Australia, 1939–1970* (Nelson, Melbourne, 1978), pp. 267–8.

Transportation

Transportation, as a form of punishment, was used in Britain from the seventeenth century until 1868. Most of the convicts were sent to Britain's American and Australian colonies. Transportation to America began in the mid-1660s. It ceased in 1776, because of the American War of Independence. About 161,700 convicts (of whom nearly 25,000 were women) arrived in the Australian colonies between 1788 and 1868. Three-quarters of them came from England, Scotland and Wales, a little under a quarter came from Ireland, and a few hundred came from India, Canada and other British colonies. The most common crime for which they were transported was theft. There were about 1000 political prisoners, including the *Scottish Martyrs, the *Tolpuddle Martyrs, some of the *Canadian Rebels, and a number of *Chartists. About half of the convicts were sent to New South Wales (including *Moreton Bay and the *Port Phillip District) (1788–1840). A further 3000 *exiles were sent there during the 1840s. *Van Diemen's Land (1803–53) and Western Australia (1850–68) also received convicts. In the early years of white settlement in New South Wales and Van Diemen's Land, convicts were used mainly on public works. Assignment (allotting convicts as unpaid servants to colonists) was used extensively, especially during the 1820s and 1830s. Various forms of probation were used, especially in Van Diemen's Land during the 1840s and early 1850s. Additional punishment of convicts included corporal punishment, solitary confinement, hard labour, confinement to *female factories for women, transportation to *penal settlements, and capital punishment.

Treaty of Versailles: *Versailles, Treaty of

'True patriots all': A now-famous phrase, which was used to describe convicts in the early years of *transportation. It comes from the following stanza of a prologue written by 'a Gentleman of Leicester' (now believed to have been Henry Carter, who was *not* a convict):

From distant climes o'er widespread seas we come,
Though not with much éclat or beat of drum,

258

True patriots all; for, be it understood,
We left our country for our country's good;
No private views disgrac'd our generous zeal,
What urg'd our travels was our country's weal;
And none will doubt but that our emigration
Has prov'd most useful to the British nation.[1]

For many years the prologue was attributed to George Barrington, a renowned pickpocket, who had been transported to New South Wales for stealing a gold watch and chain. He was reputed to have spoken the words of the prologue at the opening of the first Australian theatre in 1796.

Trugernanner (often spelt Truganini, sometimes Trugernanna, Trugernini) (1812?-76), Tasmanian *Aborigine, was born on the western side of the D'Entrecasteaux Channel, *Van Diemen's Land. Her father Mangerner (or Mangana) was an Aborigine on Bruny Island. She met *Robinson at Bruny Island in 1829, and assisted him when he travelled around Van Diemen's Land, rounding up Aborigines, during the 1830s. Trugernanner moved to the Flinders Island settlement in 1835, where she remained, except for one trip back to the mainland in 1836, until she went to the *Port Phillip District with Robinson in 1839. In 1841 she was one of five Aborigines charged with the murder of two white *whalers near Portland Bay. Two of the Aborigines were hanged, and Trugernanner was returned to Flinders Island in 1842. The settlement was moved to Oyster Cove, on the east coast of Van Diemen's Land, in 1847. After the other Aborigines had died, Trugernanner left Oyster Cove in 1874 and went to live with a white family in Hobart, where she died. Her skeleton was displayed in the Tasmanian Museum, Hobart, between 1904 and 1951. Her bones were cremated, and her ashes spread over the D'Entrecasteaux Channel, in 1976. Trugernanner has often, but

---

[1]This stanza is from the original version, which was published in the *Annual Register* (1801). It is cited in *The Australian Encyclopaedia*, volume 1 (The Grolier Society of Australia, Sydney, third edition, 1977, revised 1979), p. 273. Other versions were published elsewhere.

inaccurately, been described as the last Tasmanian Aborigine.

Turner (née Burwell), **Ethel Sibyl** (1872–1958), writer, was born in England. Her father, a merchant, died when she was two years old. She and her sister took their stepfather's name after their mother's subsequent remarriage. After the stepfather's death, the family left England for Australia in 1879. Ethel attended the Sydney Girls' High School, before she and her sister Lilian founded and ran the *Parthenon*, a monthly journal, between 1889 and 1892. Ethel Turner then contributed articles for children to the *Illustrated Sydney News*, and later to the *Town and Country Journal*. She wrote many children's books, the best-known of which is *Seven Little Australians* (1894), now a classic among children's books. It has sold widely, has been translated into a number of languages, and has been adapted for film and television. Ethel Turner (whose married name was Curlewis) died in Sydney.

'Two-airline Policy': *Trans Australia Airlines

Tyson, James (1819–98), pastoralist, was born in New South Wales. His father was a free settler, his mother an ex-convict. Tyson worked in various pastoral jobs before he and his brother William established a successful slaughter-yard and butcher's shop at Bendigo, during the *gold-rushes. After selling the business in 1855, Tyson began to acquire stations in New South Wales and Queensland. By 1898 he held 2,156,680 hectares, of which 142,585 hectares were freehold. He was a Member of the Queensland Legislative Council from 1893 to 1898, and a magistrate in New South Wales and Queensland.

U

UAP: *United Australia Party

Uniform Taxation: Popular name given to the uniform system of income taxation, of individuals and companies, that has operated throughout Australia since 1942. Under this system, the Commonwealth has an effective monopoly in the area of income taxation. The various colonies (states from 1901 onwards) introduced income taxation between 1884 and 1902. The Commonwealth did so in 1915, during the First World War. Both Commonwealth and states continued to levy income tax until 1942. Different states had different rates. The *Curtin Labor Government introduced uniform taxation, as a wartime measure, in 1942. The original legislation provided for the transfer of personnel, equipment and records from the state income tax departments to the Commonwealth; the imposition of Commonwealth income tax at a rate high enough to cover the sum formerly raised by both Commonwealth and states, making it impractical for the states to continue to levy income tax; priority to be given to payment of Commonwealth income tax; and the reimbursement of lost revenue to the states, dependent upon their not levying income tax. South Australia, Victoria, Queensland and Western Australia challenged the system's validity before the *High Court in 1942. The latter found it to be valid, and that only the transfer of departments was dependent upon wartime defence powers. Victoria and New South Wales challenged the system's validity before the High Court in 1957. The court again found the system to be valid, except for the priority provision. There have been periodic suggestions that the states should levy their own income tax again, but the Commonwealth monopoly continues in the 1980s. The introduction of uniform taxation greatly increased the Commonwealth's power, at the expense of the states.

United Australia Party (UAP): A political party formed in 1931, during the *Great Depression, when the *Nationalist Party and a group of former Labor Party members, including J. A. *Lyons, merged. The major extra-parliamentary organization behind it was the All for Australia League. The United Australia Party governed federally from 1932 to 1941; it governed alone from 1932 to 1934, and from 1939 to 1940, and in coalition with the Country Party for the remainder of the period. It also governed at state

United Nations Organization

level, in coalition with the Country Party, for periods in New South Wales and Victoria. The federal parliamentary leaders of the United Australia Party were Lyons (1931-9), *Menzies (1939-41, 1943-5) and *Hughes (1941-3). The United Australia Party was dissolved and absorbed into the newly formed *Liberal Party of Australia in 1945.

United Nations Organization (UN): An international organization established in 1945, shortly before the conclusion of the Second World War. Its aims—to solve international disputes peacefully and to foster international co-operation—are similar to those of the *League of Nations, which it superseded. Australia was one of the UN's fifty-one founding members. The UN has six main parts—the General Assembly, the Security Council, the Economic and Social Council, the Trusteeship Council, the International Court of Justice, and the Secretariat. Related organizations in the late 1970s included the Food and Agriculture Organization of the United Nations, the General Agreement on Tariffs and Trade, the Inter-Governmental Maritime Consultative Organization, the International Atomic Energy Agency, the International Bank for Reconstruction and Development, the International Civic Aviation Organization, the International Development Association, the International Finance Corporation, the International Labour Organization, the International Monetary Fund, the International Telecommunications Union, the United Nations Educational, Scientific and Cultural Organization, the Universal Postal Union, the World Health Organization and the World Meteorological Organization.

Universities were first set up in Australia during the 1850s. The Universities of Sydney, Melbourne, Adelaide, Tasmania, Queensland and Western Australia were established respectively in 1850, 1853, 1874, 1890, 1909 and 1911. The numbers of universities increased greatly after the Second World War. The Australian National University was established, originally as a postgraduate institution, in 1946, and subsumed the Canberra University College (formerly affiliated with the University of Melbourne) in 1960. The University of New South Wales (known as the New South Wales University of Technology until 1958) was established in 1949, Monash University (Melbourne) in 1958, Macquarie University (Sydney) in 1963, La Trobe University (Melbourne) in 1964, Murdoch University (Perth) in 1973, Griffith University (Brisbane) in 1971, and Deakin University (Geelong, Victoria) in 1976. The University of New England (Armidale, New South Wales), Newcastle University, Flinders University (Adelaide), the James Cook University of North Queensland (Townsville) and the University of Wollongong, all formerly branches of other universities, became autonomous in 1954, 1965, 1966, 1970 and 1975, respectively. Total numbers of students enrolled in Australian universities increased from 14,236 in 1939 to 133,126 in 1973.

V

Van Diemen's Land: The name previously given to present-day Tasmania. *Tasman, the Dutch mariner, was the first white person to discover the island, in 1642, and he named it Anthony Van Diemen's Land, after the Governor-General of the Dutch East India Company. Other Europeans, including Marion du Fresne (1772), James *Cook (1777), Joseph-Antoine Raymond Bruny d'Entrecasteaux (1792–3), *Bass and *Flinders (1798–9) and *Baudin (1802), followed. British convict settlements were established in the south and north of the island. John Bowen, sent from New South Wales, established a short-lived settlement at Risdon Cove, on the Derwent River, in 1803. *Collins, sent from England, after abandoning an attempt to settle on the coast of Port Phillip, near present-day *Sorrento, established a settlement at Sullivan's Cove, also on the Derwent River, in 1804. He named it Hobart Town. Collins was the first Lieutenant-Governor of Van Diemen's Land. William *Paterson, sent from New South Wales, established a settlement at Port Dalrymple, in the north of the island, in late 1804. Two years later he moved the settlement to the site of present-day Launceston. The settlements in the north and south were administered separately until 1812, and Van Diemen's Land was separated administratively from New South Wales in 1825. Convicts were sent to Van Diemen's Land, originally from New South Wales and then directly from Britain, until 1853. *Responsible government was proclaimed in 1855, the first responsible ministry taking office the following year. The colony's new name, Tasmania, was proclaimed in 1855.

Van Diemen's Land Company: An agricultural and pastoral organization, formed by a London syndicate in 1825. Its first agent, Edward Curr, chose land in *Van Diemen's Land the following year. The company eventually was granted about 141,000 hectares. Its major activities in the mid-1980s were agricultural and pastoral.

Versailles, Treaty of: A treaty between the Allies and Germany in 1919. It was one of a number of treaties whose provisions were determined at the *Paris Peace Conference, which was held at the conclusion of the First World War. Its main provisions included redrawing of the boundaries of European countries; the redistribution of German colonial possessions; the determination of the war reparations to be paid by Germany; and the establishment of the *League of Nations. The Australian Commonwealth Parliament ratified the Treaty in 1919. Australia was granted a mandate by the League of Nations to administer former German *New Guinea and associated islands south of the equator; a share, with Britain and New Zealand, in a mandate over Nauru; and reparations from Germany, of which £5,571,720 (much less than Australia was promised, which in turn was much less than she had claimed) ultimately was paid before the system collapsed in 1932. Australia also became a member of the League of Nations.

Victoria, a state of the *Commonwealth of Australia, is located in the south-east of the continent. In its early years of white settlement it was known as

the *Port Phillip District and formed part of New
South Wales. Early convict settlements there were
short-lived (1803–4, 1826–8). Although *sealers and
*whalers visited, the first permanent white settle-
ments did not begin until 1834 and 1835. The area
was separated from New South Wales, and named
Victoria, in 1851. *Responsible government was proclaimed in Victoria in 1855, and Victoria became a
state of the newly created Commonwealth of Australia in 1901. *Melbourne is the capital city of
Victoria.

Victoria (north Australia): *Port Essington

Vietnam War: This term generally refers to the
period of conflict between North Vietnam, supported
by China and the Soviet Union, and South Vietnam,
supported by the United States of America and other
countries, culminating in victory for the North Viet-
namese in 1975. Australia, as a member of the *South-
East Asia Treaty Organization, sent a small number
of army instructors to support South Vietnam in 1962
and 1964, and then began to send combat forces in
1965. *Holt, the Australian Prime Minister, used a
now-famous phrase, 'All the way with LBJ', to pledge
Australia's support for the United States of America,
in general and in relation to its participation in the
Vietnam War, in a speech to the President, L. B.
Johnson, during a visit to the United States in mid-
1966. The full sentence was:

*And so, sir, in the lonelier and perhaps even more
disheartening moments which come to any national
leader, I hope there will be a corner of your mind
and heart which takes cheer from the fact that you
have an admiring friend* [Australia], *a staunch friend
that will be all the way with LBJ.*[1]

By 1968 there were more than 8000 Australian men,
from the three armed services, in Vietnam. They
included conscripts. The main area of Australian
involvement was Phuoc Tuy Province. The Australians were withdrawn from Vietnam during 1972, by
which time some 47,000 Australians had served

---

[1]*Australian*, 1 July 1966.

there. More than 400 Australians had been killed, and approximately 2400 had been wounded. During the late 1960s and early 1970s, Australia's involvement in the Vietnam War, and the *conscription issue, became the focus of bitter public debates.

W

Wakefield, Edward Gibbon (1796–1862), colonial theorist, was born in London. He was educated at Westminster School and Edinburgh High School, before pursuing a diplomatic career. He eloped with, and married, an heiress. She died in 1820. Wakefield abducted and married another heiress, a fifteen-year-old schoolgirl, in 1826. The marriage was annulled and Wakefield was sentenced to three years' imprisonment. While serving his sentence in Newgate (1827–30) he began to develop theories on colonization, which eventually covered such aspects as penal reform, land policies, migration and forms of government. He is remembered as the chief exponent of *systematic colonization. Wakefield has been credited, some would say inaccurately, with having influenced migration and land policies for *New South Wales; the ending of *transportation to New South Wales; the colonization of *South Australia, *Western Australia (for example, the *Australind settlement) and *New Zealand; and colonial government policy, through Durham's *Report on the Affairs of British North America* (1839). Wakefield never visited Australia. He pursued political careers in Canada and New Zealand; he was elected to the Canadian General Assembly (1842–4), and to that of New Zealand (1853). After retiring, he lived in New Zealand until his death. Wakefield's publications (some of which were published anonymously or under other names) include *A Letter from Sydney, the Principal Town of Australasia* (1829), *Sketch of a Proposal for Colonizing Australasia* (1829), *Statement of the Principles and Objects of a Proposed National Society for the Cure and Prevention of Pauperism by Means of Systematic Colonization* (1830), *Facts Relating to the Punishment of Death in the Metropolis* (1831), *Plan of a Company to be Established for the Purpose* *of Founding a Colony in Southern Australia* (1832), *England and America, A Comparison of the Social and Political State of Both Nations* (1833), *The New British Province of South Australia* (1834) and *A View of the Art of Colonization, with Present Reference to the British Empire in Letters between a Statesman and a Colonist* (1849).

Wallace's Line: The name given to an imaginary line, running between Bali and Lombok, said to divide the fauna of Asia from that of Australasia. T. H. Huxley named it in 1868, after Alfred Russel Wallace, an English scientist, who had earlier made this distinction.

'Waltzing Matilda': One of Australia's most popular songs. A. B. *Paterson wrote the words, which tell the story of a *swagman's adventures ('waltzing matilda' means carrying a swag), while staying on a station near Winton, in Queensland, in 1895. The tune is an adaptation of a Scottish song named 'Thou Bonnie Wood of Craigielea'. 'Waltzing Matilda', which was first sung publicly in a Winton hotel in April 1895, has periodically (but unsuccessfully) been proposed as Australia's national anthem.

Warburton, Peter Egerton (1813–89), was born in England, and joined the Royal Navy at the age of twelve. He attended the Royal Indian Military College, Addiscombe, Surrey, from 1829 to 1831, and then served in the Bombay Army until 1853, when he retired with the rank of major. During his term of office as the South Australian Commissioner of Police, which lasted from 1853 until 1867, Warburton explored a number of parts of the colony's interior. He became chief staff officer and colonel of South Australia's Voluntary Military Force in 1869, remaining in the force until 1877. Warburton left Adelaide in September 1872 in charge of an expedition, financed by Thomas Elder and Walter Hughes, to explore from central Australia to the west. The party, comprising Warburton, his son Richard, two other Europeans, two Afghan camel-drivers and an Aboriginal tracker, left Alice Springs in April 1873, and had to cope with harsh country, lack of water, extreme heat and illness, and eventually had to eat some of their seventeen camels. Warburton was obliged to abandon his early plan of aiming for Perth. After almost perishing, the party finally arrived at Roebourne in north-western Western Australia in January 1874, becoming the first to cross Australia from the centre to the west. Warburton, who had lost the sight of one eye on the expedition, was awarded the Royal Geographical Society's gold medal, and his *Journey Across the Western Interior of Australia* was published in 1875. He died at his property near Adelaide.

War Precautions Act: This was the 'main instrument of war-time government'[1] in Australia during the First World War.

The War Precautions Acts *1914–15–16 delegated to the Governor-General in Council a very wide power to make regulations 'for securing the public safety and the defence of the Commonwealth'. In addition to the general power, a number of specific powers were set out covering such matters as the control of enemy aliens, censorship of communications and safeguarding of docks, etc.*[2]

About 3500 cases of breaking regulations made under the *War Precautions Act* were prosecuted. The Act was later repealed.

Wartime Transport Strike: A major industrial dispute in 1917, during the First World War, and the largest strike in Australia to that time. Workers in the New South Wales Railways and Tramways Department, protesting over the introduction of a 'card system' to record the time taken for each job, which they saw as a form of 'speeding up', went on strike on 2 August. Waterside workers, coal-miners and others soon withdrew their labour in support of them. About 97,500 Australian workers (of whom about 76,000 were in New South Wales) went on strike. The New South Wales Nationalist Govern-

---

[1]Geoffrey Sawer, *Australian Federal Politics and Law, 1901–1929* (Melbourne University Press, Melbourne, 1956), p. 134.
[2]ibid., p. 135.

ment and other employers used so-called 'loyalist' labour to maintain essential industries. The railway workers returned to work in September. The 'card system' remained, a Royal Commission was promised within three months, and many workers were demoted. All of the remaining strikers had returned to work before the end of October.

Watson, John Christian (1867–1941), politician, was born in Valparaiso, Chile. His parents, who were English, were travelling to New Zealand, where Watson grew up and worked in the printing trade. He moved to Sydney when he was nineteen, worked as a compositor, and was active in the Typographical Union. Watson became president of the Sydney Trades and Labour Council, and of the Australian Labour Federation. He was a Labor Member of the Legislative Assembly in New South Wales from 1894 to 1901. He was then a Member of the House of Representatives from 1901 to 1910, and led the federal parliamentary Labor Party from 1901 to 1907. He became the first, albeit short-lived, Labor Prime Minister and Treasurer (1904). In 1916 Watson was expelled from the Labor Party for supporting *conscription.

Wave Hill: A Northern Territory pastoral station that was the scene of significant events in the Aboriginal *land rights movement. In 1966 Gurindji people at Wave Hill station, which was leased by a large British firm, went on strike over low wages and poor conditions, and occupied station land at Wattie Creek. In April 1967 they petitioned the Governor-General, asking for some 1300 square kilometres of their traditional land around Wattie Creek. The petition was rejected. In 1975 the Gurindji people were granted leasehold title to about 3280 square kilometres of the land, known as Daguragu; an Aboriginal land trust has since been granted freehold title to most of Daguragu.

WCTU: *Woman's Christian Temperance Union

Welcome Stranger: The largest gold nugget found in Australia. John Deason and Richard Oates found the nugget at Moliagul, near Dunolly, Victoria, in 1869. Its gross weight was 78,381 grams; its net weight was 71,040 grams. Deason and Oates received £9534 for it.

Wentworth, William Charles (1790-1872), politician, was the son of Catherine Crowley, a convict, and D'Arcy Wentworth, a surgeon. His parents had both sailed to New South Wales with the *Second Fleet. Wentworth lived on *Norfolk Island and in New South Wales before being educated in England between 1803 and 1810. He returned to New South Wales and became the acting Provost-Marshal in 1811. Blaxland, Lawson and Wentworth found a route that led to the crossing of the *Blue Mountains in 1813. Wentworth worked on a schooner for some time before returning to England in 1816. He won second prize with his poem 'Australasia' in a competition for the Chancellor's gold medal, while he was at Peterhouse, Cambridge. Wentworth pursued a legal career; he entered the Middle Temple in 1817, and was called to the Bar in 1822. His *A Statistical, Historical, and Political Description of the Colony of New South Wales and its dependent Settlements in Van Diemen's Land, With a Particular Enumeration of the Advantages which these Colonies offer for Emigration and their Superiority in many Respects over those possessed by the United States of America* (1819) was influential. In 1824 Wentworth returned to New South Wales, where he led the *emancipists, campaigned for political and legal reform, established the *Australian* newspaper with Robert Wardell, and continued his legal career. He became involved in the *Sudds and Thompson affair, and was active in the *Australian Patriotic Association. He also became a large *squatter. In 1840 Wentworth and some associates tried to buy about one-third of New Zealand, but were foiled in the attempt by *Gipps. Wentworth played a part in drawing up the draft bill forming the basis for the Act of 1842 that established a partly-elected, partly-nominated Legislative Council in New South Wales. He entered the Legislative Council in 1843, and led the opposition to Gipps, especially over the latter's attempts to control the squatters. Wentworth, who had become increasingly conservative, chaired the Select Committee that drafted the New South Wales Constitution in 1853. He and Edward Deas Thompson, the Colonial Secretary, went to England, where they saw it become law in 1855. Wentworth spent the rest of his life in England, except for one brief period in 1861-2 when he returned to New South Wales and was President of the Legislative Council.

Western Australia is a state of the *Commonwealth of Australia. *Hartog, a Dutch mariner, is the first European known to have landed on the west coast of Australia, in 1616. *Dampier, an English explorer, visited the north-west coast in 1688 and 1699. Early reports were unfavourable. In 1826 *Darling, acting on British instructions, sent soldiers and convicts to King George Sound, where they established a settlement named Frederickstown, later renamed *Albany. In 1829 Britain annexed Australia's western third and founded the free colony of Western Australia. The new colony's main settlement was established at *Perth, on the Swan River. About ten thousand convicts, all male, were transported to Western Australia between 1850 and 1868. *Responsible government was proclaimed in Western Australia in 1890, and the colony became a state of the newly created Commonwealth of Australia in 1901.

West Irian: *Irian Jaya

***Westminster, Statute of*:** A British Act of Parliament in 1931 that gave equal status to the self-governing Dominions (including Australia) of the British Empire. It was based on resolutions of the Imperial Conference of 1926 and 1930. In 1926 Lord Balfour's committee had defined the United Kingdom and the Dominions as:

autonomous communities within the British Empire, equal in status, in no way subordinate to one another in any aspect of their domestic or external affairs, though united by a common allegiance to the Crown

Westpac Banking Corporation

and freely associated as members of the British Commonwealth of Nations.[1]

Australia ratified the *Statute of Westminster* in 1942.

Westpac Banking Corporation: *Bank of New South Wales

Whalers from Australia, Britain, America and elsewhere operated around Australia from the 1790s. Whales were hunted for oil and whalebone, and whale and seal products were Australia's main exports until the 1830s. Numerous whaling stations were established in Van Diemen's Land (which had forty-one bay-whaling stations by 1841), New South Wales, the Port Phillip District, South Australia and Western Australia. Whaling declined during the latter half of the nineteenth century, but continued throughout much of the twentieth century. Australia's last whaling station, in Western Australia, closed in 1978.

White, Patrick Victor Martindale (1912-), writer, was born to Australian parents in London. His father was a grazier. White was educated at Tudor House in Moss Vale, New South Wales, Cheltenham College in England, and King's College, Cambridge. Before going up to Cambridge, White jackarooed at Monaro and Walgett; after coming down, he travelled in Europe and the United States of America. During the Second World War he was an intelligence officer with the Royal Air Force in the Middle East and Greece. He returned permanently to Australia in 1948. White won the Nobel Prize for Literature in 1973. His novels include *Happy Valley* (1939), *The Living and the Dead* (1942), *The Aunt's Story* (1946), *The Tree of Man* (1955), *Voss* (1957), *Riders in the Chariot* (1961), *The Solid Mandala* (1966), *The Vivisector* (1970), *The Eye of the Storm* (1973), *A Fringe of Leaves* (1976), *The Twyborn Affair* (1979) and *Memoirs of Many in One* (1986). His other publica-

---

[1]Cited in Geoffrey Sawer, *Australian Federal Politics and Law, 1901–1929* (Melbourne University Press, Melbourne, 1956), p. 290.

tions include stories, poetry, plays, a screenplay and
an autobiography.

White Australia Policy: A restrictive *immigration
policy pursued by Australia for many years. All Australian colonies restricted Asian (particularly Chinese) immigration at times during the second half
of the nineteenth century. The term 'White Australia'
was in use by the 1880s. In 1901 the new Commonwealth Parliament legislated to exclude non-
Europeans. The main device used was a dictation
test in any European language (any 'prescribed'
language from 1905). This policy of exclusion continued, virtually unchanged, until the 1950s. Since
then the policy has been abandoned. Entry permits,
based largely upon economic criteria, replaced the
dictation test in 1958.

Whitlam, Edward Gough (1916–   ), politician, was
born in Kew, Victoria, and was educated at Knox
Grammar School in Sydney, Telopea Park School,
Canberra Grammar School, and the University of
Sydney, from which he graduated in Arts in 1938,
and Law in 1946. His father was a lawyer. During
the Second World War Whitlam served with the Royal
Australian Air Force from 1941 to 1945. He was admitted to the New South Wales and Federal Bars in 1947,
and was appointed Queen's Counsel in 1962. He was
a New South Wales Labor Member of the House of
Representatives from 1952 to 1977. He led the Opposition twice (1967–72, 1975–7), was Prime Minister
from 1972 to 1975, and Minister for Foreign Affairs
in 1972–3. The Whitlam Government's achievements,
some of which were controversial, include the abandoning of *conscription and withdrawal of Australian troops from the *Vietnam War, the granting of
diplomatic recognition to the Chinese People's Republic, the abolition of university fees, and the introduction of a national health system known as
Medibank. The *dismissal of the Whitlam Government in 1975 caused great controversy. After Labor's
defeat in the 1977 elections, Gough Whitlam resigned
from his party's parliamentary leadership, and from
parliament. He was a Research Fellow at the

Australian National University before being appointed Australian Ambassador to Unesco in Paris in 1983. Whitlam has written a number of books.

Williamson, James Cassius (1845–1913), actor and entrepreneur, was born in Pennsylvania, and gained theatrical experience in various places, including New York and San Francisco, before he and his first wife, Maggie Moore, having been engaged by *Coppin, appeared in *Struck Oil* in Australia in 1874 and 1875. After touring elsewhere with the play, they returned to Australia, with rights to *H.M.S. Pinafore*, in 1879. Williamson turned increasingly to management, forming a comic-opera company in 1880, and another organization (originally in partnership with George Musgrove and Arthur Garner), which eventually became known as 'the Firm', in 1882. 'The Firm' presented many plays, comic operas and musical comedies, mostly English and American, in Australia and New Zealand. Williamson, who has been described as 'Australia's most successful theatrical entrepreneur',[1] died in Paris. The organization (which had become J. C. Williamson Limited in 1907) continued to exist for much of the twentieth century.

'Wobblies': *Industrial Workers of the World

Wolseley, Frederick York (1837–99), inventor, was born in Ireland, arrived in Melbourne in 1854, and worked on, and eventually owned, various sheep stations in eastern Australia. He experimented with sheep-shearing machines, taking out several patents (one with R. Savage, another with R. P. Park) for such devices in 1877 and 1884. John Howard (who sold the rights to his horseclipper to Wolseley, and was employed by him) improved them. A number of Australian shearing sheds began to use Wolseley's shearing-machine in 1888. In 1889 Wolseley went to England, founded the Wolseley Sheep Shearing

---

[1] Helen M. van der Poorten, 'James Cassius Williamson', in Geoffrey Serle and Russel Ward (eds), *Australian Dictionary of Biography*, volume 6 (Melbourne University Press, Melbourne, 1976), p. 407.

Machine Co. Pty Ltd in Birmingham, and was its managing director until 1894. (The firm later also manufactured Wolseley motor cars.) He died in London.

Woman's Christian Temperance Union (WCTU): A women's organization, with branches in each state. The organization was founded in the United States of America in 1874. It then spread to other countries. The first Australian branch began in Sydney in 1882. Branches in the other colonies followed during the 1880s. The WCTU's primary objective has been the restriction, and eventual abolition, of the use of alcoholic beverages. Its other objectives have included social reform such as the introduction of women's *suffrage. The Woman's Christian Temperance Union played an active role in the campaign for women's suffrage in Australia, although some historians have suggested that this role may have been over-emphasized.

Woomera is a town in South Australia, about 180 kilometres north-west of Port Augusta. It lies within the Woomera rocket range, which extends over a large area in South Australia and Western Australia, and to which public access is restricted. Both were developed as a result of the United Kingdom–Australia Long Range Weapons Agreement (also known as the Joint Project Agreement) of 1947. (A woomera is an Aboriginal spear-throwing stick.) Various countries have been involved in programs conducted at the range. Maralinga and Emu, two of the sites of British *nuclear tests in Australia, lie within the area, as does the United States Joint Defence Space Communications Station at Nurrungar. The population of the town of Woomera in 1981 was about 1800.

World War I: *First World War

World War II: *Second World War

Wybalenna: *Furneaux Islands

Z

Zeehan, a town in western Tasmania, lies some five kilometres to the north of Mount Zeehan, a peak sighted in 1642 by *Tasman, the Dutch mariner. (*Flinders later named the peak after the *Zeehaen*, one of Tasman's ships.) Silver-lead deposits were discovered in the area in 1882, leading to the establishment of Zeehan. It developed rapidly during the 1890s, becoming a town in 1898 and a municipality in 1906, and its population reputedly reached about 8000 in the early 1900s. Mining in the area (and consequently the town itself) declined before the First World War, but a new lode of ore was discovered in 1949. The renewal of tin mining at Renison Bell, seventeen kilometres to the north-east, during the 1960s, also assisted Zeehan. The population of the town in 1981 was about 1750.